MIDDLE EAST

SAND-DUNES, MERSA MATRUH

MIDDLE EAST

A RECORD OF TRAVEL IN THE
COUNTRIES OF EGYPT
PALESTINE, IRAQ
TURKEY AND
GREECE

by

H. V. MORTON

WITH ILLUSTRATIONS
AND MAPS

DODD, MEAD & COMPANY
NEW YORK   1941

INTRODUCTION

The most interesting letters I have received since the War have come to me from soldiers serving with our Army in the Middle East. My correspondents tell me that they have found my three books about the Near East and Middle East useful in their moments of leisure, and I am glad to know that I have stimulated their interest in history and local custom. But a large number of these writers complain bitterly of the combined bulk of the three books, and ask insistently for editions on thin paper, which could be carried about in a haversack. I am told that in war-time such a venture is not possible.

I have nevertheless done my best to get over this difficulty by taking out of the three books those portions which deal in the most general way with travel in Egypt, Palestine, Iraq, Turkey, and Greece, and making one book out of them, which is more than even the thinnest of paper could have done. In *Middle East* will therefore be found passages from *In the Steps of the Master, In the Steps of St. Paul,* and *Through Lands of the Bible,* as well as impressions here printed for the first time of that heroic and beautiful country, Greece, and the ancient capital of Turkey, Istanbul.

I have taken the opportunity of revising and re-writing numerous portions of this book.

H. V. M.

April 1941

CONTENTS

ILLUSTRATIONS

All the illustrations are from photographs by the Author and Mary Morton

MAPS

ix

ILLUSTRATIONS

Drawn by Edward Stanford, Ltd.

EGYPT

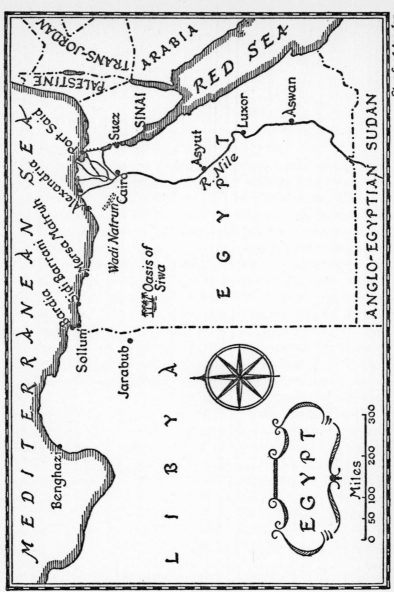

MEDITERRANEAN SEA

PALESTINE

TRANS-JORDAN

ARABIA

RED SEA

SINAI

Port Said

Suez

Alexandria

Cairo

Wadi Natrum

Asyut

R. Nile

Luxor

Aswan

EGYPT

ANGLO-EGYPTIAN SUDAN

Marsa Matruh

Sidi Barrani

Bardia

Sollum

Jarabub

Oasis of Siwa

Benghazi

LIBYA

EGYPT

Miles
0 50 100 200 300

Stanford, London.

I

MERSA MATRUH

I

ONE warm spring morning I found myself in a train that was moving along the North Western Desert of Egypt towards a place called Mersa Matruh. The rains were now over, but those portions of the track that become washed away once a year had been so recently repaired that our locomotive could make only a cautious progress that never exceeded a speed of twenty miles an hour.

I was the only European in the train, and my fellow passengers preferred to sit on the floors rather than on the seats of their compartments. Every now and again we pulled up with much shouting and whistling at some bare little station where groups of peasants would descend with the bulky objects they had acquired in Alexandria, and walk away across the desert to bleak little villages that appeared to be constructed of rusty kerosene tins.

When twenty miles or so from Alexandria the train, now almost emptied of its travellers, continued its journey with the air of having crossed a frontier. The infrequent stations lay in bleaker and browner solitudes, and the human beings upon them, who gathered to gaze with mournful appraisement at the train, were no longer Egyptian *fellahín* but men of Berber stock, the descendants of the ancient inhabitants of Libya. Instead of the *tarbush* and the *gallabía* of the Egyptian, those people wore little blue caps with red tassels and a white garment called a *jurd,* which they carried with great dignity cast over one shoulder like a Roman toga.

3

The landscape grew intensely monotonous, and curiosity alone prevented me from pulling down the slatted shutters with which all Egyptian railway carriages are provided. A thin brown dust as fine as talc powder filled the carriage and found its way even into my packet of sandwiches. There was nothing for the eye to seize on, only a shapeless stony wilderness that hardly as yet bore promise of the antiseptic solitude of the real desert; and it was with pleasure that now and again I saw the sea, as hard and blue as a sapphire, shining between a gap in brown hills.

Egypt, I reflected, is the easiest country in the world to see as long as you remain in the Nile Valley, which was made by the hand of Nature and Thomas Cook for the easy transport of the wealthy and the curious to certain well-established ruins. It is necessary only to take a Nile steamer to Luxor or Aswân and to keep awake, whereupon an ancient civilization will conveniently reveal itself at regular intervals on both banks of the river. But the traveller who is not content with an itinerary that was already well worn in the lays of Strabo is faced with a number of difficulties the moment he decides to leave the beaten track; and not the least of these is the bewilderment of the Egyptian Government official who is unable to conceive how any person in his right mind could wish to invade some hideous desert when he might drift comfortably up the Nile in a floating hotel. It must be said, however, greatly to the credit of the Egyptian official, that, once he encounters a person determined to be uncomfortable, his pride is stung; and he sends him off into the wilds with a despairing shrug of the shoulders armed with introductions to remote administrators, who will prove to him that Egyptian deserts are well run; as indeed they are.

When I expressed a wish to visit the Oasis of Siwa, my proposal had much the same effect on the department concerned as that which might be caused in the Ritz Hotel if a

guest petulantly tossed aside the menu and insisted upon or-
dering a plate of winkles or a dish of jellied eels. With the
whole of the Nile Valley and its splendid treasures organized
for the reception of visitors, here was a perverted appetite de-
manding an outlandish oasis from which any reasonable person might well pray to be saved. Nevertheless they made
plans for me. I was to present myself at Mersa Matruh, two
hundred miles to the west of Alexandria, where the Governor
of the Western Desert would send me southward to the oasis
in a patrol wagon. That suited me very well; and as the day
wore on, and the desert blazed on either side, I lay back and
told myself that this was no dream, and that I was really upon
my way to a place which has always seemed to me to be
among the most mysterious and romantic in the world.

The Oasis of Siwa was famous centuries before the time of
Christ as the seat of the Oracle of Jupiter Ammon. Remote,
mysterious, hidden in a dense palm grove surrounded by thousands of miles of burning sand, the sanctuary of the god attracted to it from all parts of the civilized world individuals
and embassies anxious to read the future.

Then from the year A.D. 20, when the oasis was described
by the Roman historian, Diodorus Siculus, the place disappeared from history for nearly seventeen centuries until an
Englishman, W. G. Browne, went there in 1792 disguised as
an Arab, the first European to gaze upon the site of the Am-
monium since Roman days. His visit was cut short when the
Siwans, penetrating his disguise, attempted to murder him,
and he was forced to fly. But he had replaced the Oasis of
Ammon on the map. The remoteness of the situation, the
strange history of the place, the difficulty of getting there and
the danger from a violent and fanatical population, who were
determined that no stranger should ever visit them, gave the
oasis a peculiar fascination for a small and daring band of
travellers.

Not more than twenty men visited Siwa between 1792 and 1914–18, and most of them had a lively time, some seeking safety in flight; others barricading themselves in mud houses and putting up a siege which lasted sometimes for months until a body of Turkish troops arrived from Cairo to set them free. Oddly enough, it was left to Great Britain to tame Siwa during the Great War. At that time the oasis was the head-quarters of an austere Mohammedan sect, the Senussi, which had been founded about a century ago by Mohammed Ben Ali es Senussi, who claimed descent from the Prophet. When the War broke out the sect, headed by a kinsman of the founder, known as the Grand Senussi, were numbered by the million, but they lacked cohesion because they were scattered about the remote oases of Libya—Siwa, Kufra, and Jarabub.

The tribesmen had given considerable trouble to Italy by opposing her attempt to colonize Tripoli, which had been evacuated in her favour by Turkey in 1912. It was natural that Germany should have seen in them a hopeful "revolt in the desert" that, if successful, might have swept us out of Egypt. Therefore German agents, moving among the Senussi, worked them up against our allies, the Italians, while German officers, eluding the Italian Navy, were landed with arms by submarines from Constantinople. It was not long before the Senussi were on the move.

The plan was to march against Egypt along the coastal strip of the Western Desert to the Delta, and, by way of the group of Oases, Siwa, Bahariya, Farafra, and Kharga, to invade the Nile Valley. We evacuated Sollum and Sidi Barrani and based our small mixed force of Yeomanry, Territorials, Australians, New Zealanders, Indians, and Egyptians on Mersa Matruh. We gained a notable victory over the enemy on Christmas Day, 1915.

The Senussi, led by a capable Germanized Turkish officer, Jafar Pasha, had assumed that, as it was Christmas Day, the

SIWA

British forces would be feasting and drinking in Mersa Matruh, and that the place might then be easily captured. It has
been recorded that there was not even a bottle of beer in
Mersa at that time, and our troops were not thinking about
Christmas at all. On Christmas Eve the British force stole
out of Mersa Matruh and, supported by aeroplanes—something entirely new in desert warfare—and by shell fire from
naval ships, destroyed the Senussi camp and inflicted a crushing defeat upon the enemy which lack of troops and transport,
and the descent of the rains, prevented us from following up.

It was not until February that another equally successful
engagement took place near Sidi Barrani when, during a dash-
ing charge of the Dorset Yeomanry, Jafar Pasha was captured.
From that point onward the history of the campaign became
the retreat of the Senussi from oasis to oasis, leaving behind
him gramophones, alarm clocks, brass bedsteads, and members of his harem. In the concluding months of the campaign
the Libyan Desert, which had seen the first dive-bomber, saw
with terror the first application of mechanized troops to desert
war. These were armoured cars that struck fear into the hearts
of the enemy. After a remarkable two hundred mile dash over
the desert, the cars captured Siwa and concluded the war.
The Senussi escaped to Constantinople, where he remained
in exile.

Since the defeat of the Senussi, Siwa has no longer revolted
against the Egyptian Government but has become a more or
less law-abiding portion of the Western Desert Province.

All through the hot afternoon the train shed portions of its
inhabitants at desolate desert villages and struggled on again
into the sand emptier than ever. As dusk fell, I seemed to be
travelling alone through a moonless night of stars. The cool
air was blowing in over hundreds of miles of Mediterranean;

and I could smell the sea. Eventually, with a low, mournful, yet triumphant whistle, we arrived at the end of the railway line—and Mersa Matruh.

II

As I stood in the dark on the small station, the smart figure of a Sudanese soldier detached itself from the shaggy crowd of Arabs and Berbers. He stood to attention and saluted. So my hours of waiting in Cairo ante-rooms, and countless interviews which seemed to me to have ended only in frustration, were, most surprisingly, bearing fruit. He took my bags and led me to a military car, which was soon bumping over a sandy road. He told me we were going to "the hotel"; and I feared the worst.

Having known hotels in lonely parts of Syria, Turkey, and Greece, I was of the opinion that no hotel could ever surprise me again, yet when we stopped outside a white building that rose starkly out of sandhills near the sea I was surprised. I saw a hotel that might have been plucked from any plage in the South of France and set down on the fringe of the Libyan Desert. I noticed that some one with a sense of fitness had called it "The Lido."

Entering, I found it empty of guests, nevertheless an Egyptian in a white jacket presided over a cocktail bar, and a waiter moved about a *salon* set with spotless dinner-tables. I was taken upstairs to a room with a little balcony overlooking the bay. A door led into a bathroom. I cynically turned on the taps and, to my surprise, a thin stream of water fell from them. There was electric light, and I could hear an engine popping somewhere, making it.

It is always rather touching to discover some small yet ambitious touch of Europe planted in an unlikely patch of desert, and I could not imagine how "The Lido" came to Mersa Matruh. I found afterwards that it is patronized in summer by rich Greeks who seek refuge there from the heat of Alexandria. Still in the off season there was a strong touch of "Alice in Wonderland" about the place: it was completely improbable.

Sitting in the lounge later that evening, I learned that the hotel was not empty: there were two other guests, both English. One was a vigorous elderly man with an ear trumpet. His companion spent his time in placing his mouth in the opening of this instrument and shouting at the top of his voice. If the man with the trumpet was not interested, he would lower the instrument and thus cut himself off from contact with his friend, a final and disconcerting act.

As both men could be heard all over the hotel, I could not be charged with eavesdropping when I gathered that both were geologists, and were evidently engaged on a Government survey of the water-supply of the Libyan Desert. With so many of Mussolini's troops a short way over the border of Tripoli, the talk in Egypt since Sanctions and the Abyssinian venture has been of the possibility of war and an Italian attempt to march on Egypt across the desert. Indeed the importance of Mersa Matruh is that of a military station, as it was during the Senussi campaign. In Cairo I had often met people who were alarmed by what they called the Italian "threat" to Egypt, and I was glad to discover in that lonely outpost two expert geologists probing a question of such importance. Then, further to my surprise, the door opened and four Royal Air Force officers in khaki shorts walked in. Before dinner officers, geologists, and myself came together in one noisy group, and I was told by the airmen that they had left Cairo that afternoon and had flown to Mersa Matruh, where they would stay a night before flying on to Siwa at the break of day.

I dined with the officers and heard from them what a "godforsaken" spot Mersa Matruh was, but how important it might become if "the balloon ever went up." It seemed to me intensely depressing to be discussing such possibilities in the year 1937 with the last War so near.

The Wing Commander was an interesting man who had seen service during the War and, afterwards, in India. At one time, he told me, Lawrence of Arabia, serving as Aircraftman Shaw, was something of an embarrassment to him. Shaw strongly resented any attempt to offer him any privilege, no matter how small, that might be construed as a tribute to his former military rank and distinction. Once, however, the Wing Commander felt himself obliged, with the exercise of great tact, to offer Shaw a place in which he might write in peace.

"It was when he was writing his prose translation of the *Odyssey*," he told me. "He worked in an ordinary hut full of men whistling, playing a gramophone, cleaning equipment, and telling yarns. He would sit with a pile of reference books and a Greek dictionary, and every now and then some one who was writing home to a wife or a mother, would interrupt him, and ask him how to spell a word. Lawrence would put down his pen, answer the question, and continue with his work. I simply couldn't imagine how he could write in that din, so one day I said to him: 'Look here, Shaw, I can give you an empty hut to work in where you won't be bothered by noise and conversation. What do you say about it?' He looked hard and stubborn. 'No,' he replied curtly, 'I don't want any favours, thank you all the same. I prefer to work in noise.' There was nothing more to be said! He was an extremely difficult fellow. . . ."

Before I went to bed I stood on my balcony and heard the sea breaking on miles of sand. The stars, brilliant as they always are in Egypt, hung in a sky like blue velvet. There seemed to be nothing else at Mersa Matruh but the hotel among the sand-dunes and a mosque, whose minaret lifted itself like a white candlestick some little distance away.

III

Mersa Matruh was the Parætonium of ancient times. It was famous for a good harbour, but one difficult to enter. It was the usual port for ships carrying pilgrims or embassies bound for the Oasis of Ammon. In Ptolemaic times Cleopatra built a summer palace there, a place to which she could go, as the modern Greeks of Alexandria go to "The Lido," to escape the heat of the city.

When "the world's debate" was settled at the Battle of Actium, Antony and Cleopatra arrived at Parætonium in despair in the first ship to touch Egypt with news of the defeat. Antony seems to have given way to hopelessness, and even to have contemplated suicide, but Cleopatra behaved with courage. Decking her ship as if for victory, she set sail for Alexandria and entered the harbour with minstrels playing. Having obtained control of the garrison, she allowed the news of Actium to leak out.

The Romans stationed troops at Parætonium for the defence of Egypt, and in late times the Emperor Justinian built there one of his many frontier fortresses as a defence against the tribes of Libya. . . .

Although I knew I had arrived at a lonely and romantic spot, no one had told me that Mersa Matruh is one of the most beautiful places in Egypt. When I opened the shutters in the morning, I looked upon a scene that sent my mind back over the years to Ballantyne's *Coral Island* and Stacpoole's *Blue Lagoon*. Here was the perfect desert place of romantic fiction: white breakers curling in the morning sunlight on a half-moon of gold; sandhills, white as snow, rising above lagoons as blue as grape hyacinths; and some way to the east a little harbour where a few ancient rigged ships rode at anchor.

A land-locked lagoon lay about twenty yards from my balcony. Even in Iona I have never seen such colours. Light, striking through the lagoon, turns the water in its deepest parts to the colour of an emerald, and in the shallows to a delicate shade of apple-green. And there were many other colours: sudden vivid streaks of mauve and purple, where beds of weed were lying, and curious, pale patches of amethyst, and even touches of amber, as if dyes had been poured on the water. And beyond the coloured shallows and white hills, a hard line of Prussian blue was drawn across the sky: the deeper waters of the Mediterranean Sea.

The hotel stands by itself, about a mile from the town which after breakfast I set off to explore. The treeless little outpost cowered in the sunlight, on the edge of the sea. It reminded me of those wild-west townships of the early films, where horses were always tethered to posts until their owners slouched out of a saloon easing the pistols in their holsters. But some one has ambitions for Mersa Matruh. Wide and optimistic roads with firm, rectangular convictions run here and there, but only three or four little bungalows stand along them, smiling nervously behind their garden fences.

The most permanent-looking structures are the shops of Greek grocers, for the wily Ulysses sells soap, biscuits, chocolate, teapots, and always *ouzo* and *retsinata*, where even a Jew would starve. He is to-day, as he has been since Hellenistic times, the enterprising commercial adventurer of Egypt. I noticed above some of the Greek shops the half-effaced words in English, "Out of bounds," a memory of the Abyssinian trouble, when British troops were stationed at Mersa Matruh which is only two hundred miles from the Italian frontier of Tripoli.

I was surprised to see a small modern Greek church and a
Greek cemetery. The half-dozen Greek grocers in the town
must be extraordinarily devout men to build such a church,
I thought. Seeking an explanation, I entered a Greek shop
and, before I knew where I was, I had bought some chocolate, a tin of biscuits, a supply of matches, and a fly-whisk. I
believe those up-country Greeks are the best salesmen in the
world: no wonder they grow rich in the desert. The man in
this shop was a square little brown man from Andros. He wore
a felt hat on the back of his head, and he stood in his shirt-
sleeves among a truly amazing stock which not only covered the counters and shelves, but was also suspended from
the ceiling like the astrologer's crocodile. He gazed at me
with brown eyes full of an uncanny intelligence, and was delighted to show off his English.

"This church," I asked, "why is it here?"

"Ah," he replied, "it is the church of the sponge-fishermen.
Mersa Matruh is a famous place for the sponge-fishing. Greeks
come from the islands every year—many, many ships—and
fish for sponges as far up the coast as Sollum. The best sponges
in the world come from here, not the little brown sponges
that men sell in Athens, but the big, soft sponges that make
much money in England."

"Have you got any for sale?"

He put his head on one side, shut his eyes, and lifted up his
hand with the palm held level with his shoulder, which in
the Greek sign language, understood all over the Near East,
means "no": but not a nasty "no," a soft, deprecating, apolo-
getic "no"; a wistful "no," a "no" full of genuine regret.

"It is not permitted," he explained. "The merchants, they
come and buy all the sponges and take them away to Alexandria. We cannot buy here."

He told me that the few rigged ships which I had seen
from my balcony were the only sponge-ships left; for the sea-

son was over.

"And the cemetery?" I said. "It is for Greeks only?"

"Ah," he replied, "sponge-fishing is much dangerous. There are always much dead men."

And here again he made another of those signs which Greeks make everywhere in the world. He pursed up his lips and lightly fanned the air with one hand in the direction of his face. This means riches, abundance, much, many, and at this particular moment it meant "much dead sponge-fishers." When I left the shop, the little man bowed himself almost under the counter in humble gratitude.

The largest building in the town is the headquarters of the Western Desert Province of Egypt. This wonderful department, half military, half police, and entirely nursemaid, mother, doctor, and detective of the desert, was once a British organization, but under Egypt's new status it is now run by Egyptians. If the Bedouin's camels die, if his wife runs away, if his crops fail, if some one bewitches his donkey or his camel, he treks sometimes a hundred miles to tell the frontier post all about it. In fact he tells the frontier post everything except the name of the man who murdered his best friend. That is something which every one in his own circle knows, but the police must find it out for themselves.

Having heard a lot about the benevolent activities of this force I was not surprised to find the headquarters surrounded by hundreds of Bedouin waiting for a free gift of barley. They had come from miles around.

I was told a sad story by the officer who was doling out grain. There had been no rain for six years. The tribes were famished. Their horses and camels had died of hunger and thirst. The people themselves were hardly more than skin and bone, as I could see for myself. And now the blessed rain had fallen and the Bedouin had come in from every part of the desert, crying for barley to sow. Soon, if the rain continued,

MERSA MATRUH

the edge of the desert would be covered with green crops.
The tribes would stay camped in the coastal areas until the
barley was ripe in April or May, and then, their pitifully
meagre needs satisfied, they would disappear southwards
into the metallic blaze of heat.

I entered the Frontiers Office to pay my respects to the
Governor of the Western Desert. He was a newly appointed
Egyptian colonel, who had arrived only the day before to
take up his duties. He had, however, received a letter about
my journey to Siwa. A map of his district, an area about the
size of Wales, hung on the wall. A Sudanese orderly appeared
with cups of coffee and we began to talk of my journey.

I explained that I was having a car sent on from Cairo,
which should arrive at any moment, and in that car I pro-
posed to travel. He approved and added that he would send
a patrol wagon to escort me and show the way, because it is
a rule of the Frontiers administration that no car crosses the
desert alone.

He suggested that I should start at five o'clock on the following morning, if my car arrived in time, and a young Egyptian officer who had been to Siwa was called in. He told us
that if everything went well, and we had no breakdowns, we
should do the journey in one day. This surprised me, for I had
expected to spend at least one night in the open. The journey
which cars can now perform in one day used to take eight to
ten days by camel.

In the afternoon I walked to the harbour to see the sponge-
fishermen. I noticed in the low, limestone hills on the way
to the harbour signs of ancient terraces on which vines and
olives once grew, and many a Greek marble pillar has been
dredged from the lagoon or dug up from the white sandhills.
Such relics are all that remain of the small Greek port of
Pa;rætonium.

Until a year or so ago every drop of water was brought to

Mersa Matruh by sea in large tankers, and it was puzzling to understand how a town could have stood there in Ptolemaic times. The mystery was solved by the recent discovery of underground tunnels half a mile in length, and full of fresh water. Twenty-five manholes give access to the conduit, and when first discovered, there was something like 78,000 tons of sweet water lying underground waiting to be used. This is the ancient water-supply, and it is now being used again and still runs through the old channels.

I hired a rowing-boat and went out to look at the sponge-ships. The scene might have been an illustration from *Treasure Island*. The ships lay in a sheltered bay as if on a sheet of blue glass. So clear was the water that I could see fish, coral, and living sponges lying on the sand and rocks thirty feet below. Four wooden sailing-ships lay at anchor, their rigging festooned with the crew's washing, a happy touch which reminded me that when pirates reach a hidden and sheltered bay, they always indulge in such cheerful domesticity. As I drew nearer, I saw men who might have sailed the seas with Captain Kidd, blue-chinned, hairy, and half-naked, lounging about the decks or sprawled in sleep. I noticed that most of the ships came from Rhodes and Ægina.

The men answered my questions with surly suspicion. I could see their Greek minds wondering why I had taken the trouble to row out to them in the heat of the afternoon. They told me that the season was over. Most of the ships had gone home.

Sponge-fishing is a dangerous occupation. The men told me that a sponge-diver does not often live to be over forty, but a hundred pounds for a few months' fishing is real money in the Greek islands. If a diver is not killed by a defective helmet—and both masters and men are criminally careless—he may get diver's paralysis, caused by working under the water.

The most primitive method of sponge-diving, and probably less dangerous in the long run than a bad diving suit, is to plunge naked into the water, roped to a heavy stone. In those few seconds while he is on the sea-bed the diver detaches a sponge or two and, letting the rope go, shoots up to the surface of the water. Some divers are able to stay below for several minutes.

Another method is to hack at the sponges with a spear or trident, but that often damages the sponges. A third method is the use of a diving suit, but I was told some horrible stories of the badly fitting helmets in use and the capricious supply of air.

The sponge-divers' cemetery at Matruh tells the tragic story eloquently enough. Hardly a season passes but some divers leave their bones in Egypt. Some are killed by sharks, others die of paralysis or of diseases caused by under-water pressure on lungs and heart.

Standing in this lonely little graveyard, I remembered the small brown boys who dive for pennies round the lovely islands of Greece. They swim beneath the water like seals and come up with a penny in their white teeth, shaking the water out of their eyes and laughing with triumph. That is how the sponge-divers begin their short and dangerous lives.

Late that afternoon my car arrived from Cairo. It was driven by a dusty and exhausted Armenian named Mikhail. He had done a lot of desert travel and was the kind of Armenian who would take a brand new American limousine into the mouth of hell. I noticed with approval that he had brought picks, shovels, and sand boards. When I told him to go and have the car overhauled at the Frontier Department garage because we were starting off at five o'clock in the following morning, he bowed slightly and said: "As you please."

II

ACROSS THE WESTERN DESERT TO SIWA

I

A MAN came into my bedroom with a cup of tea. The stars were shining and waves were breaking on the sand below the window. It was cold, and I hated the idea of getting up.

Two cars were waiting in the darkness below to set out across the desert: my car and the patrol wagon driven by a Sudanese soldier. There were two other figures wrapped to the eyes in drapery: one was a Sudanese cook and the other a young Egyptian servant.

I was delighted to discover that the cook, the waiter, and Mikhail were as excited as I was at the prospect of travelling to Siwa. That lovely oasis was as strange to them as it was to me.

"Have you ever been there before?" I asked the lorry driver.

He sloped arms, brought his hand smack down on the butt of his rifle, and said:

"Yes, sir. Me go one time."

"When do you think we shall get there?"

"If no breakdowns," he said, casting a reproachful look at Mikhail's car, "we arrive to-night."

"Right. Let's start."

The patrol car roared off in the darkness and we followed its tail-light into the desert. In two hours the sun came up and we looked out over a high tableland as bare and featureless as the sea.

The Libyan Desert, or rather that small part of it between the coast and Siwa, must be among the most monotonous

18

portions of the earth's surface. It is unlike the conventional
idea of a desert. There are no picturesque, undulating hills of
golden sand. No palm-trees strike the horizon. As far as you
can see there is nothing but a brown plain like an ocean-bed,
scattered with millions of stones. It is a dirty khaki colour.

At first we saw camels grazing on the thorn bushes that
grow here and there; then life ceased as we journeyed on into
the wilderness, and there was nothing but the sun beating on
thousands of miles of brown sterility.

The road was merely a track made by the wheels of lor-
ries. The wheel ruts turned and twisted among boulders and
would suddenly run off at a tangent to avoid dips in which
water gathered in the rainy season. At more or less regular
intervals we came across hard sandy stretches as flat as a race
track, on which it was possible to travel at sixty miles an hour
for a minute or so before the "road" began again with its jolts
and sudden crashes on axle springs.

At first we looked forward to the crest of ridges, hoping
that when we reached them there would be a different view,
something—anything—on which the eye could linger with
interest, but it was always the same: a stone-scattered khaki
plain, treeless, shrubless, lifeless.

The fate of the fifty thousand Persians who perished in this
desert on the way to Siwa is too awful to contemplate. They
were sent out by Cambyses in 525 B.C. to sack Siwa and wreck
the shrine of the Oracle. They did not arrive and were never
seen or heard of again. It is conjectured that they were either
overwhelmed in a sand-storm, or, losing the way, wandered
over the desert until they went mad or perished of thirst.

Will some fortunate archaeologist ever solve the mystery
of that lost army? Somewhere along the road to Siwa fifty
thousand Persians lie beneath the sand with their armour
and equipment, just as they fell five centuries before Christ.

Noon came . . . one o'clock, two o'clock, three o'clock,

and we continued to journey through the same nightmare land. I called a halt so that we could eat our sandwiches at one of the five wells that lie at distances of about forty miles from each other along the route. Although there is water, there is no vegetation.

As Mikhail stepped from the car, he gave a howl of terror, and looking through the window, I saw that he had almost stepped on the most deadly snake in Egypt—the horned viper. It was long and thin, almost the colour of sand, with a small flat head and a tail ending in a thin pale point. I have been told that its bite can bring death to a man in twenty minutes. It is one of the few snakes that will deliberately attack a man, and among its horrible peculiarities is the speed with which it can travel not only backwards and forwards, but sideways as well.

Fortunately for Mikhail, the reptile had been driven out of its hole during hibernation and was in a comatose condition. We shouted to the soldier to bring his rifle, but he did not understand. So taking the first thing that came to hand, which happened to be my photographic tripod, we took our courage in both hands and killed the viper. We then congratulated Mikhail on being alive and had our frugal lunch in the shadow of the cars.

We continued our journey: I to bump unhappily from side to side, and the patrol wagon, with its better springs, to dart ahead with surprising speed. There were no birds. Incredible as it may sound, there were no flies. We were in a dead portion of the world.

Some thirty-five miles to the east of the track is a slight hill which the Bedouin call Jebel Iskander, the Hill of Alexander. They do not know that Alexander's guides lost their way to Siwa: the name has just come down from mouth to mouth through the centuries. After the War a British officer, who had been told by the Arabs that pots were to be found on this

hill, went there and unearthed eight perfect amphorae of the
Hellenistic period. I saw one in a garden at Mersa Matruh.
It was made of red clay and was about four feet high, with
a pointed base, a bulbous body, a long neck, and two handles.
If they are water-jars of Alexander's expedition, as it seems
they may be, one wonders what other relics might be found
on that lonely spot.

As the sun was setting, we left the plain and entered one
of the most fantastic bits of country imaginable. I think the
mountains of the moon must look like this. It seemed that
Nature, conscious of the bleakness of the past two hundred
miles, had crowded all the fantasy of which it is capable into
a small space. The valley was surrounded on all sides by weird
dead hills, each one carved into some improbable shape, a
cone, a cube, a queer isolated pinnacle, a ridge that from
a distance looked like a battlemented castle with turrets.
Other hills rose up like the ruins of old cities. In this strange
valley we cried out:

"Look! A bird!"

It was the first bird we had seen since early morning, and
a sign that we were approaching Siwa.

For an hour or so we travelled slowly downhill through
the moon mountains: then emerging suddenly from the gorge,
we saw below us thousands of date-palms standing in the pink
flush of the sunset.

As we drew near, the superb fantasy of Siwa revealed itself:
a rock covered with mud dwellings piled up like skyscrapers,
like some queer African Manhattan Island. The date-palms
formed a green sea from which this hill of houses rose against
the sky.

Soon we were running in the shadow of this hill, and we
realized that there was something uncanny about it. No people came out on the roof-tops to look at us. There was no
movement at the small square windows which pierced the

high walls.

We learned afterwards that the old town had been condemned as unsafe a few years ago and is deserted. The inhabitants have built a new village round about it, a cluster of low, flat-roofed, white houses made of mud and roofed with palm branches.

I went to the police station, where the Mamûr, the district Government official, was expecting me. The Mamûr, the doctor, and the officer of the local camel corps, all Egyptians, are the only resident officials. There are no Europeans in Siwa.

The Mamûr said that he had opened the Government resthouse for my reception. It stands about a mile away through a palm grove, a gaunt building of whitewashed mud, alone on a hill. Every window was closely meshed with mosquitonetting, which delighted me, for I am one of those people whom mosquitoes attack in and out of season.

A sad air of departed grandeur hung about the house. The late King Fuad had stayed there when he had visited the oasis, and a memory of that visit remains in a regal hand-rope covered with frayed blue velvet which still hangs, though a trifle listlessly, beside the stairs. There is also a bathroom, doubtless the strangest sight in Siwa, but its capabilities would not deceive the most callow or optimistic wanderer.

I was given the royal bed-chamber, where a brass fourposter rose in the shadows, and from this room a step led into a pleasant living-room furnished with a wooden table and two canvas chairs. The usual portrait of his late Majesty, wearing a tarbush and a frock coat, gazed from the wall. A long window covered in wire-netting ran along one side of the room and afforded a superb view of Siwa beyond the palm grove.

Sounds of dismay and confusion from the courtyard below indicated that the cook, the waiter, Mikhail, and the patrol-car driver were attempting to coerce a reluctant paraffin stove in the kitchen. Glancing out of the window, I saw the cook walking below, holding a dead cockerel. Soon I smelt a strange chorus of smells which indicated that the cook, with the passionate enthusiasm of one who finds himself alone and on his mettle, was preparing a tremendous meal.

The sun sank and darkness descended upon this lonely place. Stars snapped above the palm-trees, the bats were flying; and a mile away the weird outline of the dead town rose on its hill, grey and ghostly.

The waiter entered with a paraffin lamp, and a dinner was served which only a Sudanese cook could have prepared in that remote place. There was soup, an omelet, fish from Mersa Matruh, roast chicken, tinned peaches, a cheese savoury, and oranges.

As I went to bed that night, I saw a big gold moon sail into the sky and hang above the dark palm groves. No dog barked; no jackal cried; no night-bird called. The oasis lay in a pool of green light, frozen in silence like a land under snow.

II

In the early morning Siwa is like a Gaugin or a Van Gogh. It is a reckless exercise in hot colour: ochre-brown hills; golden sand; vivid green trees; a hard sky of blue untouched by any cloud. Heat throbs in the open places. Goats run in blinding light to the welcome shadow of the palm groves. White pigeons rise from feathery tree-tops to wheel sparkling in the sun. All the sounds are little sounds: the note of a bell on a goat's neck, the lazy song of a man working in one of the water-gardens, the bright click of a donkey's hoof against a stone, and the padded sound of camels walking.

From the window of the guest-house I could see to the west a narrow lake of intensely blue water, streaked with bands of snowy white. This is a salt lake which dries up in summer, so that it is possible to walk across on bricks of sparkling salt. In ancient times the priests of Ammon exported salt, to be used in the temples of Egypt and Persia. The natives say that the sword, the seal, and the ring of Solomon lie hidden on an island in the lake. One of Siwa's early explorers, the French engineer Colonel Boutin, took with him a collapsible canvas boat in the hope of reaching that island, but the Siwans would not let him launch it. Had he gone there in the summer, he could have walked across without difficulty along a causeway of solid salt.

As I was dabbing a mosquito bite with ammonia, I wondered how many people know that they invoke the name of the Oracle every time they ask for ammoniated quinine or salammoniac; for it was here in Ammonia, near the temple of Ammon, that ammonia chloride is believed to have first been made from the dung of camels. I wondered, also, as my nose approached too near the bottle, whether the asphyxiating fumes of this chemical had anything to do with the Oracle. The Delphic Pythia sat on a tripod directly over a chasm which was supposed to emit vapours, and Plutarch believed that fumes stimulated the prophetic frenzy, just as diviners among certain tribes of Hindoo Koosh, the Dainyals, are said to work themselves into a prophetic condition by first inhaling the smoke of burning cedar wood.

The Mamûr arrived while I was having breakfast, a large man in a suit of khaki drill and a sun helmet, and we sat down to talk about Siwa.

The population is about five thousand, and there are more men than women. There is no polygamy, but divorce is so frequent, and so little thought of, that a proportion of the female population is in constant circulation; and one Siwan has been known to divorce as many as forty wives. The Siwans still hold to the Senussi faith, but their fanaticism and hatred of outsiders has broken down since the War. Cairo does not seem so far away now that aeroplanes can reach the oasis in a few hours, and the motor patrol cars bring it within a day's journey of Mersa Matruh, instead of a week or ten days. But the Siwans are still difficult, and ready to quarrel among themselves.

They are riddled with superstition and firmly believe in all forms of witchcraft. The Government doctor has a hard time to convince them that his knowledge can be more useful than the spells and poultices of witch doctors and wise women. Most of the work is done by the descendants of Sudanese slaves and by the poorer Siwans who are not paid in money but in food, which is given to them every six months. The Government pays for work at the rate of 3s. 6d. a week which is considered lavish. But there is nothing to spend money on in Siwa, except green tea, the only extravagance of the oasis. Coffee is forbidden to the Senussi, therefore the Siwans have taken to tea, which they drink in enormous quantities and on every possible occasion. The only real object of money is to purchase a wife, and the price of a wife has been stabilized for many years at 120 piastres, which is about twenty-four shillings. As women are in a minority and are always sure to find suitors, and as large numbers of the men receive no money and could never save twenty-four shillings, a proportion of the population is resigned to lifelong bachelorhood.

The rulers of Siwa are the sheiks, who own large date groves. The oasis possesses 600,000 date-palms, which produce some of the best dates in Egypt. Each tree is taxed, and the oasis pays an annual tax of just under two thousand pounds to the Egyptian Government. This has caused a certain amount of bloodshed in the past, but like most people under the influence of civilization, the Siwans are now becoming resigned to taxation.

The dates are sold in an open market and are taken away by motor lorry. The old date caravans, which once used to come to Siwa from Egypt every year, are no longer seen, although merchant caravans do sometimes come from Tripoli. The end of the camel caravan traffic has had one curious effect on the Siwan exchequer. One of the main sources of revenue was derived from the sale of the camel manure left on the public square during the date market season. This has now ceased and the budget is down accordingly. The only industry in Siwa is a Government date-packing factory, recently established, where the dates are dried, washed, and sent away in boxes to Cairo and Alexandria.

The absence of dogs and cats in Siwa is due to the fact that the Siwans eat them. They also eat the jerboa, the rat, and the mouse. They make an intoxicating drink called *lubchi* from the sap of palm-trees, under its potent influence they become violent, and in times now past the east and the west ends of the town, which have always been at enmity, used to drink *lubchi* and engage in pitched battles in the main square, which invariably resulted in a marked decrease in the population.

The Mamûr and I set off to see the wonders of the oasis, and, as we passed through narrow streets between rows of mud houses, I asked him why so many skulls, bones, and inverted pots were built into the walls and set above the doors.

"Every one believes in the Evil Eye," he replied. "It is thought that any possessor of it will look at things like the skull of that donkey over there, and so avert it from human beings."

We came into the wide main square above which rise the fantastic battlements of old Siwa. Nothing more crazy has ever been erected. For many centuries house has been built on top of house in a casual, haphazard manner, until the outside walls are in places nearly two hundred feet high. The streets that tunnel through this human ant-heap run in complete darkness and wind up to the top, giving through an occasional airhole a bright snapshot of the world outside.

When the old town was inhabited it must have been an eerie experience to pass crouching along the dim, narrow streets, more like shafts in a coal-mine than anything else, and to hear nothing but women pounding corn in the dark, or the voices of invisible people in the houses on either side.

There were once nine gates to the town, which were guarded day and night, and when darkness fell all unmarried men were expelled to spend the night in huts outside. They were not admitted until morning.

I had heard that there was some excitement in Siwa that morning, for a caravan had arrived from Italian Tripoli, the first for many months. That sounded romantic, and I expected something rather spectacular. But when we came to a small market-house roofed with palm trunks and branches, I saw four Bedouin squatting on the floor, with knotted handkerchiefs in front of them. This, I was told, was the caravan from Tripoli. They opened their handkerchiefs and exposed a few poor silver trinkets. They had travelled for days and nights all the way across the desert, moving from well to well, striking camp and moving on, to bring those pitiful little things to the oasis. I thought what an admirable insight this was into the grim energy of primitive commerce. Archaeologists often wonder how a silver ring could have got here or there, and evolve long and ingenious theories to explain why an object should be where it has no right to be. I suppose the true explanation is that there have always been men like those merchants from Tripoli, who would bring a ring across the whole world just for the pleasure of having a cup of tea and a gossip at the end of the journey.

The market itself was an object lesson in the simplicity of life in the oasis. There were not more than ten merchants, and each sat cross-legged, with a sack in front of him. One sack would hold about four pounds of granulated sugar, another two or three pounds of tea; in a third would be some beans or lentils. To people accustomed to such a frugal market, no doubt the handkerchiefs of the Tripolitan Bedouin must have looked like Cartier's window in Bond Street.

We entered the date market not far away, a large open space floored with dates drying in the sun: some were a rich gold, some yellow, and some the colour of horse chestnuts. The Mamûr explained that the dates are of many kinds, each with its own name. Some Siwans are so expert in date culture that they can tell from which garden—almost from which tree —a particular date has come.

It is a custom that any one may enter this market during the date harvest and eat as many dates as he likes. But he must never put one in his pocket.

The date is to Siwa what the olive is to Mediterranean people. The poorer inhabitants live almost entirely on dates. The trunks of the date-palm provide the builder with wood. Palm wood is used as fuel. Fences are made of palm fronds, and houses and huts are roofed with them. From the fibre of the palm-tree the women make beautiful mats and baskets so closely woven that they will hold water.

The Siwan donkeys, which are remarkable for strength and size, are said to owe their perfect condition to a diet of dates, and in a corner of the market I saw a donkey eating his date ration with enjoyment.

We passed again through the streets of Siwa, and small brown girls about ten or twelve years old, each one like an ancient Egyptian statuette, stood frozen in curiosity as we approached, waiting until we were within a few yards before

running to cover. They were the belles of Siwa. Their faces
were mature, but their bodies were those of children. Their
plaited hair gave them a curiously archaic look, as if they were
wearing the festival wigs of the women in ancient Egypt.
They wear their hair in a number of tight plaits, and a fringe
of them falls over the forehead in a straight line. It is dressed
with an oily, scented unguent in which fig-leaves have been
pounded.

Each little girl wore round her neck a hoop of silver, to
some of which were attached silver disks about the size of a
saucer. These are "Virginity disks," which the girls wear until their marriage. On the marriage eve the bride, attended
by girls, goes to bathe in one of the springs of Siwa. She takes
the disk from her neck and flings it into the spring; then,
slipping off her garments, she dives into the water. One small
boy is generally allowed to be present at such ceremonies,
and as soon as the ritual is over, he dives down and retrieves
the silver disk, which is preserved for the bride to hand on to
her daughter.

When in full dress, these little girls are loaded with barbaric
jewellery. Enormous ear-rings are attached to their hair, carrying long chains to which bells are fixed, and round their necks
are to be seen rows of mummy beads taken from the tombs.

I saw such children everywhere, but not once did I see a
woman between the ages of sixteen and thirty-five. Nowhere
are married women more rigorously secluded, and it is only
when you glance up at the houses that you sometimes see
from an upper window an eye gazing inquisitively into the
street.

III

When I came to know Siwa better and could find my way
about, I never became weary of sitting beside the springs.
There are about two hundred, some of fresh water, some of

salt, some sulphurous, some warm, and some cold: a little Harrogate in a setting by Gaugin.

This varied volume of water has been pouring itself through the desert sand for centuries, and the explanation I like best is the theory that an underground river from the Congo shoots up through cracks and holes in the desert's crust. Nearly all the springs look like circular swimming-baths full of green and blue water, for it is green in the sunlight and blue where palm-trees cast their shadows. Most of the springs are lined with hewn stones, and have parapets on which you can sit and gaze through fifty feet of limpid blue-greenness to floors of tinted stalagmites.

Gazing into still water is the historical occupation of the vain, and there is not much to be said for it unless you are fond of your own face; but in Siwa the springs hold your attention hour after hour because they are alive with ascending strings of pearls. These quicksilver bubbles come at times in such numbers that the whole surface of the spring will move with escaping air, as if hundreds of invisible fish are mouthing the water. Then for no apparent reason the movement ceases, and you look down into still, green cellophane. I can understand how those springs excited the imagination of antiquity, as indeed they still excite the superstitions of modern Siwans, for there is nothing mechanical about their queer aerated vitality: the bubbles are blown as if at the whim of some underground giant who becomes tired and starts again, or who goes away for a rest and returns, sometimes blowing chains of little silver peas and sometimes sending up one as large as an orange.

The clearings in which the springs lie are hot, sunny openings in green jungles. All around, like masts in harbour, rise the jointed, matted boles of date-palms. Bright green leaves are spotted with the flushed rind of ripe pomegranates, or the delicious green-yellowness of sweet limes. And as you look into the springs, you can see clusters of dates reflected from the trees overhead, lying in the water like swarms of polished brown bees.

Dragon-flies of red, green, and orange dart and quiver over the springs, and sometimes a hoopoe, which is tame here, as elsewhere in Egypt, will fly down and look at you with a speculative eye, head cocked sideways, its plume of feathers rising like a question mark.

The springs of Siwa are of course the life-blood of the oasis, and the little channels carry the water into the gardens. Each spring has a watchman or guardian, who keeps a book in which is written the amount of water due to every strip of land. The guardians preside over toy canal systems of water tracks, some of which are carried over others through hollow palm trunks. When the time comes for a certain garden to be watered, the guardian approaches the water channel leading to it and kicks down a mud dam, which thus allows the water to flow in the right direction. And that is how the Israelites watered their gardens in Egypt as described in *Deuteronomy* xi. 10: "Where thou sowedst thy seed, and wateredst it with thy foot, as a garden of herbs." The guardians of Siwa, who have no watches or clocks, take their time from the sun, and when the sun sinks they listen for the muezzin, whose clear call they can hear in the still air; and when there is no sound from the mosque, they have the stars.

The Fountain of the Sun is the most famous and the most beautiful of Siwa's springs. Herodotus said that it was cold at midday but grew warmer towards midnight, a story which the Siwans repeat. There is also a legend that black, sightless fish once lived in the spring and were connected with the worship of the Oracle of Ammon, whose temple was not far away. While I was sitting by this spring, a dignified figure in a Roman toga, for that is how all Libyans wear their white robes, came towards me through the trees. He wore a little red cap from which hung a blue silk tassel, and he grasped a black umbrella. He was the sheik of the village of Aghourmi, and he had come to show me the ruins of the temple of Jupiter Ammon.

IV

First we went to see a ruin not far from the Fountain of the Sun, which must be the remains of the smaller temple mentioned by Diodorus. There is nothing left now but a few stones which once formed a gateway or a pylon. They are covered with figures pictured in the act of making offerings to the god Ammon. From the broken character of the ground, it is evident that a large building once stood in that place. Leaning gracefully on his umbrella, the sheik told me that long ago a Turkish governor had blown up the temple with gunpowder in order to get stones for the police station.

We ascended a small hill towards the old village of Aghourmi, which I thought even more impressive and interesting than Siwa. Its mud houses completely cover a rock that rises abruptly above the palm forests. From a distance it looks like a brown, mastless hulk drifting on a sea of palm fronds and, like Siwa, this village is now abandoned as unsafe, and the villagers have built new houses some distance away.

The main street wound steeply up between mud walls, losing itself now and then in an incredible rat-run of narrow tunnels which led to dark little houses now inhabited only by jackals and snakes.

We emerged on the ramparts, where we had a superb view of the oasis. The feathery heads of the palm forests lay below us mile after mile, and beyond them the Libyan Desert stretched to the horizon like a gold ocean.

Climbing in darkness over steep piles of rubbish and fallen walls, the light of an electric torch revealed the splendid stones

of an Egyptian temple and the remains of a massive gateway.
Some of the stones were as large as the stones of the Pyramids
of Giza.

This temple on the hill, lifted so high above the palm groves,
was the shrine of the Oracle, and somewhere beneath the
mass of mud buildings and tunnels is the place where Alexander the Great stood face to face with Jupiter Ammon.

The Siwans believe that an underground tunnel connected
the temple of Aghourmi with the lesser temple near the Fountain of the Sun. They say that a monarch called King Meneclush lies buried with his horse underneath Aghourmi. Who
Meneclush was they do not know. They say he was a king
who lived long ago and kept four speaking statues in his palace. Those images spoke when the sun touched them. This
surely must be some old memory of the Oracle.

The oracular god of Siwa, like the Oracle of Amûn-Rē at
Thebes, of which he was a duplicate, was a statue of a god
with a man's body and the head of a ram. As the ancient
Egyptians thought of the sky as an ocean on which the sun
and the moon sailed in their barks, the god was exhibited
either standing or seated in his shrine, which was placed
amidships of a slender canoe-like ship covered with plates of
hammered gold.

At Siwa the god's golden bark was covered with silver disks
which hung down on each side, and when the curtain was
drawn away from the shrine Ammon was seen inside, shining
with green malachite, which is a word that is often mistrans-
lated as emeralds. There were rings at the corners of the boat
through which poles were thrust, so that on festival days the
priests might shoulder boat and deity and carry them in procession round the temple.

The Oracle ranked with Delphi and Dodona as one of the
chief spiritualistic spas of antiquity; one of those places in
wild and remote parts of the earth where the divine wisdom

was believed to bubble up for the benefit of mankind. It should not be difficult for us, who belong to an age that has devoted so much study to psychic matters, to understand the effect upon the mind of antiquity of organized mediumship; certainly it should not be possible for us to scoff at those who confessed their belief in oracles; and they included both Socrates and Cicero. So great was the belief in the divine guidance to be obtained from those sacred places that hardly any colonial expansion was considered in Ancient Greece until the Oracle of Delphi had been consulted, and at one period the advice of Jupiter Ammon was so highly prized that the Athenians maintained a trireme, named Salaminia Ammonias, always ready to pass the seas to Egypt, whence envoys crossed the desert to the Oasis of Ammon with some current problem of statecraft.

It would be interesting to know as much about the process of divination at Siwa as we do of the procedure at Delphi and Dodona; but, alas, nothing has come down to us. It is probable that instead of the ecstatic trance of the medium at Delphi, and divination by the interpretation of the sound of wind in a tree, as practised in early times at Dodona, the statue of Ammon at Siwa was capable of marking some movement of its head and arms, or even perhaps of speaking with the voice of a priest, who was recognized as the god's interpreter. Whatever happened when visitors came face to face with the god in the gloom of his remote sanctuary, we can be sure that the experience was solemn and convincing; and his audiences departed over the burning sands satisfied that the veil had been withdrawn between the visible and the invisible.

In the year 321 B.C., the most interesting and important of all Ammon's visitors approached the oasis, the young Alexander the Great, who had just conquered Egypt. He could hardly conceal his impatience to come face to face with the god, and so, no sooner had the ground-plan of Alexandria

been approved by him and marked out by the architects, than
he set off for Paraetonium, and then struck inland to Siwa. So
great was his anxiety to see the god, and so undeniable the
wishes of the young master of the world, that the priests ex-
empted him from the period of probation usual before a man
was permitted to present himself to a god. Straight as he came
from the desert with the ten days' dust of his journey upon
him, he was led into the sanctuary while the members of his
entourage bathed and changed their clothes. And in the darkness of the sanctuary one of the most interesting of history's
unknown conversations took place: the conversation between
Alexander and Jupiter Ammon. All we know about it is that
the ram-headed god proclaimed Alexander to be his son, and
the recognition, preposterous as it may seem to the modern
mind, had an immense influence upon Alexander's life and
upon the future course of kingship. As every coin collector
knows, the beautiful silver tetradrachms of Alexander after
that date shows his handsome head crowned with a couple of
ram's horns that curve downward over his ears, evidently
a crown that he devised for himself to be worn on state occasions in memory of his divine parent.

Many of Alexander's biographers have been puzzled by the
visit of the hero to the god, and try to explain it rationally as
a cynical political act. It was the fiction in Egypt that the
pharaoh was a divine being, the son of the Sun God, Ammon,
and what more natural, they ask, than that Alexander, having
conquered Egypt, should wish to regularize his position in the
eyes of Egyptians by claiming the throne by divine right?
That, reasonable as it sounds, is not a satisfactory explanation. Alexander was not cynical: he was a lonely, romantic
young man who was, at the same time, intensely conscious
that he was an exceptional character. Furthermore, had he
wished only to gain priestly authority for the assumption of
the crown of Egypt he could have received it more easily at

the god's headquarters at Thebes, and have saved himself a long journey to a remote and outlandish sanctuary. Why, if he were anxious only to impress the Egyptians, did he not instantly publish the result of his interview as soon as he returned to Memphis, where an Egyptian audience would have been impressed by it? Why, too, if, as some argue, his visit was designed to impress the Greek world, which venerated the Oracle of Ammon so deeply, did he not send envoys posthaste to Athens to announce his divine parentage in the temple of Ammon, which had been established there only a year or so before his pilgrimage? Surely his silence in Egypt, as in Greece, proves that his visit was a private matter between the god and himself.

I find it easier to believe that Alexander really did believe that he was divine, a belief in conformity with the ideas of the age in which he lived. I find nothing extravagant in the thought that he went to Siwa with one desire in his mind, and one desire only: to hear from the lips of the god himself proof of his divine parentage. The clue to all this, in my opinion, is to be sought in the life and character of Alexander's mother, Olympias, a woman of a strange, passionate, and ecstatic nature. She was the daughter of the King of Epirus, in whose state was to be found the famous Oracle of Dodona. That shrine was linked by legend with Siwa, both having been founded, as one story has it, by two black doves which flew from Thebes in Egypt. Thus before Alexander was born there existed an association in his mother's mind between her native land and the far-off oasis in the Libyan Desert. The oracular influences of Dodona and Siwa were linked as closely as they could be.

Olympias was no stranger to the religious mysteries. She is said to have met Alexander's father, Philip of Macedon, at the secret rites of the Cabeiric Mysteries in Samothrace, and that rather weird and frightening woman, whom Philip soon

neglected for less puzzling companions, is believed to have
had a dream in which it was revealed to her that a god, and
not the earth-bound Philip, was the father of her mighty son.

Alexander never admired his father and grew up, as usually
is the way with such sons, with a passionate regard for his
mother; certainly he never showed the slightest interest in any
woman of his own age. His marriage to Roxana was entirely
political. Thus it would seem to me entirely reasonable to suppose that the mystery of Alexander's visit to Siwa is really the
simple story of a man, the son of a neurotic, imaginative
woman, who had been told since childhood that he was the
offspring of a god, a man who, living in a world where such
ideas were accepted, simply took the earliest possible opportunity of paying his "father" a visit.

After all, how entirely in character with Alexander's pre-
posterously romantic nature it was. We may recall how upon
one occasion, as his warships set out for Troy, he dramatized
the situation by standing in full armour beside the helmsman,
and, when the ship drew near, cast a shining spear towards the
empty shore as if the ghost of Achilles, his hero, had returned
to life. Then, again, he ran naked round the tomb of Achilles,
and carried with him into later battles a battered shield, which
those who knew his love of such antiquities told him was a
genuine relic of the siege of Troy.

The touch of poet and visionary in Alexander was his
mother's gift to him; and the blend of poet and soldier is always irresistible, even when a man is a poor poet and not a
very good soldier. But when the man is a world conqueror
and still a poet, still able to yearn for Humanity, as Alexander
did, the complexity of his nature, given full expression by unlimited power, shines god-like in success. If Alexander had
lived long enough to become an eccentric middle-aged man,
or a failure, perhaps we should think differently of him; for
it is probably true to say that only after failure do men dare

to pick such characters to pieces, analysing their component parts and finding the mixture a trifle ludicrous.

v

The sheik invited me to drink tea at his house. I have already said that drinking green tea is an inevitable act in Siwa, so I rose and followed him through the ruins into a palm grove.

His house was a short walk away, a large, square mud house from whose upper windows I caught a fleeting glance of sharp feminine eyes. We climbed a flight of mud stairs and emerged on a square roof exposed to the blaze of the sun. Several doors led from the roof to rooms built around it, and in one of them we found a table covered with food. There were English biscuits, sweet limes, pomegranates, bananas, plates of nuts, and a soft, delicious date called Shengbel, which must be eaten straight from the tree.

Two or three young men came in, the sons of the house, and after polite conversation, I was asked to help myself to dates and pomegranates, while the sheik performed the solemn rite of tea-making.

I watched his preparations with interest. It is a great compliment to be asked to pour, but it is not etiquette for a newcomer to accept; he must throw up his hands in feigned dismay and say that he is unworthy to do so. The man who makes the tea is called the "Sultan," and when Siwans gather together on social occasions, they elect one of their number to be the "Sultan" of the party.

The sheik first rinsed little glasses in boiling water from a kettle that stood on a brazier of charcoal. He then opened a chest that contained several compartments. One was full of green tea, one full of black tea, a third held soft sugar, and a fourth mint leaves.

He carefully and judiciously measured a small quantity
of green tea, added a pinch or two of black tea, and poured
a little boiling water into the pot. He smelt the aroma and
poured the whole brew away. His next attempt was more
successful. He added more boiling water and poured himself
a small quantity of the tea, which he sipped critically once or
twice. At the first sip he appeared doubtful, and I thought
he was going to pour it away again; but a second sip reassured him, and he handed me a little glass full of the scalding
liquid.

The ceremony was immediately repeated. A second glass
was given to me, and this time the tea was sweet with sugar.
When, with many compliments, I had drunk this, tea-making
took place for the third time. The third glass was sweet and
flavoured with mint.

It is etiquette always to drink at least three glasses. You
must never refuse. The Siwans believe that tea is good for
you, but should you feel ill after too much of it, they recom-
mend the eating of sweet limes.

A gilded scimitar, which King Fuad had presented to the
sheik, was produced for my admiration. I sat with it across
my knees and was given first a sweet lime and then a red
pomegranate, a fruit I cannot remember eating since I was
a child. It is a difficult and disappointing fruit. When you
open it, you might have opened a box of rubies, but the ulti-
mate result is a mouthful of pips and mildly scented water.

The sheik sat fanning away flies with a palm frond and
pressing upon me chocolate biscuits made in Reading, whose
appearance in Siwa struck me as one of the romances of
commerce.

Our conversation was so trivial that we might have been
a couple of visiting kings on some formal occasion. I did not

ask the questions about the oasis which I wanted to ask, and after a number of compliments I departed at the moment which was, I felt, indicated by etiquette.

VI

I looked out of the guest-house window one afternoon and saw a group of men putting up what I thought was a gibbet. They told me that, as I was departing in the morning, a dance had been arranged in my honour, and the gibbet was to hold an acetylene lamp.

About nine o'clock that night, with a moon silvering the palm groves and lying green over the desert, the sheiks and notables began to arrive on donkeys. I had sacked the guest-house for chairs, which I arranged in a row opposite the gibbet. The largest chair had been reserved for the Mamûr, and the three next best chairs for the doctor, the officer of the Camel Corps, and myself. On either side of us sat the sheiks and village notables.

I had already sent down to the village for a pound of tea, and by this time I knew too much about local custom to ask my cook to prepare it. When the sheiks had all gathered, I suggested that the time had come to elect a "sultan." There followed a ridiculous scene of social hypocrisy, first one sheik pretending to be unworthy of the honour, then another, and again a third, until finally it was necessary to lead the elected one—who happened to be the most important and would have been deeply insulted had he not been chosen—almost by force to the brazier. He wasted quite a lot of my pound of tea in concocting brews which he tasted and poured away, and I began to wonder if we should have enough to go round.

At last his palate was satisfied, and he produced a large tin pot full of bitter fluid which every one seemed to think the best cup of tea ever brewed in Siwa. Holding little glasses which I had borrowed from the police station, we sat in the moonlight waiting for the dancers to approach from the distant village.

Coming nearer across the stretch of sand we heard the beat of a tom-tom. Some one lit the acetylene lamp and it threw a circle of white light brighter than the moonlight.

As the dancers drew nearer, we could hear a flute as well as the tom-tom, and every now and then the dancers gave a wild cry, a rhythmic repetition of the same sentence, a wailing, plaintive sound which ceased as suddenly as it began. Into the circle of lamplight came a barbaric gathering escorted by a *gaffir* with a long whip and a policeman with a rifle across his shoulders, strange guardians for a dance party!

Before the Siwans dance, they drink deeply of *lubchi,* and it sounded to me as though the men and boys, for there were no women in the crowd, had worked themselves up into a state of suitable exhilaration. They advanced clapping their hands and gyrating as they surrounded the drummer and two flute players.

Seating itself on the ground, the band played a monotonous but attractive air. I wished I had enough musical talent to write it down. I believe the technical term for such music is "hot jazz." This, however, was several degrees hotter than anything I have ever heard, even in Harlem. It had the pathos and savagery of the Libyan Desert, and also a plaintive beauty, and a hunger which is the hunger and splendour of the desert.

At a certain point in the tune the whirling dancers sang the verse which we had heard as they were approaching over the sand. It was in the Siwan language, which the Egyptian doctor could not understand. I asked one of the sheiks to tell me what it meant.

"It is a love song," he said. "The dancers say that the beauty of the loved one is so great that their eyes do not close at night. . . ."

The dance itself was the most barbaric posturing that can be imagined. The men circled round the musicians, suddenly leaping in the air with wild cries, or revolving in a curious crouching attitude. There was also a bounding forward step, and now and again the whole horde of dancers, as if animated by the same insanity, crouched and took three forward leaps. It was done with a meticulous regard for rhythm, and none of the steps was essentially more ridiculous than the dance steps made popular in the last twenty years. During the War there was a step which consisted of three quick runs and a dip, that compares not unfavourably with the Siwan technique.

The dreary thing about this dancing, in London, as in Siwa, is its monotony. As the *lubchi* began to work, the dancers became absolutely tireless. I was told that they could keep it up all night.

I talked to the young doctor. He was an Egyptian who had spent many years in the desert and had come to Siwa from the oasis of Bahariya, where, he told me, the women dance instead of the men. They perform a peculiar and ancient dance. Standing with backs to their audience, they move only their hips in time to drums and flutes. The Bahariya women are kept in the strictest seclusion, except on dance nights.

"I remember," said the doctor, "that once I had to go to a sheik and tell him that unless his wife saw me she would probably die.

"'All right,' he replied. 'See her; but as soon as she is well again, I shall divorce her.' And he did so."

"What impression have you formed of these desert people?"

"They are —— primitive man. If an anthropologist wants to study primitive man, why should he dig up skulls that are thousands of years old when he can come out to the oases and study the living human being? Customs and beliefs going back beyond ancient Egypt into an unknown past have been handed down in these places, and every doctor is up against witchcraft in some guise or other."

There now arrived in the pool of lamplight a remarkably coy elderly woman. Her hair was dyed a bright auburn, her cheeks were rouged, and her hands were loaded with jewels. She wore a shapeless bunch of rather garish garments, and her feet were encased in delicate little heelless Arab boots of soft crimson leather.

"Who is she?" I whispered to the doctor.

"She is a dancer," he replied. "She came from Tripoli long ago, when she was so very beautiful that men contended for her charms."

As soon as she arrived, a rival dance ring was formed. Another drummer and flute-player appeared and squatted in the centre. After many coy preliminaries, the dancer glided into the circle with a queer, undulating movement and with a black veil completely hiding her face. As she had appeared unveiled, I was surprised.

"No woman must dance without a veil. It is the custom," explained the doctor.

I was hoping that the beauty from Tripoli would infuse a little charm into the proceedings, but her motions, which were just a rhythmic sideways movement of the hips, became as tedious as the movements of the rival dance ring. She kept this up for nearly an hour, after which a man leapt into the ring and danced with her. If the origin of dancing is, as some say, sex, then I saw one of the first of all dances.

I began to feel that the evening had outlived its first careless rapture, but the Siwans were as fresh as ever. The sandflies were now biting without mercy, and I suggested that perhaps the time had come to break up the party.

The policeman with the rifle and the man with the whip

instantly flung themselves into the dance, but the dancers declined to stop. They said that they would dance as long as the music went on playing. The band said that they would play as long as any one wanted to dance. I seemed to have heard such sentiments before, but far from those desert sands!

Eventually a happy compromise was reached. The band was persuaded to return, still playing, to the town. As they moved away, the dancers clustered round them like a swarm of bees about the queen.

The sound of the tom-tom and the monotonous chant faded in the distance: but all that night the tom-toms beat in Siwa, and only in the hours before the dawn did the dancers fall down exhausted.

VII

I was awakened at a quarter to five. The moon was still up and I could hear the servants packing in the courtyard below. Looking out of the window, I saw Siwa laying hushed in a wash of green light, the tracks running across the sand, the dark trees standing motionless, and the old village on its hill, silent and dark as a place of tombs.

We had managed to buy a couple of eggs the night before, and these came to the table in the light of a paraffin lamp. The moon was still shining, when we started at six o'clock, though the first hint of dawn was in the air. A bird flying near in the darkness uttered a sweet note, but though I looked everywhere, I could not see it. Some one said that it was the Haj Mawla, a bird known only in Siwa.

The patrol car roared off across the sand, and we followed into the silent, sleeping village. We stopped at the police station, where the driver of the patrol car had left his rifle. The Sudanese cook and the waiter sat crouched together in the patrol car, their heads swathed in white cloths like peo-

ple with toothache. Their dark faces peered out at the fretted
walls and the black shadows, and up to the old village which
lay massed in inky darkness, its turrets touched with green
moonlight; and they were strangely quiet. The driver came
down the steps of the police station carrying his rifle and
bandoleer. He slung the bandoleer across his shoulder, leaned
the rifle against his seat, and climbed up. The police sentry
sloped arms and wished us a good journey, and we sped off
into the white moon mountains. I looked back and saw Siwa
lying dark among its palm-trees, with the stars burning in a
sky that was growing lighter with approaching day. Then
for some time we went on through the pass with the moon
on our left and daylight coming in a pink pulsation on the
right. Soon all the east was throbbing in livid incandescence,
and when we reached the plateau we saw for one second a
burning rim rise over the desert's edge, then the sun was shining and the air grew warm.

All that day we journeyed to the north through the heart-
less land. We saw the sun cross the sky. We became tired, hot,
and thirsty. We saw the stars come out. In the first hour of
darkness a camel ran across our headlights and we knew that
we were nearing the end of the plateau and the long descent
to the sea at Mersa Matruh. Suddenly we looked down and
saw the lights of the town shining on the edge of the sea.

In the morning, while another dawn was rushing upward
from the east, I got into Mikhail's car and we drove along
the coast to Alexandria. The villages through which we passed
rose treeless on a brown plain, and sometimes we saw to our
left the blue line of the Mediterranean shining across a mile
of sand. We bought petrol in a village made of petrol tins and
inhabited by men who wore their *jurds* like Roman togas. The
man who lifted the cover of our radiator was draped like a

statue of Augustus.

As darkness was falling, we saw the lights of Alexandria covering the flat land for miles, and we were soon running through the confusion of its streets.

III

ALEXANDRIA

I

ALEXANDRIA was looking her best that night. Her pearl necklace of lights was reflected in still water, the air was warm, and palm-trees in the gardens rose in a windless silence.

The first act of the traveller who has come in from the desert is to call for a bath and a barber. My barber, it is perhaps unnecessary to say, was a Greek. Alexandria is still one of the largest Greek cities in the world, and if some one who had never seen Athens were taken there blindfold and told that he was in the capital of Greece, it might be some time before he discovered his mistake. Names are written above shops in what is more or less the alphabet which Plato knew. Greek newspapers are sold everywhere, and you can try to read them in Greek cafés while you sip a glass of *ouzo* or *retsinata*.

My Greek barber was a lively, bright-eyed man who professed an undying love for England. I positively blushed as I listened to the virtues which he attributed to us. There was nothing to be done, for a man armed with a razor is obviously a privileged conversationalist. He had at one time worked in the shop of a London hairdresser not far from Piccadilly, and the fact that I had sometimes had my hair cut there seemed, to him, to establish a unique bond of sympathy between us. He talked of "dear old London." He asked me whether I had ever used a special kind of hair lotion sold in that shop, and I said that I had done so. We agreed that the

47

price was fantastic. Suddenly, with a dramatic gesture, for the Greeks are among the most transpontine of people, he pulled open the door of a cabinet which revealed itself to be full of bottles.

"I have taken the recipe!" he cried proudly. "Here is the same mixture . . . exactly, sir! And—to you—three shillings!"

In every Greek I meet I seem to encounter some resemblance, though it may only be a distorted one, to the wily Ulysses: of course I bought a bottle, and, so far as I can tell, it is indeed the same mixture.

Later in the evening I was sitting in the lounge of the hotel when a young Englishman sat down at the next table. I had an idea that, like myself, he was a stranger in the country and we fell naturally into conversation. As he told me about himself, I marvelled at the queer jobs some men manage to find. He was employed by a firm of chocolate manufacturers, to discover what kind of chocolate the Egyptians like, and why they like it. This, I suppose, is scientific salesmanship. But as we sat in the lounge in Alexandria, it seemed sheer fantasy that this well-dressed, educated, and expensive young man should be going about asking the Orient if it preferred nut-milk or plain. He had just received a cable, which he showed me, asking him to discover why the products of a rival firm were selling so well in Baghdad.

"Do you really mean to tell me," I asked, "that you are going all the way to Baghdad to find out?"

"Oh, it's not so very far," he replied. "I shall fly there."

"And what will you do on your return?"

"I shall fly over to Cyprus," he replied.

There was something ambassadorial about him, and I thought him every bit as strange as any character in the *Arabian Nights*.

One of the notable things about Egypt is that Alexandria, having been a ruin from the Middle Ages until a century ago, has risen from its grave, not Arab, but almost European. It never belonged to Egypt. It has always been a piece of Europe grafted on to Africa. In the Hellenistic Age it belonged to Greece, and to a great extent, to the Jews; and to-day it belongs to the Levant.

The statement so frequently made that "there is nothing to see in Alexandria" is untrue. What memories crowd round the shores of the Eastern Harbour: memories of Alexander, of Ptolemy, of Caesar, Cleopatra, Antony; of the Seventy Rabbis translating the Septuagint; of St. Mark stepping ashore from his galley; of Bishop Alexander watching the young St. Athanasius playing at baptism on the edge of the sea.

Parts of Alexandria are beautiful, but it is a little difficult to understand why other parts should be so ugly. They might have passed unnoticed if my mind were not filled with a vision of the splendid city which has perished so completely. Alexandria is entirely satisfactory from a ship at sea, for then you might be looking at the marble city which Cleopatra knew. The pressed-concrete buildings and the buildings of stucco and plaster group themselves boldly, until it seems that the great Pharos is once again standing out to sea, that the Museum is rising in pale marble above the city, and the Canopic Way, pillared from end to end, still sweeps in white majesty from the Gate of the Sun to the Gate of the Moon.

I took a walk one morning to the Isle of Pharos, which is known nowadays as Kait Bey Fort. It stands on a rocky promontory which forms the northern arm of the Eastern Harbour, and is joined to the land by a narrow causeway.

Below the foundations of the Fifteenth Century fortress may still be seen what appears to be the remains of that wonder of the ancient world, the Pharos of Alexandria. The old fort is now uninhabited and ungarrisoned, and I walked through dusty cavernous rooms and peered through embrasures and descended stone stairways, all the time hearing the crash of waves on the north wall, which faces the sea.

The fort is built on solid rock, and some of the huge granite blocks, which lie in the sea round it, may have belonged to the older building. I believe there are many huge blocks of Aswân granite, which can be seen only from a boat.

When the Arabs conquered Egypt the Pharos was still in working order. It was said to be six hundred feet in height, which is nearly twice the height of St. Paul's in London, and it was a stone building formed of several towers, each one smaller than the one below. The first story was square, the second was possibly octagonal, and the lantern was circular.

The stones were held together with molten lead, which was a better preservative than cement against the assaults of the sea. There are said to have been three hundred rooms in the Pharos, and an inclined roadway led to the lower half of the building, up a slope so gradual that chariots could be driven along it. Donkeys laden with fuel were constantly ascending, and when they had dropped their loads, the wood was lifted to the top of the building by machinery.

Ancient writers say that ships could pick up the beam of the Pharos nineteen miles out at sea, but no one has ever been able to find out whether the ancient Greeks had discovered the use of the lens. The classical writers were so eager to admire the Pharos that they did not explain very clearly how it was constructed or how the light was worked. I suppose they thought that every one knew this, and they were perhaps unable to imagine a time when not one stone of it would be left upon another.

The Arab chroniclers write with maddening vagueness about a "great mirror" on the summit of the lighthouse, which could be turned to catch the sun's rays so as to burn ships at

sea. Another story says that when you looked through the
mirror it was possible to see ships as far off as Constantinople!
Putting these stories together, we seem to have a description
of a telescope and also a lens. The mirror was reported to
be made of "transparent stone," which must surely be a description of glass.

The end of the Pharos came about in this way. During the
Ninth Century a Christian spy was sent from Constantinople
to wreck the lighthouse because of its usefulness to Moslem
shipping. The envoy set about his task in a way which leaves
no doubt about his nationality: he was evidently a country-
man of Ulysses.

Insinuating himself into the confidence of the Caliph Al-
Walid, he whispered that a great treasure of gold was concealed beneath the lighthouse. There has never been a surer
way of wrecking a building in the East.

When the Arabs had almost demolished the Pharos, they
appear to have detected the hoax. They tried to rebuild it
in brick, but were unable to lift the great mirror back into
position. This precious relic, whose existence to-day would
have solved the mystery of the Pharos, fell from a height and
was shattered to pieces.

Although neglected for centuries, the remains of the Pharos
were still visible in 1375, and if an earthquake had not tumbled them into the sea, they might still be in existence to-day.

The Arabs called the Pharos *manar*—the place where fire
burns—a word that is related to the Hebrew *menorah,* the
place of light, which was the word used for the Seven-
branched Candlestick. The word *manar* passed from the Pharos into *manaret* or *minaret,* and was applied to the prayer
towers of the mosques. I have read somewhere that the Pharos
was, architectually, the parent of the minaret, but Dr. Cres-
well, the great authority on such matters, tells me that the
earliest known minaret was a tower in Damascus.

II

I met a man in Alexandria who believes that the body of Alexander the Great is still lying hidden beneath the city and may some day be discovered. That this surprising theory is not as fantastic as it may sound, is indicated by the interest taken in it by a man who knows everything there is to know about the archaeology of Alexandria, M. Breccia, once keeper of the Municipal Museum.

After Alexander's body had been brought from Babylon, it was laid to rest in a splendid tomb in Alexandria, where in the course of time all the Ptolemies, including the famous Cleopatra, were buried. Alexander's tomb was the central feature of that extraordinary collection of defunct royalty, and was evidently a place which was freely visible. He was buried "in the Macedonian fashion"; that is to say, his corpse was placed on a stone plinth like a bed and laid to rest in a room with an open door, which led to an apartment furnished with stone benches and a central altar, where members of the family would come from time to time to eat and make offerings, just as modern Moslems do to-day in the tombs outside Cairo. A number of Hellenistic tombs of this type have recently been unearthed at Chatby, near Alexandria, and they probably reproduce, though in a less splendid manner, the tomb of the great Conqueror.

Alexander's mummy was enclosed in a golden coffin in which it remained until Ptolemy IX had the gold melted down to pay his Syrian mercenaries. The mummy was then placed in a coffin of crystal in which it was to be seen when Strabo visited Alexandria in A.D. 24. The Roman emperors showed reverence for this tomb. Augustus paid it a pious visit and Caracalla left his mantle, his belt, and his jewels there as an offering, so even at that late period the body of Alexander must have been lying in its crystal coffin.

If the tomb were rifled during the revolutions and wars of the Third Century, or when Alexandria fell into ruin some time after the Arab Invasion, there is no record of it. And it is surely unlikely that a tomb venerated alike by Greeks, Romans, and Arabs, for Alexander figures as a hero in the Koran, could have been sacked in secret.

That the tomb was lost among the ruins of the royal palaces is evident from a remark in one of the homilies of St. John Chrysostom. "Tell me," he asks, "where the Sema (the tomb) of Alexander is?" It is clear that he is asking what he feels to be the impossible. So at the end of the Fourth Century the whereabouts of Alexander's burial-place had been forgotten.

Archaeologists believe that the place known to have been occupied by the Sema of Alexander is to-day an ancient mosque dedicated to a venerated saint said to be the Prophet Daniel. Those who support the theory that Alexander's body was never destroyed, but was merely lost, believe that Daniel is Alexander: "Everything goes to show that Alexander's Tomb was in the vicinity of the Mosque of Nebi Daniel, if not under the mosque itself," says M. Breccia. The theory is that the Arabs discovered an imposing tomb containing an unknown body, which, for want of a better name, they called Daniel, and they built a mosque over it.

The ground under the mosque has never been disturbed, and every time this has been suggested religious objections are put in the way. The idea that Daniel is Alexander is not a novel theory: it has apparently been in existence for centuries. When that delightful traveller, George Sandys, whose bones now lie in Boxley Church, near Maidstone, visited Alexandria in 1610, he was told of "a little Chappell within a tombe, much honoured and visited by the Mahometans, where they bestow their almes supposing his (Alexander's) body to lie in that place."

Seventy-eight years ago considerable impetus was given

to the story when a dragoman named Schilizzi, in the service of the Russian Consulate, claimed to have descended into the tomb chamber of the mosque. He said that in 1850 he had penetrated into the vaults below the mosque and had come to a wooden door with a hole in it. Looking through this hole, he saw a "human body whose head was crowned with a diadem," preserved in a cage made of glass. The figure was not lying down, but was, so far as he could make out in the dim light, sitting bent on what looked like a throne or elevation of some sort. A number of books and papyri were scattered about.

This story has always been regarded as a dragoman's tale, and no importance has ever been placed on it. Even though we may dismiss Schilizzi as a liar, we must admit that he was voicing the tradition of centuries.

When I went to visit this mosque, which stands near the tramlines running down the Sharia Nebi Daniel, I found the building closed on account of some feast day. It is an ordinary looking mosque with a minaret and several domes, as well as a pleasant little garden at the back where a few palmtrees are growing.

IV

CAIRO

I

I TOOK the morning train from Alexandria to Cairo. As it sped south on its three-hour journey, I sat at the window of a white Pullman car and looked out on Egypt.

I saw a land, flat and low-lying, stretching to the sky, emerald-coloured with crops of maize and sugar-cane, chocolate-coloured where the plough had turned it: a land steeped in sunshine. There were dense groves of date-palms, and banana plantations where the yellow fruit lay among leaves huge and tattered like the ears of green elephants.

Embankments rising twenty feet or so above the fields carried the varied traffic of the Delta: a slow-moving string of camels, arching their necks towards some neighbouring market, or donkeys trit-trotting in the dust, bearing upon their backs, with an air of blithe servitude, a more than full-sized human being. Sometimes brown girls passed by in single file with water-jars upon their heads, followed by a herd of goats in charge of a child, both girls and goats moving in a foot-high black powder which is the Eleventh Plague of Egypt—dust.

In the fields stood the *fellah*, who has probably changed less with the centuries than any character in Egypt. He stood bent above his hoe, the same kind of hoe which is to be seen in museums, labelled 3000 B.C., or he walked behind a plough drawn by two black oxen, or by an ox and a camel, a plough like those to be seen on the tomb paintings of the Old Empire.

All the way from Alexandria to Cairo I saw young men and old men, burned almost black by the sun's rays, sitting beside the irrigation canals, ceaselessly turning the handle of an object like a slender wooden barrel, which sucked up water from the canal and directed it to a higher level.

Those poor brown men were pumping life-blood into Egypt. Day after day, year after year, century after century, they have been at their monotonous task, moving water from here to there; and if they ceased to do so the land of Egypt would dry up and become a desert. The student of ancient things looks at those water turners with amazement, for the thing they are turning all over the Nile Delta to-day is the water-screw which the mathematician Archimedes invented over two hundred years before Christ.

The train passed village after village, many of them set with exquisite picturesqueness among groves of date-palms, or beside blue canals where high-masted *giyasât* lay at anchor with reefed sails, like butterflies with folded wings.

The houses in those villages were small brown boxes of two and three stories, built of mud. Unshaped palm trunks formed roofs and ceilings, and protruded from the walls. Elaborate pigeon houses were built on the flat roofs around which thousands of blue and white birds were in a constant flutter.

Brown children, turkeys, chickens, donkeys, camels, and water-buffaloes crowded the narrow, dusty space between the houses, while the women, quite aged at twenty-five and old at thirty, sat at their house doors, or beneath acacia and eucalyptus trees, pounding maize for bread or baking flat cakes in outdoor ovens.

Even during a short railway journey in Egypt you can understand the two main factors in the life of the people: the sun and the Nile. The Nile makes life possible in the narrow strip of green which is Egypt, and the sun pulls up the crops as if by magnet.

From the beginnings of civilization Egyptian agriculture has depended on the annual flooding of the Nile, and on the covering of fresh mud which the river brings down from the Abyssinian highlands and spreads over the valley. This mud raises the level of the land four inches a century, and the general level of the Nile Valley is to-day seven feet higher than it was in the time of Cleopatra, and from twenty to thirty feet higher than it was when the Pyramids were built.

Every year Nature carefully spreads a new carpet of mud on which the Egyptians grow crops, which in ancient times was chiefly corn. It was not until a century ago that cotton was introduced into Egypt, and with it came a great change in the system of irrigation. Nile water, instead of coming down only in flood-time, is now stored in dams and released as it is required, so that, in addition to the annual inundation, there is a controlled irrigation which has made it possible to grow two and three crops a year instead of one. And that is why, as you travel in Egypt, it often seems that the seasons are all mixed up in the space of a few acres. Here a field is brown from the plough, there it is green with growing crops, and next to it is field ripe for harvest.

The peaceful countryside gave place to the outskirts of Cairo, where only the eternal sunlight redeemed from squalor an incredible assortment of shacks and houses. Palm-trees and the minarets of mosques stood up above the low flat roof-line, and kites hung in mid-air watching the earth.

II

The plaintive whistle of the kite is one of the characteristic sounds of early morning in Cairo. Those big brown birds, which sometimes measure five feet from wing-tip to wing-tip, have scavenged the streets of Cairo for centuries. No one would kill a kite in Egypt. To do so would bring bad luck, and there is also a belief that if a kite haunts a certain balcony or window, it is a sign of death. Like the ibis and the cat in ancient Egypt, the kite is privileged and protected.

I stand on my balcony every morning to watch those birds. They have no fear of human beings, and many a time I have seen them swoop among a group of street cleaners and, without pausing in their flight, rise grasping in their claws some fragment of offal. They love to perch on high places such as the tops of flag-poles, where they look rather like eagles as they keep watch on the streets below.

Some people say that a kite will never attack a living animal, but friends in Cairo assure me that they have seen those birds rising in the air with rats and snakes in their claws. One friend tells me that a kite went off with a kitten from his balcony; another told me a story of an outdoor luncheon-party that was ruined by the arrival of a kite, which ascended taking with it the fish course!

Those birds, now so rare in England, were once common to all our cities. Visitors to London four centuries ago mention their whistling, and the way they swooped down on the street garbage. There is an old English proverb which says: "a carrion kite will never make a good hawk," which is equivalent to that eloquent maxim: "you can't make a silk purse out of a sow's ear," a belief seldom heard in these democratic days, when you have only to open the purse to see a hair or two.

As I stood on my balcony one morning, a kite illustrated a line of Shakspere for me. There is a portion of Shepheard's Hotel garden which is railed off as a drying-ground for table napkins and cloths. Some of these had fallen from the line, and upon them I saw a kite dive and, with his beautiful unchecked motion, which one never tires of watching, rise into the air grasping a napkin in his claws.

"When the kite builds, look to lesser linen," says Autolycus in *The Winter's Tale*—a puzzling warning until you see a kite fly off with a linen cloth to pack between the sticks of his nest.

Having breakfasted, how good it is to find the sun warm
on the hotel terrace. Open carriages are clip-clopping through
the streets. Schoolboys, European in appearance save for the
little red flower-pots of felt on their heads, walk sedately to
school with books under their arms.

The streets of modern Cairo are wide and spacious, and the
romantic Cairo which appealed so strongly to our grandfathers is rapidly vanishing. It still exists in a warren of narrow
streets always crammed with traffic, winding lanes crowded
with little shops, and in the bazaars, with their alluring reek
of musk and attar of roses, of incense and coffee, where you
can spend a whole day, if you like, in pleasant conversation
about a possible purchase and leave without buying anything.

Embedded in the acres of tiny booths are a series of magnificent buildings constructed of immense blocks of honey-
coloured stone, much of it stripped centuries ago from the
Pyramids. They are the mosques of Cairo, whose minarets
rise above the roofs of the surrounding buildings. The most
spectacular is the Mosque of Mohammed Ali, perched high
on the rock of the Citadel, its slender Turkish minarets poised
above the city like a dream of the Bosphorus.

West of the city runs the Nile, the life-giver, the very mother
of Egypt as the sun is the father, calm and blue in the heat of
afternoon. House-boats and Nile steamers are anchored to
the shore. Flotillas of *giyasât*, their slim masts towering to the
sky, their white sails reefed, lie together in midstream. Some
of them come slowly down the river loaded with cargoes of
sugar-cane, grain, rice, and cotton.

The crowds are as varied as the city. There is the modern
Cairene in a European suit, with a tarbush on his head. You
see him sitting at the pavement cafés, eagerly reading the
latest political sensation in the newspaper, for Egyptian politics proceed from crisis to crisis, while he drinks a little cup
of Turkish coffee and slowly lifts first one foot, then the other,

towards a kneeling bootblack.

Women of the rich classes, who only a few years ago used to drive about the streets attended by slaves, now drive their own cars and attend dance teas at Shepheard's Hotel. But in the poorer streets of Cairo the women still go veiled. You can see them coming in from the country or the suburbs, seated, five or six together, on a two-wheeled cart drawn by a donkey. Sometimes the cart is stopped before the medieval gate, the Bâb-el-Mitwalli, in order that a woman may descend and attach to the massive structure some fragment of rag, or a tooth. The whole gate is covered with such relics. They are tied there in order to gain the sympathy of a spirit which is believed to live behind the gate.

Only a short walk from regions which have not changed spiritually since the time of the Caliphs is another part of Cairo where motor cars, saxophones, the radio, the film, and other superficialities of modern life, are assessed at more than their true value.

III

I was in Egypt in 1923, which seems so long ago, when the mummy-chamber of the tomb of Tut-ankh-Amûn was opened. I was privileged to enter the tomb while the treasures were standing with the dust of three thousand years upon them. Those wonderful objects, to which a floor of the Cairo Museum is devoted, are now among the best-known antiquities in the world. Visitors go to the Museum as soon as they arrive in Cairo, and return saying that it was worth while having come to Egypt to see them.

I had my doubts. I was almost afraid to go there. Fifteen years ago I used to sit day after day in the sunlight outside the tomb, watching the treasures carried out to meet the sun after thirty centuries of darkness. How could they be wonderful to me now, in the glass cases of a museum, with people peering

at them while custodians sauntered about, gazing at their
watches, hoping it was nearly closing time?

However, I went to the Museum one morning, and, climbing a short flight of stairs, I came to the great floor which the
Museum has devoted to the treasure; and my first impression
was of gold. Gold shining, gold gleaming, gold almost rose-
red and dull, gold in solid masses, gold hammered paper-thin;
everywhere, as far as I could see right down to the end of the
sunlit corridor, gleamed the metal for whose sake men have
betrayed and enslaved their fellows since the world began.

As I looked in amazement—for the first impression of this
treasure is something almost impossible to convey to any one
who has not seen it—the uncompromising words of St. Paul
came into my mind:

"We brought nothing into this world, and it is certain we
can carry nothing out. . . ." This pharaoh tried hard to do so.

When I saw the inside of the tomb fifteen years ago, very
little had been touched. The treasures lay in confusion, some
on top of others, just as they had been piled up three thousand
years ago. And my most vivid memory is of two life-size,
black-faced statues of the dead man which stood guarding
the unbroken wall, as if saying: "Stop; go no farther!"

Those two figures, now in glass cases, are the first objects to
be seen in the Museum. They still guard the treasure as they
guarded it in the tomb for three thousand years, standing with
left foot advanced, a wand in the left hand and a gold mace
in the right. As I looked at them, I remembered all kinds of
little things: the feel of the shallow limestone steps leading
down into the tomb, the hot, stuffy air, and the indescribable
smell of age. Although their beauty and majesty remained,
the drama had gone from the two statues now that they were
in the Museum; and how impressive they once were, in the
dark of the tomb, among the tumbled vases and the chariot
wheels, defying men to desecrate the body of the king.

How well they have been cleaned and brightened. When I first saw them, the gold was tarnished and stained with streaks of red like dried blood, the result of standing in the hot air of that limestone vault while Athens rose, while Rome rose, while London rose, while Constantinople rose—a long time to stand on one spot.

And I remembered, too, that three thousand years ago some one had cast linen shawls around them, and this linen had turned dark brown after so many centuries in the tomb, and hung like cobwebs from their arms, the lightest touch sending it to dust. They wear no shawls now. They stride boldly forward, gazing, as the Sphinx gazes—as all Egyptian statues gaze—firmly, almost defiantly, into the eye of Eternity.

I moved from case to case, thrilled by what I saw in them. Even photographs in colour can give but a poor idea of the beauty and the delicacy of these objects. The skill of the artists, goldsmiths, silversmiths, and the workers in wood, ivory, and alabaster, who lived in Egypt three thousand years ago, has never been surpassed.

I saw a little loaf of bread which some one baked three thousand years ago to feed the Ka, or double, of the king; and it is still lying in the little form of palm fibres in which it went into the oven.

There are wreaths and bouquets of flowers which look like brown paper and are as brittle as sealing-wax. The mourners picked them one morning three thousand years ago in the gardens of Thebes, and carried them into the valley of death to cast on the king's coffin when at last the moment should come to leave him to the silence of centuries.

Scientists have examined those leaves and flowers. Some fell into dust when touched, but it was possible to find others strong enough to stand for a few hours in warm water. Some are cornflowers—which grow no longer in Egypt—some are olive-leaves, some the petals of the blue water-lily, some are leaves of wild celery, and some the berries of the woody-nightshade, or bitter-sweet. Those were the flowers cast on the coffin of Tut-ankh-Amûn so long ago; and they tell us that he was buried either in mid-March or in April.

There is a fascinating room reserved only for those objects which were found on, or about, the king's mummy. Here is to be seen the finest thing of all: the portrait of Tut-ankh-Amûn as he was at the time of his death, a wistful boy of eighteen. This mask was found in position over the head of the mummy. The face is of burnished gold, and the striped head-dress is of alternate bars of dark blue glass and gold. The two emblems of his Kingdom, the vulture and the cobra of Upper and Lower Egypt, both of solid gold, lie upon his forehead.

This is without doubt one of the great portraits of antiquity. I have been told by a man who has seen the uncovered face of the mummy that the mask is a superb portrait of the king. There is something ineffably sad and lonely about the face, as if the boy knew that he was fated to die before his time. He gazes at us across thirty centuries, a human being, and not a happy one, his eyes charged with the touching pathos of young manhood.

When they found Tut-ankh-Amûn each finger and toe was carefully cased in a separate little sheath of gold. They took these from him, and you can see them, curious little finger and toe stalls, lying together in a glass case. I cannot tell you why they look so pathetic. Surely enough has been taken from him. I wish they could have left him with ten gold fingers and ten gold toes.

IV

Were it possible to bring to life the mummy of an ancient Egyptian, one of the things which would surprise him about modern Egypt would be the absence of wild animals.

Centuries ago, as the pictures on the tombs and sculptures in the temples prove, Egypt was a country in which the hippopotamus, the crocodile, and the lion were frequently hunted. To-day those animals have deserted Egypt, although they are still found in the Sudan. This is probably because a greater area of land is now under cultivation, and also because the Nile in flood no longer creates every year new marshes in which such animals love to make their lairs.

The cat, which in Egypt kills snakes as well as rats and mice, occupies a curiously privileged position. No Egyptian would dream of killing a cat. He might refuse to pull a drowning cat out of water, for a Moslem cannot interfere with the decrees of Allah, but he would never throw it in. In the atmosphere of almost superstitious awe which surrounds cats, we may see no doubt a relic of the cat worship of ancient Egypt.

The cobra, which in ancient times was the symbol of royalty, is still found in town and country all over the Nile Valley. Although it is frequently killed—I have seen a policeman shoot one with his revolver—I have been told that in certain villages a cobra that takes up its abode in the cellar of a house is sometimes venerated as "the guardian of the hearth," and is fed on eggs and chickens. The peasant attributes extraordinary intelligence to the cobra. A country police officer, whom I met outside Cairo, told me a story which I do not believe— although I am sure he did—which illustrates the *fellah's* attitude to this snake.

He said that in a village in Upper Egypt, in which he was once stationed, two cobras hatched a family of young snakes in the cellar of a mud house. One day the children of the house discovered the little cobras lying in the sun and began to tease them with sticks. The female cobra appeared and coiled herself round the body of the youngest child, and the cries of the infant brought out the man and his wife.

The parents were terrified, but to have made one move against the cobra might have caused the death of the child. Suddenly the woman cried out:

"Perhaps if *our* children stop tormenting *her* children, she will go away!" The father ran over to his children and gave them a sound thrashing, whereupon the cobra quietly uncurled herself and went away. Such stories cannot fail to suggest that a reverence for the royal snake has come down to modern Egypt from ancient times.

One morning I went to the Cairo Zoo.

A taxi took me in about fifteen minutes to a beautiful garden on the west bank of the Nile. Among fifty-six acres of tropical vegetation, the animals are kept in open pens which reminded me of Regent's Park. The gardens were once the private property of an opulent pasha who, it is said, built the unnecessary suspension bridge over an artificial lake in answer to his wife, who once asked him what a suspension bridge looked like. It is fortunate that she never asked questions about Euston Station or the Arc de Triomphe.

What impressed me about Cairo's Zoo was that the animals were of a size, cheerfulness, and condition unknown to us in Europe. I have always thought the hippopotamus to be one of Nature's more sombre jokes, and I have often felt sorry for this lumbering creature with his vast jaw, his swollen body, and his small legs. As we in Europe know him, he is a sorry sight. In his native Africa, however, he is cheerful and full of surprising vitality. The hippo in the Cairo Zoo is a royal beast, mighty of muscle, with a wicked and roving little eye, and a pinkness under his skin.

Giraffes in Europe are poor, puny things compared with the huge animals in Cairo, whose hides are like spotted velour.

The ostriches in the Cairo Zoo are so much at home there that ostrich eggs are sold in the ticket-office. They cost £2 each.

The one tragedy of the Cairo Zoo is the polar bear. Although a sympathetic authority has arranged a perpetual cold shower in his cage, that poor creature suffers agonies from the heat and should not be in Africa at all. It is a mangy and pitiable object, pointing the moral which would, I suppose, defeat the first object of all zoological societies, that wild animals should not be shown out of their natural climates. I wish the miserable polar bear of Cairo could be exchanged for some unhappy hippo from Europe.

The visitors to the Cairo Zoo interested me. I saw Egyptian boys aged about ten dressed in European clothes with the exception of the little red tarbush on each small head. Those children were just as excited about an elephant ride as little boys are in Regent's Park.

Numerous country sheiks and peasant farmers were wandering round the Zoo, men who had obviously come up to Cairo from the country. They would not dream of going to look at the mummies in the museum, but were thrilled to see the crocodiles, the hippopotami, and the lions. When they came to some unfamiliar animal they would often smile with pleasure, and, as I watched them, I thought that people who love and understand animals often regard them with affectionate amusement.

The English are always doing so. The first books which our children read are animal fantasies like those by Beatrix Potter in which the humour of the animal characterization is always delightful because it is based on observation and understanding. I am sure that Mickey Mouse would have been popular in ancient Egypt, for the people who built the Pyramids are the only people of antiquity who saw the humour of animals and attributed human characteristics to them as we do.

Some of the most amusing tomb paintings of ancient Egypt are animal caricatures, one of which shows lions starting back in terror as a stately domestic cat walks across the road. Another shows a lion playing chess with a gazelle. Another shows a jackal who might have come from Harley Street paying a visit to a ludicrously sick hippopotamus, and a fourth shows a leopard playing a flute to a flock of geese.

Even if the tomb paintings of birds and animals were not so full of life and so obviously the result of loving observation, we should know that the ancient Egyptians were fond of animals simply on the evidence of these few charming little caricatures, the work of some far-off Beatrix Potter.

As I watched the modern Egyptians in the Cairo Zoo, it seemed to me that they were touching hands across long centuries with the people who once lived on the banks of the Nile.

V

INSIDE THE GREAT PYRAMID

I

HAVING fallen a victim to a sharp, painful illness well known as "Gippy tummy," I was sent by the doctor to recuperate at Giza. I have slept in many strange and interesting places in the course of a fairly varied life, but I shall always think of my room at Giza as one of the most remarkable. Lying in bed, I could see the Great Pyramid only about two minutes' walk away. Its colossal triangle exactly filled the space of my balcony.

At first it inspired me with awe, especially by moonlight. Then, becoming used to it, I would wish that it could move away a bit and give me a better view of the desert; and finally the sweat and blood of the unknown thousands who had slaved to build it, and the whistle of the lashes that drove them to their labour, began to haunt me; for the Pyramids are surely the monument of a vanity both cruel and futile. Even so, they did not do their job properly—which was to guard the body of the Pharaoh in death—because they were broken into and robbed thousands of years ago.

I was not allowed to go out for the first few mornings. Instead, I would get up and lie on the balcony until the sun became too hot, watching the curious daily routine of the Pyramids. The first thing that happens every morning is the arrival of police at seven a.m. Some march up to the Pyramids, others ride on smart little Arab horses; and they patrol the area until sunset, to see that nobody is robbed or pestered. There is little danger of robbery.

Then the guides assemble and with them come the little pestering boys, and the men who draw with an air of tremendous secrecy some incredible fake antiquity from their shabby robes; and they all go up the road and wait for the visitors.

Men appear from various points on the sandhills leading camels and donkeys and converge on the corral near the tram terminus. They, too, wait for the visitors. From eight o'clock onwards the visitors arrive. There are earnest Germans in sun glasses and pith helmets, French, and Egyptians, and English, who, to the annoyance of the camel and donkey men, sometimes insist on walking up the hill.

One morning an air of excitement was noticeable below the balcony. A great day had evidently dawned. More camels, more donkeys, more sand-carts than usual, emerged from the dunes to wait near the tram terminus; and at last a string of cars arrived from Cairo from which stepped about a hundred tourists, dressed as if for the exploration of Central Africa. Some wore jodhpur breeches and open-necked shirts, others wore field boots and breeches, with pith helmets and spine pads, and many were even more strangely clothed.

While the camels bubbled and groaned with hatred, and the donkey and sand-cart men screamed and waved their arms in the ordinary way of business, the weird cavalcade mounted and slowly wound its way up the hill. A liner was passing through the Suez Canal. Her passengers had seized the chance of landing at Suez and, rushing to Cairo and the Pyramids, returning in time to catch the ship in the evening at Port Said.

It is clear that the traditions of Nineteenth Century travel die hard. All those people were convinced that a visit to the Pyramids and the Sphinx involved moments of hardship, if not of physical danger. And, as I watched them going up the hill, I could tell how the ship's courtships were progressing from the way the young men tried to urge their cynical beasts within protective distance of the young women. More often

than not they were forced to cry from the humiliating distance
of ten yards:

"I say, Miss Robinson, are you all right?"

And the ship's funny man always turned round on his camel
and shouted with irritating inevitability to some member of
the rearguard:

"Come on, Steve!"

II

When I actually stood beneath the Pyramid of Kheops, it
looked even larger and more improbable than any work of
man's hands that I had ever seen. It was once sheeted from
top to bottom in the finest white limestone, smoothed after
the blocks had been placed in position, so that the immense
structure looked as if made of one solid slab of polished stone.
That was how the ancient world saw it, and the reason why
the Pyramid is now a series of steep stone steps, narrowing to
the summit, is because the Arabs stripped off the casing and
used the stone to build Cairo.

The entrance is about forty feet from the ground, on the
north side, and was made centuries ago by treasure-hunting
Arabs. When you walk round the Pyramid, you notice that
several attempts have been made to break a way in; but the
present entrance is the only successful one, because the Arabs
drove their tunnel immediately below the original entrance,
and joined their passage with the main corridor along which
the mummy of the Pharaoh had been dragged to the burial-
chamber.

This entrance is a big black hole in the hill of stone. I
climbed up to it over slabs of limestone, where one of the
Arab guardians took charge of me. I walked upright for a
few paces and then had to bend double and crawl for about
twenty yards. I did not expect to find that the Pyramid is
lit by electricity. When an Arab turned a switch, a row of

naked electric lights shone in the darkness. After twenty yards
the robbers' tunnel joins the main corridor which rises steeply
into the Pyramid, a narrow stone passage about thirty feet
high, looking like a shaft of a moving staircase in a tube station.

The electric lights illuminate limestone walls whose ma-
sonry is so perfect that it is difficult to find the joints in the
stones. Steps and a handrail have been fixed to one side. There
was a steep climb for another fifty yards, when once again I
had to crawl on hands and knees through a stone tunnel not
more than three and a half feet high. This led to a really astonishing sight—the room in the heart of the Pyramid where
Kheops was buried.

It was one of the most sinister apartments I have ever entered, a really horrible place, and I could well believe that
it might be haunted. The air was stale and hot, and the foul
reek of bats so strong that I kept glancing up, expecting to
see them hanging on the corners of the walls.

Although this room is a hundred and forty feet above the
level of the sunlit sandhills outside, it gives the impression of
being in the depths of the earth. The Arab, who had followed
me, suddenly switched off the light and said with a horrid
laugh:

"Dark—*very* dark!"

It was indeed the darkness of the grave, and joined to the
darkness was the silence of death. I have never known what
claustrophobia is, but as I thought of the way up to this completely enclosed prison I was conscious of a faint feeling of
panic.

The only object in the burial-chamber is a massive granite
coffin without lid or inscription. The Arab went over and
tapped it with his hand. It gave out a metallic, bell-like sound.
It was the sarcophagus in which the Pharaoh Kheops was
buried seven thousand years ago.

One of the remarkable things about the Pyramid, which very few people know, is that it was built round this coffin. When the structure had reached the height of the mummy-chamber, and while that apartment was still open to the sky, the coffin was brought in, and the top portion of the Pyramid was built over it.

Herodotus tells us that one hundred thousand men worked for three months every year, and that it took ten years to prepare the site and twenty years to build the Pyramid. How often, I wonder, during that time did the king visit the site to see how his tomb was getting on. He must have stood in this chamber when it was still open to the sun, with his coffin standing in the corner. He may have struck it with his hand to hear the sweet, bell-like note as the Arabs do to-day. He may have come again when the room was closed, dark, and ready. Then one day he came for the last time, with a gold mask on his face, to the straining of ropes and the chanting of priests.

In spite of the ingenuity of the architects, those narrow tunnels blocked with granite slabs after the funeral, and the single stone swinging on a pivot known only to the priests, robbers entered the tomb within two hundred years or so of Kheops' death.

We shall never know who levered the lid from the great stone coffin and stripped the Pharaoh of his gold, strewing his bones about the floor. But we know that centuries after his tomb had been desecrated, men continued to smite the Great Pyramid, unable to believe that it did not still contain riches. Persians, Romans, and Arabs attacked it with battering-rams; they tunnelled and they mined. When gunpowder was invented, they even tried to blow it up. Now and then some would enter its dark passages and creep along them with beating hearts. Instead of piles of gold, they came to an empty coffin and the twittering of bats.

VI

THE COPTS

THE history of Egypt is the story of a patient, docile race of red-brown men on the banks of a river who century after century have accepted new masters much as a man in the course of a long life might acquire a large number of different hats. The only thing that ever changes in Egypt is the ruling race: forty odd centuries of divine pharaohs; three centuries of synthetic Greek pharaohs; three centuries of Roman prefects; three centuries of Byzantine emperors; nearly nine centuries of Arab caliphs; over three centuries of Turkish sultans, then a brief period of British rule and now a dynasty of home-made monarchs. So the long procession of Egypt's masters winds its way down the ages.

While such changes have been going on at the top, the common people of Egypt, chained to the Nile as slaves to their galley, have continued to lift water with which to fertilize a few miles of desert on each bank of the long river, and have continued to plough the dark soil and to harvest the green crops. They are the same red-brown men, whether their master was a noble of 3000 B.C. in a pleated white robe or a man of A.D. 1900 with a pink face and an Oxford voice.

While the general background of the Egyptian's life remains the same to-day as it was when the Pyramids were built in the sense that his daily agricultural tasks remain the same, he has experienced two sharp mental, or spiritual, changes which have profoundly affected him: the first, the introduction of Christianity, which destroyed his old gods, and the second the introduction of Mohammedanism, which has obscured the fact that Egypt was once the most devout Christian

73

country in the world.

The death of the old gods of Egypt, the disintegration of the mighty priestly colleges and the crash of the vast temples that had been in existence for nearly fifty centuries, is by far the most interesting thing that ever occurred in that conservative land; and it came about slowly during the Roman period of mastership. From 332 B.C. to 30 B.C. when Cleopatra died, an ancient land had seen its historic capitals, Memphis and Thebes, fall into shadow while a blaze of light was focused upon its new capital, Alexandria, the New York of the Hellenistic World. How appropriate it was that the ancient Egyptians should have portrayed some of their deities as creatures with the bodies of men and the heads of animals; for that is a perfect symbol of Egypt when her native pharaohs ceased to rule her: a country which retained the same body upon which a strange head, or ruling class, was grafted that bore no real relationship to the body, and was indeed as strange as the head of the Ibex on the body of Thoth, or the head of the ram on the body of Amûn-Rē.

So, had we visited Alexandria in the Ptolemaic time, we should have found ourselves in a brilliant, rich, slick, busy, intellectual Hellenistic city, full of Greeks, Jews, and Levantines. But how easily the Nile would have taken us into an entirely different world: the mysterious native Egypt of the red-brown men, where sacred crocodiles were fed in temple ponds and where the old gods were still carried in procession by shaven priests round huge, painted halls. In that old world were large, impoverished estates whose Egyptian owners spoke, no doubt, of "the good old days" long ago when their families were related to the gods.

The Greeks were awed and mystified by the age and the weirdness of Egypt, and it was fashionable for rich tourists to leave the marble bathrooms of their Greek New York to sail up the Nile, to stand lost in wonder as they saw the deities of

the land through the smoke of sacrifices. The Greek pharaohs
supported the priesthood for their own political reasons, and
sponsored an archaeological and self-conscious revival of the
old religion, but the spirit of ancient Egypt was dying and
artificial respiration hardly postponed the end.

Unlike the Greeks, the Romans saw nothing in the local
deities of Egypt except an irritating source of riots and faction
fights, and it was their policy to persecute both the old religion and the new Christianity, which now began to take root
among the Greeks of Alexandria. The new faith spread slowly
up the Nile, among the native population, finding nothing but
rivals, dying of old age, that one vigorous belief sent crashing
from their plinths. It found also a people mentally prepared to
accept the new Greek faith, having been for centuries dream-
ing of the life hereafter. So temple by temple fell, and soon
small Christian churches were railed off in vast hypostyle
halls, while the Virgin Mary was revered in sanctuaries for-
merly dedicated to Bast and Amûn-Rē.

At first the Church of Egypt was Greek, and Greek was its
language. Then an inevitable change took place. As long as
the Egyptian had worshipped the old gods of Egypt, he had
lived in a different world from that of his Greek masters.
When both became Christians, they inhabited the same spiritual world, and the result was an intensely violent racial clash
and a demand from the Egyptians for a national church, not
a Greek one. The Church of Alexandria, ruled by a Greek
Patriarch, was at that time the second in authority to Rome,
and at one period her superior in intellect. Such names as St.
Clement of Alexandria, St. Athanasius, Origen, and St. Anthony, the founder of monasticism, give some indication of
Alexandria's contribution to Christianity during the first great
period of her Church.

But it was not possible for the Greeks and the Egyptians to
agree theologically. National and political riots and disturb-

ances, disguised as religious convictions, turned Alexandria into an intermittent battle-ground for centuries, and the end came in the Fifth Century when the two races parted company, the Egyptians to form their own national Egyptian Church, which exists to-day under the leadership of the Coptic Patriarch of Alexandria. From that moment the liturgy and the Gospels were translated into Egyptian, and to this we owe the fact—one of the greatest romances in the history of languages—that the Egyptian Church to-day celebrates the Korbân or Mass, in the language of the Pharaohs, or rather in that debased form that was spoken in the Fifth Century.

When the Moslems conquered Egypt in the Seventh Century and drove out the Greeks, the new Arab masters turned almost with affection to the native Egyptians, who, of course, were now a Christian race. They gave to them the name of Copt, an Arabic contraction of the Greek *Aegyptus,* and if we spelt it *Gypt* or *Gupt* we should be nearer the proper Arabic pronunciation of it. The Copts were as useful to the Arabs as the Christian Greeks to the Turks when Constantinople was captured. And the Arabs had the good sense to let the Christians run the country for them, build their mosques, add up their books, and make their jewellery. It was, however, not long before religious persecution crept into the relationship.

Copts were tortured and persecuted in every possible way. They would recover during a lull in the storm with extraordinary resilience, only to be flattened out by the next gale. Enormous numbers of them turned Moslem, but always a proportion was ready to suffer and die for the Faith. "The wonder is rather that any Copts at all kept faith during these hideous centuries," wrote Adrian Fortescue, the Catholic historian. "When the last day comes, weightier than their theological errors will count the glorious wounds they bore for Him under the blood-stained banner of Islam."

There are now about a million Copts among the fourteen

million inhabitants of Egypt, and they are the direct descendants of the race that built the Pyramids and the Sphinx. Those Christian Egyptians are outwardly indistinguishable from the Moslem Egyptians; both wear the same kind of clothes and speak Arabic. Now and then, however, one notices a small blue cross tattooed on a man's wrist, a sign that he is a Copt, and a custom that goes back to ancient times when small children were tattooed in that way so that they could never deny that they had been born Christians.

In the villages of Egypt, Copts and Moslems till the earth together with nothing to show which of them profess belief in Christ and which Mohammed, but in cities the Copts tend to become bank clerks, book-keepers, jewellers, merchants, and artificers, in which they probably show a resemblance to their remote forefathers of Ancient Egypt, who were also good at such tasks.

But it must not be thought that because an Egyptian is a Moslem and goes to the mosque he is of pure Arab ancestry, and that no trace of ancient Egyptian blood runs in his veins. The Arab Conquest of Egypt, like the Norman Conquest of England, was the work of a small military expedition that displaced only the upper classes. It left the red-brown men on the Nile banks, just as the Conqueror's invasion left the Anglo-Saxon at his plough. But when intense religious persecution of the Copts began in Egypt many thousands of Christians renounced Christ and, joining the Moslems, earned for themselves that unhappy and inaccurate designation—Arab.

It is intensely interesting for the traveller in Egypt, with such facts in his mind, to look for, and discover, among the modern Egyptians, Copts and Moslems alike, physical and mental resemblances to the ancient inhabitants of the land. While there may be a larger element of doubt about the ancestry of the Moslem, whose chances of inter-marriage have been enormously greater than that of the Christian Egyptian, who has kept himself to himself from motives of safety, there can be no doubt whatsoever that, in the Copt, we have one of the most interesting survivals the world can show of an ancient people.

It is strange indeed that so little has been written in English about the Copts and their religious observances. Separated from the rest of Christendom for fourteen centuries, and hidden away in their own misfortunes since the Arab Conquest, their one object has been to preserve and hand down intact their ancient religious life and customs. This causes them to be archaeologically the most interesting of all the Eastern churches. They observe to this day customs once common to the Universal Church, which now have died out everywhere except in Egypt. In many of these customs the beautiful voice of Primitive Christianity can be heard. If it should be said that the Copts are ignorant, and that some of them have no clear or elevated idea of the faith they profess, it should be remembered that they can boast as many martyrs as any community of their size in history.

Their virtues and their faults spring alike from the fact that for many centuries their whole energy has been spent in an effort to survive.

Until recently the Coptic Patriarch had to be chosen from the simple monks of the desert monasteries, a good rule in days when the monasteries were seats of learning. For many centuries, unfortunately, it has resulted in the elevation to the Chair of St. Mark of an ignorant and generally reluctant recluse. In 1928 the rule was cancelled, and bishops have now become eligible for the position of Patriarch. The head of the Coptic Church must be over fifty, must never have been married, and must abstain from meat and fish. He ordains the bishops, of whom there are seventeen, and consecrates the holy chrism, or sacred oil. The bishops are celibate, but the priests, who are drawn from the artisan class and are often uneducated, must be married before their ordination. The language of ancient Egypt, which is the liturgical language, is now dead, and few of the priests understand it. About thirty per cent of the Coptic vocabulary consists of Greek words which crept into the Egyptian language at the time when the native Christians embalmed it, so to speak, in their liturgy fourteen centuries ago. There are two reasons why this ancient language died. After the Arabs had conquered Egypt, Arabic became the spoken language of the country; also, the Church Coptic was the Alexandrian dialect, the Boheiric, which was not spoken by the country at large. Upper Egypt spoke the Sahidic, which differs from the official Church Coptic about as much as Cockney English differs from broad Glasgow. Therefore the last vestige of the old language of the Pharaohs died gradually as a spoken tongue, and it is difficult to say how much of the Boheiric Coptic spoken nowadays in the churches would be understood by a Fifth Century Egyptian of Alexandria.

Nevertheless, if any one should wish to hear the sound of the voice of Ancient Egypt, he has only to go down to Old Cairo any Sunday morning and attend the Korban at any of the furtive little Coptic churches that are hidden away in its narrow lanes.

VII

A COPTIC WEDDING

I HAD been invited to attend a Coptic wedding at night in a church in the Mouski. The Moslem driver did not know where it was and we were soon lost in narrow, crowded lanes, where the horse nosed his way over the shoulders of the crowd to an accompaniment of maniac cries and much whip-cracking. The Cairo cab-drivers use their whips, I am glad to say, not so much on their steeds as on their compatriots.

Once we had to stop, for the lane was so narrow, while a man moved from our path a bright rampart of the superb vegetables which the black soil of Egypt produces in profusion: majestic cauliflowers which would win a prize anywhere at home, leeks as thick as one's wrist, fat purple aubergines, and lizard-green cucumbers. Any one unfamiliar with the East might have expected murder at any moment, as greengrocer and driver flung themselves into an ecstasy of vituperation. Their faces became distorted with rage. They waved their arms, their indignant palms lay upward in the lamplight, their fingers outstretched, and at the precise moment when Englishmen would have knocked each other down the contest in abuse concluded and, with a smile which indicated that he had enjoyed it all very much, the greengrocer politely removed his cauliflowers. And we went on.

I enjoyed the feeling of gliding peacefully through dark canyons full of life. Each lighted booth was a vivid picture framed by darkness: in some, men sat cross-legged at coffee or commerce; in others, Syrians or Armenians sat like spiders in their webs in shops loaded with Persian rugs; and sometimes, when we came to a standstill and the faces seemed to

close in on me, I would see three or four black, veiled ghosts
gazing into the carriage, their dark eyes ringed with *kohl*,
placid and expressionless. We came to a corner where several
streets met. A minaret, rising from the deeper darkness below,
lay against the sky, washed in a green light of its own, and the
driver, pointing down a lane with his whip, told me that even
he could not venture there: it was filled from side to side with
cars, taxi-cabs, and *'arabîyât*.

The wedding guests were dodging round the bonnets of the
cars, making for the end of the lane, where a large crowd had
gathered outside the church door. They were waiting for the
bride. Facing each other in two lines from door to street stood
a choir of dark young men. They wore white gowns like night-
shirts, with stoles crossed on the left shoulder. On each head
was a stiff little cap of white with a silver cross on the top; in
each hand was a lighted candle. One man held cymbals, another held a triangle. As they stood in the darkness, the candle-
light moving over their dark, clean-shaven faces, I thought
that I might be looking at priests of Isis.

There was some commotion as a car ploughed its way
among the spectators, and from it stepped a girl like a dark,
full-blown peony. She wore an evening dress of cream-coloured lace. Her raven-black hair shone from recent treatment. Her plump, good-looking face was flushed beneath the
rouge that sits so feverishly on dark skins. Four bridesmaids,
likewise in evening dress, took their places beside her, whereupon the choir, suddenly breaking into a harsh chant punc-
tuated by a clash of cymbals, led the way into the church.

In the confusion of the arrival, I was aware only that we had
entered a hot, crowded place in which lights from pendulous
candelabra blazed everywhere. Presently a young usher took
me away from my modest seat at the back, and, to my confusion and embarrassment, gave me a seat among the officiat-
ing clergy. There was, however, nothing to be done about it.

The bride and bridegroom sat a few yards from me on red and gilt chairs placed before the haikal screen. The bridegroom sat at the bride's left hand, wearing an expression of self-consciousness which is probably an international one at such a moment in a man's life. Candles burned all round them, so that they sat in a pool of golden light. The bridegroom wore evening dress, over which was draped a richly decorated cope. He wore a tarbush on his head, and gazed uneasily through horn-rimmed glasses beyond the fence of candles.

Here, I thought, we have a typical Coptic mixture of past and present, of East and West. The choir was singing an anthem in the tongue of the Pharaohs, the bridegroom wore a head-dress which suggested Mohammedanism, with a cope that might have been worn by St. Athanasius, and the evening dress of modern civilization, with a pair of glasses that once suggested America. The bridesmaids, on the other hand, were as near Paris as they could be. And it was upon this fantasy in origins that the saints and fathers of the Egyptian Church gazed from their aged ikons through an ascending mist of incense.

Among the dignitaries with whom I sat were the Bishop of Tanta, the Bishop of Jerusalem, and the acting Bishop of Khartum. They wore black soutanes with silver pectoral crosses, and on their heads were the tight black turbans of the Coptic priesthood. The ceremony was a long and interesting one. The bishops rose one after the other to say prayers or to deliver long and powerful exhortations. A member of the laity read from the Scriptures in Arabic with considerable dramatic force; and I thought how strange it was to see a man in a tarbush reading lessons in a church. Between every prayer, and at the conclusion of the lessons, the choir, led by a young man who quietly beat time with one finger, plunged into long, harsh anthems. The sound of the triangle and the rhythmic beat of cymbals, which accompanied all the quicker anthems, lent an air of paganism to the scene. There were two choirmen in particular who might have come straight from a painting in any tomb of ancient Egypt. They had the same lips, noses, and almond eyes, and their hands, I noticed, were extraordinarily slender and well-shaped.

The bride was fanned throughout the ceremony by one of her maids. This bridesmaid was dark and slender, her face neat, round, and slightly negroid, with pouting lips, a type seen on the walls of certain 18th Dynasty Theban tombs. The dancers in the tomb of Nacht are of that type, and so are the women in the festive fresco in the British Museum, the one which depicts the full-face figures and the two naked girl tumblers. As this girl stood moving the ostrich feathers and gazing beyond the candle-light with dark, deer-like eyes, I thought that Charmian probably looked like that when she fanned her mistress in Alexandria.

To a solemn chanting, the bride and bridegroom were anointed with oil, and then came the culminating moment of the ceremony. Two golden crowns were produced and, as the bishop took them in his hands, he uttered the following prayer in Arabic:

"O God, the Holy One, who crownest Thy saints with unfading Crowns and has joined heavenly things and earthly things in unity, now also, O our Master, bless these Crowns which we have prepared for Thy servants; may they be to them a Crown of glory and honour. Amen. A Crown of blessing and salvation. Amen. A Crown of joy and gladness. Amen. A Crown of delight and pleasure. Amen. A Crown of virtue and righteousness. Amen. A Crown of wisdom and understanding. Amen. A Crown of strength and confirmation. Amen. Grant to Thy servants who shall wear them the Angel of Peace, and the bonds of love, save them from all shameful thoughts and base desires, and deliver them from all evil assaults and all temptations of the devil. Let Thy mercy be upon them, hear the voice of their prayer, let Thy fear fall upon their hearts, watch over their lives, that they may be without want until old age. Gladden them with the sight of sons and daughters and bring up those that shall be born to them as useful members of Thy one and only Holy Catholic Apostolic Church; and let them be established in the Orthodox faith to the end. Watch over them in the way of truth, according to the will of God."

Here he paused a moment and placed one crown over the tarbush of the groom and one on the dark hair of the bride, saying, as he did so:

"With glory and honour thou hast crowned them, O Lord; the Father blesses, the Son crowns, and the Spirit comes down upon them and perfects them. Worthy, worthy, worthy, place, O Lord upon thy servants a Crown of grace that shall not be overcome. Amen. A Crown of high and abundant glory. Amen. A Crown of good and invincible faith. Amen. And bless all their actions, for Thou art the giver of all good things, O Christ our God."

Two rings were brought tied together by a red ribbon. The bishop untied them and placed one on the finger of the groom and the other on that of the bride. He then pronounced a benediction and, drawing their heads close together, touched them with his hand-cross. A beautiful and ancient ceremony was over.

All the wedding guests now approached to congratulate the enthroned couple as they sat together in the yellow light like Pharaoh and his queen. The ostrich fan moved all the time over the bride's head, and the bridesmaids, in modern taffeta dance-frocks of mauve and yellow, rustled and whispered behind the throne, making large eyes at the court.

As we left the church we were each given a little present. It was hard and knobbly, and when I unwrapped mine in the hotel, I found a small gilt casket, velvet-lined, full of sugared almonds and silvered sweets.

It occurred to me that I had seen a faithful version of a marriage in primitive Christian times. Like all ceremonies of the Coptic Church, it had come down almost unchanged from the Graeco-Roman world, unvaried by the emendations, the omissions, and the alterations which Western churches have introduced into the ceremony.

All pagan and primitive Christian weddings were in two parts: the Betrothal and the Wedding. I had seen only the Wedding, or the second part, for the Betrothal had taken place weeks, perhaps months, before. This is a solemn business, as the attending priest reminds the contracting parties. The parents of the bride and bridegroom settle the bride's dowry, draw up a marriage contract, and choose the date of the wedding. That corresponds with ancient custom in Greece and Rome. The pagan and the early Christian bridegrooms all gave the bride an engagement ring at that stage of the proceedings. We have inherited our "ring finger" from the Romans, who wore an engagement ring on the fourth finger of the left hand because, as Gellius said, it is connected to the heart by a nerve. The solemn character of this contract, and a memory of its religious solemnity in Christian times, is still preserved in Coptic custom by the fact that it is the priest, and not the bridegroom, who hands the bride her engagement ring.

The marriage at night is an obvious survival of a custom which goes back into a remote past, for no marriages were celebrated by daylight in the ancient world. Again, the crowning of bride and bridegroom is another pagan custom adopted by the primitive Church, although only the Eastern Church still observes it: the wedding veil, which is Roman, was always more symbolically important in the West. As in ancient times, the Coptic Church regards the crowns as symbols of virtue and purity and, as in the earliest times, they are the property of the Church and are solemnly returned when a stated interval after the wedding has elapsed.

It is still the custom, though not among the modern members of Coptic communities in the cities, to take the bride from her own home to that of her husband by torchlight, attended by musicians, and a noisy crowd in which walks a man carrying a lighted candle in a bunch of flowers. This is an extraordinarily interesting survival of the pagan "marriage pomp" that was sometimes condemned by the early Christian Fathers because it tended to become riotous. In the lighted candle we can see, no doubt, the nuptial torch of the Roman wedding, which was lit by the bride's mother before the procession set forth on its way. St. Gregory of Nazienzus wrote a charming little letter in the Fourth Century, in which he excused himself from the gaiety of a wedding on the plea that a gouty old gentleman would be out of place among dancers, though in his heart he would be with them in their amusements. Therefore some of those routs, although high-spirited, were among the functions to which saints were sometimes invited, and it is indeed pleasant to think of the Early Fathers of the Church smiling benevolently on such celebrations.

The casket of sugared almonds was clearly a token from the ancient world, for it was the custom of Roman bridegrooms to cast nuts among the crowd as the procession passed through the streets, while in ancient Greece sweetmeats were thrown over the bride as she entered her new home. Therefore sugared almonds are a happy blend of Greek and Roman custom. It is obvious that our *confetti* and rice are a variation of this old custom, though real *confetti* is, as the name tells us, a sweetmeat.

All the venerable customs embalmed in the Coptic wedding have come from Hellenistic Alexandria in an unbroken chain of observance. But older than any of them is the scene at the bridegroom's door after the church ceremony, when the bride must not only witness the sacrifice of a calf but must step over its blood into her new home. That is neither Greek nor Roman; Christian nor Moslem: it is something that has come down to the Copts of to-day from their ancestors of Ancient Egypt.

VIII

THE MONASTERIES OF THE WADI NATRÛN

I

It was perhaps natural that the Egyptians, when converted to Christianity, should have taken an extreme and gloomy view of the faith. Although in pharaonic times they were a gay, laughter-loving people, who liked to feast and dance and play music, they were also a people whose thoughts were directed upon the tomb and upon the life of the soul in the hereafter.

By an entirely natural process of thought the Egyptian contribution to Christianity was monasticism, which in its earliest form was a selfish attempt to save the individual soul by self-denial and pain. The first Christian monks were Egyptians of the Fourth Century who turned their backs on life and went out into the desert to be alone with God, and to lead lonely lives of prayer and fasting. What made this movement so extraordinary was its national character. Within a generation the land was covered with hermit's cells and monasteries in which a large proportion of the population was segregated. Young and old, rich and poor, went out to seek a spiritual life. Sometimes whole towns, like Oxyrhynchus, were inhabited by monks and nuns. Everywhere up and down the Nile the temples of the old gods had been turned into monasteries. On the slopes of desolate and inaccessible mountains, and on flat wastes of burning sand, stood still more monasteries; and caves and tombs were tenanted by hermits, who gazed with fear and horror at the pictures which their ancestors had painted on the walls.

Towards the end of the century the Government was seriously embarrassed in its attempt to raise levies because so great a proportion of the young manhood of the country had embraced the monastic life and claimed to be exempt from military service. Indeed, the administrators of that day saw whole cities and districts pledged to celibacy, and must have feared the possibility that the race might end, extinguished by its own fear of the physical.

I think the influence of taxation, anarchy; and a good climate upon early monasticism might be a fruitful study, for it is obvious that such enormous numbers of people could not all have had a vocation for the solitary life, neither is it likely that they would have left their wives, families, and possessions unless life had little to offer them. Reading the history of the Fourth and Fifth Centuries, one sees a world tottering to its fall in anarchy, civil war, and barbarian invasion. Taxation was crushing, the tyranny of a swollen bureaucracy unendurable; the middle classes, overloaded with unpaid social services, were disintegrating; the upper classes had seen their fortunes go to a State whose demands were no longer satisfied by ordinary taxation; the small farms were breaking up; the labourers were flocking to the cities; the standards of art and morals were declining, and side by side with this picture of a society in its death throes was a vulgar display of wealth by the few in whose hands money had accumulated, vast public doles and festivals, huge building enterprises, which became bigger and more pointless the poorer became the State.

In the absence of firm authority, and the peace that goes with it, civilization could no longer flourish, and may it not therefore be possible that large numbers of people, finding no hope or security in the present world, were only too happy to turn their backs upon it and bend the whole force of their thought upon a world to come?

And what a remarkable turning away from life it was! As

we look at the deserts of Scetis and the Thebaid, we see a nation there in sackcloth and ashes. Half-naked hermits lift emaciated arms to God in the lonely places of the land. Thousands of men and women vowed to poverty and hardship live in caves and holes in the ground. It is a nation striving to stamp out the desires of the body in order that the soul may rise triumphant. Such was the Egypt of the Desert Fathers.

The ancient Egyptians believed, as the moderns do, that the desert was haunted by evil spirits and that was one of the reasons why the hermits went to live there: they deliberately entered Satan's country in order that they might pit the strength of their faith against the evil which they felt to exist all round them. It is wrong to believe that these men entered the desert to escape temptation. It was the exact opposite, for, to an Egyptian of that time, the desert contained infinitely greater temptation than a city, and, as the tempters were supernatural, they were more difficult to fight.

The hermit guarding his soul in the desert might not relax his vigilance for one instant, or the devils would be at him. He was on perpetual sentry duty, pacing the ramparts of his soul, ever on the watch for the enemy and for the spies of the enemy, for Satan was always sending out scouts. They came in disguise, sometimes even in the habit of holy men and speaking in a voice of hypocritical sanctity; therefore it behoved every hermit to look beyond the exterior and the fair face of words into the soul of things, if he would not be lured away. A dangerous adversary was Satan's daughter, in whose existence the early hermits firmly believed. She was a woman, more than presentable, who, like all the fiends of hell, had the freedom of the desert and would often be sent out by her parent when other more obvious troops had failed to carry an objective.

There was only one way to keep evil at bay: by unceasing prayer. All the fiends together, led by Satan himself, were powerless against the pure soul of a truly holy man. Thus the great hermits, though they were encompassed by clouds of devils, remained safe and secure in the strongholds of their sanctity. Every hermit was surrounded by a wall of prayer which grew higher and stronger with the years. Every day and night spent on the knees in communion with God added another stone to the protective rampart.

St. Anthony, the first of the hermits, though so mighty a man of prayer, was one of the most devil-pestered of them all. And that, of course, was natural, for the greater the man the greater Satan's triumph in his capture; the higher, the more impregnable the fortress of faith, the greater the satisfaction of the enemy in the fall of such a citadel of God. The name of Christ and the Sign of the Cross were two infallible protections against the attacks of devils. When St. Anthony saw them prowling round the ramparts, looking this way and that for a possible breach in the defences, he would often blow a puff of wind at them and make the Sign of the Cross, and, lo, they would vanish into thin air, although a moment before they had seemed solid creatures of the earth.

In order to become a monk, it was necessary to take nothing into the desert but love of God, humility, and a determination to stamp out every bodily desire. "As the body groweth the soul becometh weak; the more the body becometh emaciated the more the soul groweth," was a saying of Anba Daniel, and another holy man, Anba Poemen, use to say, "the Spirit of God never entereth into the house wherein there are delights and pleasures."

Dry bread, baked perhaps once in six months or a year, and softened in water before use, salt, and herbs, were the diet of a monk, but the more advanced ascetics did not eat every day. An ordinary monk would eat in the evening, but he would strive to subdue his appetite until he could go without food for two days, then perhaps for three days, and so forth, until eventually he would be able to fast without difficulty for a week. Some of the more severe Fathers considered that even dry bread inflamed the passions. Theodotus said, "Abstinence from bread quieteth the body of a monk." Others declined to touch herbs that had been cooked, and took as their ideal the saying, "Eat grass, wear grass, and sleep on grass," a maxim which some actually put into practice.

Silence was another rule of the monastic life. Arsenius said that even the twittering of a sparrow would prevent a monk from acquiring repose of heart, while the sound of wind in the reeds would make it absolutely impossible. A naturally talkative monk named Agathon only learned silence by holding a stone in his mouth for three years. Sleep had also to be conquered. Arsenius trained himself until one hour's sleep a night was enough for him. Anba Sisoes was in the habit of spending the night standing on the very edge of a precipice, so that one moment of unconsciousness would have hurled him to death.

Yet when the great Macarius visited a sick brother and asked what he wanted, and the brother replied, "I want some honey-cakes," Macarius, without a word, set out for Alexandria, sixty miles away, and procured them. Love and charity were as important as humility and endurance.

The childlike charm of desert life is beautifully illustrated by a story told by Rufinus in his *Historia Monachorum in Ægypto*. Two ancient hermits had lived peacefully together for years. "At last one of them said to the other, simply, 'Let us have a quarrel, as other men have.' And when the other answered that he did not know how to quarrel, the first replied, 'Look here, I will place this stone in the midst between you and me; I will say it is mine, and do you say that that is not true, but that it is yours—and in this manner we will make a quarrel.' And placing the stone in the midst, he said, 'This stone is mine!' And the other said, 'No, it is mine!' And the first said, 'It is not yours, but mine!' And the other said, 'If it be yours, then take it.' And, in short, they could by no means contrive to quarrel, being so accustomed to peace."

There are only seven monasteries in Egypt still inhabited by monks. Four of them are in the Wadi Natrûn, the famous holy district of Scetis; one is at Asyût; and two are in the Arabian desert, not far from the Red Sea, Dêr Anba Bula, the Monastery of St. Paul, and Dêr Anba Antonioûs, the Monastery of St. Anthony.

These monasteries have a history which links them with the Fourth Century, and they are the oldest Christian monasteries in the world. You may imagine with what keen interest I now found myself descending the sandy slopes of the Wadi Natrûn to find out what the modern monks of Egypt are like, how they live, and what resemblance, if any, they bear to their famous predecessors.

II

The desert slopes gradually to the natron lakes, where the red chimney of a chemical factory lifts itself in a great expanse of sand. A factory in the desert is an unusual sight. It looked to me rather like a prehistoric monster that had come to drink the turgid natron water; a creature that, aware of its vulnerability in open country, was lifting its tall red neck with a certain apprehension.

The factory workers live in a village near by, in which there is also a post of the Frontiers Administration. Hearing the sound of a car, the post, and that part of the village which was not at work, which included all the children and dogs, turned out to greet us. The captain of the post politely asked where I was going, and then offered to send the local sheik and a sergeant with me. The sheik was a middle-aged man with the moustache of a Guards sergeant-major. He had a heavy gold *egal* binding his *keffieh,* such as I have seen before only on the brows of Arabian royalty, and at his belt was a leather holster from which protruded the butt of a revolver. The sergeant was a six-foot Sudanese in khaki, who grasped a camel-whip.

These two climbed into a desert patrol wagon and led the way across the slopes of sand which rise into the bare fastness of the Desert of Scetis, a desert which stretches without a break westward to the boundary of Tripoli, and then, still westward, into the Sahara, with its three and a half million square miles of desolation.

As we mounted the sandhills, we saw three touches of white on the desert, about four miles away: one was standing by itself, and there were two close together. It was like sighting ships at sea, for there was nothing else to attract the eye. These were the walls of the desert monasteries. Stopping the patrol car, the sheik pointed towards them and told me their names. That to the right, standing by itself, was Dêr el-Baramûs; then, six miles to the left, Dêr Anba Bishôi and Dêr es-Syriani stood together, a mile of sand separating them. To which should we go first? I told him to go to Dêr el-Baramûs. But where was Dêr Macarius, the most famous monastery of them all? The sheik pointed to the left and said that it was twelve miles away, out of sight.

For a time we had all three monasteries in view, and I could see that they were built on the same plan. Each one lay within a high, rectangular wall, and each had only one gateway. There was absolutely nothing round them but the flat desert, stretching as far as the eye could see. No roads led to the gates, no wheel-tracks, no footprints of man or beast lay round them. A remarkable air of alertness was given to them by the absence of any kind of outbuildings. They were

MONASTERIES OF SŸRIANI AND BISHOI,
WADI NATRÛN

three white boxes on a brown table.

At first I saw only the walls shining against the sand, but as we approached Baramûs, squat white domes and the tops of buildings and a few palm-trees showed above the ramparts, for ramparts they were. Each monastery proclaimed itself a fortress built to endure siege and assault, and to their history is due their permanent air of watchfulness. The buildings fell back within the enclosure as we drew into the long shadow of the wall.

The sheik pulled a bell-rope that hung from the top of the wall. A faint tinkle sounded on the other side. But nothing happened. The monastery remained as silent as the tomb. An earthenware pot of water stood on a flat stone near the gate, and the sheik told me that it was the custom—"from old, old times"—for the monks to place water outside for travellers and Bedouin. Every monastery, he said, had its water-jar. Thus at the gates of my first monastery, in the last abode of the Desert Fathers, I encountered a relic of that charity and thoughtfulness for others which the hermits and monks prized so highly in their Golden Age.

I was impressed not only by the strength of the wall, but also by the vast archway which formed so strange a contrast to the gate itself. The archway was made for giants, but the gate for dwarfs. There was no need to ask the reason for this narrow postern: it spoke eloquently enough of desert raids.

At last we heard a voice, and, looking up, we saw a brown old man gazing down with a puzzled expression from the top of the wall. He wore a white skull-cap and a dusty black shirt. Did we want to come in? Who were we? He asked a lot of questions and at last said that he would come down and open the gate. Eventually we heard the noise of many keys turned, of many a bar shot back, and the tiny gate opened gingerly to reveal our ancient friend of the ramparts, holding three or four immense keys, one of them a wooden-toothed *dabba* about two feet in length.

Although I was impatient to see the inside of this queer place, I spent some moments examining the door. Never have I seen one so loaded with chains, bolts, locks, and wooden cross-bars. It looked as though the inventors of such things had been practising on it for the past ten centuries. As if this were not enough, the narrow passage behind the door could be filled with stones, thus sealing up the entrance to the monastery; and in that way the last glimmer of Christianity has been kept alive in the Desert of Scetis.

The old man led us towards a remarkable collection of buildings, shining with a blinding whiteness in the sunlight. Some were roofed with clusters of domes like white button mushrooms, and all were crowded together without apparent plan or method. There was a central square, an overgrown garden where palm-trees, and a few orange-trees in fruit, rose from a mass of shrubs and plants. We passed several cells. The door of one was open. A monk sat inside, cross-legged on a mat, busy with pen and parchment as he copied a liturgical book in Arabic. Like the old man, he wore a skull-cap and a black *gallabia*.

I was led towards the guest-house, a modern, half-French-looking house with a veranda on the upper story and wooden slatted shutters to all the windows. A number of monks, some of great age, emerged like blackbeetles from their cells to look at me. There was no question about their poverty and it was also evident that, like the first Desert Fathers, they scorned soap and water as a pandering to the flesh.

In the guest-house was a plainly furnished room upstairs where I was asked to sit. Divans ran round it. A photograph of the present patriarch, and of an equally bearded and ancient man who may have been his predecessor, hung framed on the walls. Curtains of some dark material were more or less attached to curtain poles, and it occurred to me how life-

less a room can become when it has never known a woman.
It is probably natural for a man to live in a cave, but not in a
room. As soon as he has a room, it demands a woman to choose
a colour for it and to keep it clean, and to see that all the
inanimate things, which obey women, such as rugs, carpets,
chairs, tables, and fabrics, keep their proper place. The curtains of this room, hanging so reluctantly, seemed to me a
pathetic perhaps distant memory of some monk's home in
Asyût; and I wondered if the Desert Fathers ever find themselves obliged to seek the advice of the youngest brother on
the correct method of hanging curtains and the right way
they should be looped back, as the one last in touch with the
lost world of womankind.

My reflections were interrupted by the entrance of a man
not much more than five feet in height, who wore a round
black turban, a black gown, and a pair of slippers. As he
came forward and shook hands, I knew that he was the abbot.
I suppose visitors to Dêr el-Baramûs in the course of a year
might be counted on the hands, yet the abbot greeted me as
if he had been expecting me, and asked no questions; which
is one of the ancient rules of courtesy. I could tell that he
wondered why I should have come, so I satisfied his curiosity
to the full. A brother entered with little cups full of scalding
hot tea.

When I visited the other monasteries in the days that
followed, I was to discover that I had been fortunate in my
first abbot. He was more alert and intellectual than most
Coptic dignitaries. He told me that there are thirty-five monks
now in the monastery and that the word Baramûs is an Arabic
corruption of Pa Romeos, the cell, or monastery, of the Romans. When I asked him who the Romans were, he told me
an interesting story.

About the year A.D. 380, two holy young brothers, famed
for the miracles they had worked, came from Palestine to live

in the Desert of Scetis. The monasteries were not yet built, but the desert was full of anchorites living in caves and in huts of reed and matting. The young men were St. Maximus and St. Domatius.

The two brothers were known to their fellow hermits as the "Young Strangers." St. Maximus "achieved perfection," but St. Domatius, though an exceedingly holy young man, was not quite . . . and here the abbot fluttered his hand up and down to indicate that the brother saint fell short of absolute perfection only by so much as a flutter.

Whether they were carried off by plague or by the severity of their austerities is unknown, but both young men died not long after their arrival, and "all the saints gathered to welcome them into heaven." Soon afterwards the hero of Scetis, the great St. Macarius, passed that way, and he told the monks to build a church in memory of the "Young Strangers" and call it Pa Romeos.

At my request the abbot first took me up to the sentry walk that runs round the wall on the inside. Here, forty feet or so above the sand, we looked out over miles of desert, and over the vaults and domes of the monastery buildings within the walls. All the monasteries of the Wadi Natrûn are essentially the same: fortified walls with one gate, and inside them churches, cells, a refectory, a bakehouse, a mill, various outbuildings, and, most prominent of all, a high square keep called a *kasr*, or fortress, standing by itself and provided with a wooden drawbridge. The monks would barricade themselves in these keeps if the monasteries were invaded, pulling up the drawbridge behind them.

I asked if he had any swords or muskets from the days of the Arab raids, and he was astonished to think that monks should fight with arms. For something like fifteen centuries, it appears, they have repelled their enemies with boiling water and stones. The last time this monastery was attacked by the

Bedouin was during the Eighteenth Century.

To look at these monasteries to-day, one naturally imagines them to have been organized Pakhomian monasteries from the start. But this was not so. In the Fourth Century Scetis was one of the most famous haunts of the cenobite, or individualistic, monk. Thousands of them lived alone, or grouped about a leader, in cells made of stone or of reeds, which were dotted all over the desert. Many are even said to have lived in caves, but they cannot have been really convincing caves in that flat desert.

Churches were built, which the monks attended on Sunday for Mass; after eating a common meal, they returned to their cells to work out their own plans of salvation. During raids by desert tribes in the Fifth Century, towers were built beside the churches—the predecessors of the modern *kasr*—to which the monks fled for safety in time of trouble.

The next stage in the development of the desert monastery, when the raids became continuous during the Ninth Century, was the building of fortified walls round churches and towers. At that period life was so dangerous for the monks that they retired inside the walls, and thus became enclosed communities by force of circumstance.

It took me some time to realize that the characteristics of the modern Coptic monk which offend the unsympathetic observer (the words "dirty," "lazy," and "useless" convey these characteristics) are really a direct survival of the cenobite attitude to life of eighteen centuries ago. The ideal of the modern Coptic monk, as of his predecessors of the Fourth Century, is still that of individual salvation. He is interested only in the preservation of his own soul. This will seem to many people a deplorable creed.

The very squalor which repels and revolts so many Western Christians is in itself entirely in accord with the teaching of the first hermits. When the godly matron, Melania, saw a young deacon, who afterwards became Bishop of Askelon, washing his hands and feet in an attempt to keep cool during the height of summer, she rebuked him with these words: "Believe me, O my son, for I am this day a woman sixty years old, from the time when I first took upon myself this garb water hath never touched more of my body than the tips of the fingers of my hands, and I have never washed my feet, or my face, or any one of my members. And although I have fallen into many sicknesses, and have been urged by the physicians, I have never consented nor submitted myself to the habit of applying water to any part of my body; and I have never lain upon a bed, and I have never gone on a journey to any place reclining on a cushioned litter."

The dirtier the body became, the cleaner, in the eyes of the hermits, became the soul. All the tortures endured by the hermits, Stylites on his pillar, Macarius bitten into an unrecognizable state by mosquitoes, and a hundred other self-inflicted pains and humiliations, were designed simply to degrade the body and elevate the soul. We in the West have long forgotten the ancient association between dirt and sanctity which can be dated to the age of the Desert Fathers, but it seems to me that the Coptic monasteries have still got this tradition of saintly dirt in the blood. Our maxim "cleanliness is next to godliness" would have sounded in the ears of St. Anthony with the ringing clarity of Satan's voice! Until we understand this, I think we are always in danger of saying unjust and cruel things about these Eastern monks. In all my contacts with them I tried to remember that I had no right to judge them by any standards known to the modern world.

The abbot took me down to a cool, dark church like a colossal tomb, standing in a confused huddle of buildings. It is dedicated to the Virgin Mary and stands on the site of a church built in the Fourth Century. Some parts of the building probably date from that church, although most of it is, I imagine, of the Eighth Century and later.

The light filtered through small windows high up near the wagon-vaulted roof. Everything was covered with an indescribable veil of age. It was grey with antiquity as a tree grows grey with lichen, and the old men who wandered in drifted about like ghosts. A great mound of corn was heaped to a height of six feet in the nave. The monastery receives corn and oil from Cairo, the product of the monastery property at Tanta, in the Delta.

The church was divided by the wooden screens common to all Coptic churches, and one end was occupied by the customary three altars. In a recess on the left I was shown the bodies of St. Maximus and St. Domatius, sewn up in leather bolsters, and also the relics of a saint with the strange name of "Moses the Robber."

Passing through a door at the end of the church, I entered the most venerable-looking room imaginable: it was lighted by openings in the bays of the vaulted roof, and a stone table over fifty feet long and four feet wide occupied the centre. A stone bench ran the length of the table and there was a stone lectern at the end of the room. This was the refectory. Plaster was peeling from the walls, dust and dirt had collected everywhere, and the table was piled with lumps of rock salt and a mass of round brown objects as hard as brick, which might have been bread.

When I asked if it was bread, the abbot took up a handful of the brown stones and pressed them on me, telling me to soak them in water as the monks did. That is how St. Anthony ate his bread sixteen centuries ago, and St. Athanasius, in mentioning this, explains that it was the Egyptian custom to bake at one time enough bread for a whole year. That the monks of Egypt should still eat this hard bread, and flavour it with rock salt, precisely as the first hermits did, is surely an astonishing piece of conservatism.

We next entered the *kasr*, crossing the drawbridge and climbing a massive stone staircase. The two floors of the tower are occupied by a number of vaulted chambers, most of them empty, some in pitch darkness, and many of them badly in need of repair. The most interesting is a chapel dedicated to Michael the Archangel, which, I was told, is a feature of all monastery keeps. On the roof of the keep is a small cell built about twenty years ago for the last of the hermits, a monk called Serabamum, a grand survival of the Egyptian name Serap-amûn. Like a true hermit, the monastery did not suit him and he lived in a cave about half an hour's walk away. He would arrive at the monastery for Easter Week or for Christmas, but his presence cannot have added to any gaiety which Coptic monks allow themselves at such times, for he refused to speak to any one or to inhabit any of the numerous vacant cells. Instead, he insisted on living on top of the tower. During one of his infrequent appearances a small pumping engine, which had been procured in a rare moment of enterprise, went wrong, and, to the astonishment of the community, he was the only person who knew how to put it right! Some of those present no doubt regarded this as a miracle. Having exhibited this unsuspected knowledge of the Twentieth Century, the hermit gathered his rags about him and disappeared with every appearance of relief into the Fourth Century. Whether they ever sent messengers to his cave from time to time, as to an electrician or a plumber, begging him to come and look at the engine, I was unable to discover.

The whole community accompanied me to the gate and waved me along the track to Bishôi and Syriani.[1]

---

[1] A full account of the other monasteries in the Wadi Natrûn is to be found in *Through Lands of the Bible*.

IX

LUXOR

I

A TRAIN of white sleeping-cars leaves Cairo every night to go south to Luxor and Aswân.

When I glance from this train in the early morning, I see that we are steadily pounding along an embankment high enough above the surrounding land to lift it clear of the Nile's inundation. The sun is up; the sky is blue; the villages are awake. Donkeys come along the embankments with a mincing quick-step, bearing on their backs shrouded and rotund forms. I see a fox stealing home to his lair at the corner of a patch of sugar-cane. Women in trailing robes stand at the wells, their water-pots held on head or shoulder; and among the palm-trees in the villages young and old sit warming themselves on the sunny sides of walls now streaked with the black, gigantic shadows of early morning.

No sooner does the warm light pour itself upon Egypt than the whole land begins to wheeze, protest, and whine with a hundred aged voices like the sighs and groans of overburdened men, for under tattered roofs of palm-matting oxen slowly revolve as they make a circular journey which must have known a beginning perhaps before the Pyramids were built, but seems to know no end. And as they travel thus, without a hope of arrival, the wheezing, whining wheels of the *sakiyeh* turn as slowly as the mills of God, and a number of poised water-jars discharge their minute contribution to the welfare of the land.

Some day a learned man, digging in the eloquent sands of

this ancient country, may come upon a carved stone bearing the design of the first *sakiyeh*, that most involved yet most simple of all man's inventions. With a gasp of delight he will discover in the neat language of hieroglyphs the name of the inventor—He-âth Rob-in-Son. For who can doubt but that the *sakiyeh*, like the water buffalo, is really a joke that has been taken seriously?

Men whose skins are the colour of mahogany and shine with a polished glow like Chippendale furniture, stand in mud trenches and pull down the slim, curved mast of the *shaduf;* dipping the bucket in blue water, they lift it dripping to the channel above. In a few hours' time, when the sun grows stronger, they will throw off their clothes and work like living statues of bronze.

Now and again, as the train presses southward, the Nile is seen hushed and windless in the golden morning, lying among the emerald embroidery of maize and sugar-cane like a broad ribbon of palest blue. Upon the western bank the Libyan Desert rears itself in wild hills, sometimes the colour of a lion's skin, sometimes the colour of an orange; and in the valleys between these hills, and in their clefts and corries, the light is mauve, deepening to the misty blue of lavender in bloom.

The Nile twists and turns through the green land, often losing itself for a mile or two in groves of palm-trees, then shining clear again, only to disappear into the green, its presence proclaimed by the tall sails of the *giyasât,* like the wings of white birds poised above the palm-trees.

And now a man passes down the train, knocking at the doors and crying "Luxor!" Tourists crowd to the windows, first at one side, then at the other, for they are nearing the great moment of travel in Egypt: Thebes, the Valley of the Tombs of the Kings, the Tomb of Tut-ankh-Amûn, the great Temple of Karnak.

I step from the train and select a smart little *'arabîa* drawn by two dapple-grey Arab ponies. We pass with a jingle of harness and a tinkle of bells through the streets of this growing town, dreary streets even in the eternal sunlight, and we come at last to one of the most exquisite places in the world—the banks of the Nile at Luxor.

There are two hotels on the bank, one hidden in a scented garden, the other on the river-side, like a ship in dock. A row of little shops faces the Nile: souvenir shops, shops full of fake antiques, English book-shops, and a pharmacy kept by a Scotsman who used to be a chemist in Chelsea.

I go to the big hotel on the river-front. From the balcony of my room I look down on the river, which is twice as wide as the Thames at Westminster, but so smooth that the ferryboat, which is crossing to the west bank, appears to be moving on a pale mirror.

The pink Libyan Hills shine against the sky on the other side of the river, their valleys and corries filled with blue shadows as if an artist, who had been painting the bluebells at Kew, had taken his brush and made a series of delicate little downward strokes on their tawny flanks.

It is that hour of the morning when the sound of Luxor is the prickle of water on tough leaves. I see gardeners directing hoses on exotic flowers that might be stamped from red velvet, on trailing banks of blue bougainvillaea, and on thousands of red and yellow rose-trees. If they stopped for a month, the garden would wilt and go back to desert. Rain does not fall sometimes for sixteen years at a time, yet the constant effort of the men who pour Nile water on the garden makes it one of the greenest places in Egypt. No rain for sixteen years! Can you imagine what the sun is like at Luxor; how it springs into a clear sky every morning, bringing long, golden hours, day after day, year after year, sinking to rest in the evening behind the Valley of the Dead, in a symphony of red, orange, lemon, and apple-green.

The certainty that to-morrow will be as lovely as to-day explains the sense of happiness and well-being which steals over a man in this place.

II

When I was at Luxor fourteen years ago, I used to step into a boat on the east bank of the Nile, sail across to the west bank, and, mounting a donkey, ride for an hour up into the Valley of the Kings to the tomb of Tut-ankh-Amûn. It is different now. The Nile has thrown up a sandy island between its banks, and you must leave your boat, walk across this island, and take a second boat to the west bank. And—what a change awaits you!

Instead of the donkeys and sand-carts, about twenty old Ford cars now stand with engines running, turned in the direction of the Valley. The drivers lean out of their seats and shout:

"You go to the Valley of the Kings, sir, jump in, sir, and on the way back I take you to the Ramesseum, or Dêr el-Bahari, as you wish! Jump in, sir, this is the best car!"

It is a pity that the donkeys have almost disappeared, because the slow ride into the Valley of the Dead, the gradual approach to that fiery cleft in the hills, every yard becoming more grim and more desolate, was, I think, a more fitting approach than the rush in a car over a bumpy road.

The Valley widens, the road ends, and the orange-yellow mountains become higher and rise more steeply on every side. Their lower slopes are covered with small limestone chips, the refuse flung out three thousand years ago, when the tombs were tunnelled. In the sunlight this limestone is as white as snow. Sixty-one tombs have been found, but only about seventeen are open to inspection. How many more remain to be discovered, no one can tell. Most of the existing tombs were

rifled in ancient times, and the only untouched royal burial
which has ever been found is the tomb of Tut-ankh-Amûn.

There is no sound in the valley but the insistent stutter of
a small petrol engine which makes electric light for the tombs.
Gaffirs paid by the Government, and armed with guns and
buck-shot, guard the tombs day and night. There is a certain
poetic justice in the fact that these guardians are descended
from the tomb-robbers who until recent times spent their lives
searching for mummies, ready to tear them limb from limb
for the gold which they hoped was concealed about them.

The entrances to the tombs are all the same: a flight of limestone steps leading down into the mountain, ending in a black
opening hewn in the face of the rock and protected by a grille
like the door to a deposit vault. One of the first tombs on the
right is that of the young Pharaoh Tut-ankh-Amûn, the small-
est and the plainest tomb in the Valley. That its position had
been forgotten when the architects tunnelled the later tomb
of Rameses VI, immediately above, is well known. Had the
workmen deviated only a yard or so in some places, they must
have broken down into the golden treasury which, all unknown to them, was lying below.

As I descended the sixteen shallow steps into this tomb, I
remembered the last time I had done so fourteen years ago,
when the burial-chambers were piled almost to the ceiling
with the treasures which are now in Cairo.

It was a queer experience to stand beside the two guardian
statues of the king and to know that when Alexander the
Great was born they had already been there for over a thousand years, grasping their thin wands of office, and that their
incredible vigil had lengthened to nearly two thousand years
by the time William the Conqueror set foot in England. The
awe which dawns in the mind at such a moment is partly due
to the feeling that Time, whose inexorable demands cease
not even when we sleep, had somehow spared that hidden

cave under the mountain. That the gold and the wood had not perished did not seem so wonderful to me as that wreaths of flowers, brown with age and tender as ash, had still retained their shape; and from these I turned to thoughts of the hands which had plucked the flowers and had cast them in the places where they still lay.

I remembered, too, how I had sat waiting on the wall outside and had heard, muffled by the rock, the sound of hammers and chisels breaking in upon the king's silence. Bit by bit the wall which separated the ante-chamber from the tomb-chamber was broken sufficiently for those who were watching to see, in the darkness beyond, the tall, gleaming tabernacle which rose over the nest of coffins in which the mummy of the king was found.

I stood again in the tomb of Tut-ankh-Amûn. By the pale radiance of an electric light I mounted a wooden platform and looked down into another chamber, where I saw a beautiful sarcophagus of red granite. Inside is a gold coffin shaped to the human figure, which encloses the badly preserved mummy of a youth of eighteen; for that was the age at which death overtook Tut-ankh-Amûn.

The gold face gazes calmly with open eyes towards the roof of the tomb. The king is portrayed wearing a close-fitting war-helmet of gold, with the symbols of his country, the Vulture and the Cobra, rising from his forehead. His gold hands are crossed on his breast; in the right he grasps the Flail, in the left the Crook, emblems of royalty. Tall figures painted on the wall show him, followed by his Ka, or spirit, embracing the mummied figure of Osiris, the God of the Dead.

In that silent tomb, where many thoughts crowd into the mind, one thought perhaps comes first: gladness that the discoverers have not taken away the mummy of the king to Cairo, but have left it in the tomb where it was placed over three thousand years ago.

III

I spent the morning descending into the tomb of pharaoh
after pharaoh. Painted corridors slope gently into the rock
so that the king's mummy could be dragged downward on a
sledge. The passages end in lofty halls whose walls, seen by
a dim light, are a theological tapestry of figures and scenes
still as bright as on the distant day when they were painted.
Ever downward the shafts lead, and into an ever stuffier
darkness until, at last, you stand perhaps five hundred feet
from the tomb entrance, in the burial-chamber of the pharaoh.

The floor is inches deep in black dust, and is scattered
with chips of stone. Some are fine white limestone, others
are red granite or alabaster; and they tell you that at some
time treasure-hunters smashed everything in their frenzy to
reach the gold. The electric light casts only a pale glow,
leaving the corners in shadow. It is switched on and off as
is required, and when it goes on suddenly, various dark
objects, like black rags attached to the ceiling, swiftly detach
themselves and go flapping noiselessly in the hot, still air.

The big bats in the tomb of Amenophis II, which filled me
with such repugnance fourteen years ago, are still performing
their *danse macabre* above the dead face of the king. He who
was once master of all this fair land now lies in the dark
hall, gazing up through a sheet of plate-glass at their flicker-
ing wings.

While I was exploring one of the royal tombs, the light
which fell from the shaft was obscured by the bodies of two
descending human beings, one an American and the other
his dragoman. When the American had mopped his brow and
removed his coat, he turned to me and said:

"How do you suppose they painted these pictures on the
walls? Had they gotten electric light, do you think?"

Many people have wondered how the artists painted such exquisite scenes deep down in the earth, without leaving behind a trace of lamp-smoke. I told him I had read that a smokeless oil was used, but there is another theory that sunlight was trained round corners into the darkness by means of a series of reflecting disks.

"And now, gentleman, if you please," chipped in his guide, "here is the Eye of Horus and over there you see the sacred ape. . . ."

I stayed just long enough to observe on the face of the visitor the bewildered but attentive expression which the features of Herodotus probably wore on such occasions; and, leaving him to follow the explanations of his guide as best he could, I climbed up into the sunlight. Hardly a day passes now on which you may not stand above a pharaoh's tomb and know that in the darkness below stands a perplexed Christian, an inaccurate Moslem, and all about them the confident theology of ancient Egypt.

I went on to El-Qurna and saw the Tombs of the Nobles. Instead of the puzzling and conventional glimpses into the Underworld, here are amusing and infinitely touching little pictures of real life. You can see people who lived in Egypt thirty centuries ago, dressed in their best clothes, seated at banquets, listening to music, watching dancers, fishing, hunting, gathering the harvest, and sitting together in affectionate happiness, with their families around them.

What a chill gulf separated the pharaoh from ordinary men. The convention that he was divine is nowhere more obvious than in the Valley of the Tombs of the Kings. He was not allowed to take with him into the other world any charming wall paintings of his past life. His wife could not sit beside him, hand in hand. No children were allowed to

play about the throne. The lovely days he had spent in his
garden, or boating on the palace lake, were not considered
fit subjects for his soul's comfort. He was obliged to walk, a
god among gods, his soul nourished by no memories of earth,
but by the grim comradeship of forbidding fellow-deities
who, having asked for his credentials like passport officials,
passed him onward to the chill realms of the Osirified. Even
home-sickness, so common with the ordinary soul, was denied
the pharaoh. A god was simply returning home, and could
not therefore retain any interest in his sojourn on earth. But
how different it was with common men. How clearly the walls
of ordinary tombs—those snapshot albums for the soul—express the belief that the lonely Ka would return many times
to dwell upon the days that were gone.

I think the most attractive couple in any of the tombs are
Ramose and his pretty little wife at Qurna. They sit together
at a feast. She places her left hand on his shoulder and grasps
his right arm in that affectionate and charming pose seen so
frequently in the marital couples of Ancient Egypt. He holds
a badge of his rank, a wooden baton, and they both gaze
sedately in front of them in the direction of their guests.

What a delightful pair they are, and what a model of con-
jugal companionship to have come down to us from 1300 B.C.
It is not until early Christian times that we are again privileged to see the lord and his lady sitting together in their hall
in dignity and in peace; each supreme in his and her own
sphere, as, no one can doubt, Ramose and his wife were in
theirs.

IV

When I came out of the tombs at Qurna, and before my
eyes had become used to the light, I was aware that people
were running towards me. One of the first to arrive thrust
something into my hand. I looked down and saw that I was

holding the hand of a mummy. I did not wonder to whom it had belonged, or whether it had once been a beautiful hand or an ugly one: I was anxious only to get rid of it. It was dry, black, and claw-like, and was even more hideous than it need have been by the loss of one finger.

The man to whom it belonged refused to take it back, believing that as long as I held it there was a chance that I might give him the shilling he was asking in preference to all the other things that old and young were thrusting on me. While I was wondering what to do, I saw a man who looked as old, as brown, as dried up, and as horrible as any mummy, coming slowly in my direction, leaning on a staff. Although his eyes were closed and he seemed to be blind, he found his way nimbly over the stone-scattered ground, and when he came near he cleared a way for himself by making savage swings with his staff at the legs of the crowd. Several children ran away howling, but I noticed that not one of those who received his blows showed any resentment, for such is the respect for age in the East.

The old man evidently had something important to say to me. When a few yards away, he slowly opened his eyes; and they were white. A desire to get away from this terrible old man came over me, but I waited to see what he wanted. Slowly he thrust his hand into the body of his shirt and drew forth a piece of coffin. It was horrible to see that old man, himself a walking mummy, trying to sell me a bit of coffin, and a nausea for this disgusting trade in tomb relics swept over me until I was ready to put distinguished archaeologists, and all others who have dug up Egypt's dead, on the same level with this dreadful apparition.

I looked down at the mummy's hand, which I was still holding, and decided to buy it for a shilling and bury it, or get rid of it somehow to put it out of its misery. My purchase seemed to astonish the crowd, and especially the man who had sold it, and they all disappeared shouting into the sand-hills, leaving only the terrible old man standing in a bewildered, half-witted way, holding a piece of yellow coffin wood.

I had no newspaper in which to wrap the mummy's hand, and when I tried to put it in my pocket its nails clawed at the edge of the cloth and refused to go in. I began to be sorry that I had bought it. To have buried it where I stood, or to have slipped it behind a rock, would have been futile, for it would have been re-discovered within a few hours and offered to some other visitor. There was nothing to do but to walk about hand in hand with it until I could find a safe place to bury it.

I had promised to take coffee with the sheik of Qurna, and while I did not relish the idea of appearing at the house of the most important man in the village holding this grisly relic, I thought it best to offer no explanations, but to behave as if I were in the habit of carrying such things about with me. The sheik led the way into a bare room on the ground floor of his house. It was teeming with animal life. A group of hens made way, rather resentfully I thought, in the passage; crickets were trilling somewhere in the mud walls; and a line of ants, like one's conception of a military expedition in Afghanistan, was proceeding along what was to them the mountainous inequality of the floor. In a corner of the palm trunks which served as rafters a swift had built a nest like a small yellow sponge. Every now and then he would fly into the room over our heads, flatten himself against the nest for a second, and curve out into the sunlight.

A barefoot boy entered with a tray of Turkish coffee, and while I was helping myself to a cup I thought I saw a movement in the corner, but I could not be sure. Looking again, I saw an extraordinary mouse. He was the size of an English rat, and his coat was of the pale fawn colour worn nowadays only by royal coachmen. His ears were large and almost round and all his characteristics were those familiar to admirers of

Mr. Walt Disney. I was astonished that a creature as large as a rat, and so nearly related to it, should have retained all its mousy charm. There was nothing sinister and rat-like about it. It came running merrily in as if on wheels, busily nosing here and there, looking round intelligently all the time, and then darting away again. The sheik saw my interest in this creature, but neither of us made any remark about it, just as we accepted in silence the mummy's hand, which lay between us on the divan.

While we sipped our coffee in the cool, dark room, I asked him if he had ever met 'Abd er-Rasûl Ahmad. He looked at me sharply, for I had plunged from the harmless triviality of polite conversation into reality. I had touched the deathless story of Qurna. He replied that he well remembered 'Abd er-Rasûl as a man of over ninety, and also the old man's mother, who used to walk about on two sticks until she died at the age of a hundred and ten years. This story of 'Abd er-Rasûl of Qurna is worth telling.

A little over sixty years ago a number of wonderful antiquities were sold quietly to tourists in Luxor. Many of them were objects associated with kings and queens of Egypt whose mummies had never been found. The authorities, scenting that a discovery of great importance had been made, set men to watch, and eventually an Arab family, whose ancestors had lived in an old tomb at Qurna since the Twelfth Century, came under suspicion. Arrests failed to drag the secret out of them, but, as usually happens in the East, some one made a clean breast of it; and so the whole story came out.

It appeared that one day in the summer of 1871, 'Abd er-Rasûl Ahmad, when climbing the hills behind Dêr el-Bahari, discovered a shaft which went down into the earth for forty feet. Having descended to the bottom, he saw that a tunnel, which proved to be two hundred and twenty

feet long, led from it into the mountain. He crawled along
and emerged in a rock-cut chamber. As the light of his torch
flickered over its contents, he caught his breath in astonishment, for he saw a scene which even he, the descendant of a
race of tomb-robbers, had not considered possible in his most
optimistic dreams. The cave was piled to the roof with coffins,
mummies, and funeral furniture, whose gold decoration glittered in the light which he held aloft. He did not know it
at the time, but he had stumbled by chance on a secret cache
in which the priests, in 966 B.C., had hidden about thirty royal
mummies to save them from the thieves who were always
robbing the tombs of Egypt even in ancient times.

His joy must have ended abruptly as he realized that, in
order to move the heavy sarcophagi and to prise open the
cartonnage cases, he would need help, and that meant admit-
ting others into his astounding secret. After thinking it over,
he confided in his son and his two brothers. Those four men
then began to visit the cave of treasures at dead of night,
rifling the mummies and removing the small and easily port-
able objects, which they unloaded gradually on the market.
Their fortunes grew, and it was necessary for them to observe
great self-control in order to prevent others from guessing that
they were sitting on the greatest gold-mine which it had ever
been the good fortune of tomb-robbers to discover. But such
treasures could not remain hidden. As soon as the purchasers
had shown them in Europe, their value and interest roused
such curiosity that it was only a question of time before the
secret of the cave was made known.

It was a bitter day for 'Abd er-Rasûl Ahmad when, having
made his confession, he was ordered to lead Emile Brugsch
Bey, of the Antiquities Service, to the cave.

"It is true that I was armed to the teeth, and my faithful
rifle, full of shells, hung over my shoulder," wrote M. Brugsch,
in describing his adventure, "but my assistant from Cairo,

Ahmed Effendi Kemal, was the only person with me whom
I could trust. Any one of the natives would have killed me
willingly, had we been alone, for every one of them knew
better than I did that I was about to deprive them of a great
source of revenue. But I exposed no sign of fear, and pro-
ceeded with the work. The well cleared out, I descended, and
began the explorations of the passage.

"Soon we came upon cases of porcelain funeral offerings,
metal and alabaster vessels, draperies and trinkets, until,
reaching the turn in the passage, a cluster of mummy cases
came into view in such number as to stagger me. Collecting
my senses, I made the best examination of them I could by
the light of my torch, and at once saw that they contained
the mummies of royal personages of both sexes; and yet that
was not all. Plunging on ahead of my guide, I came to the
chamber, and there, standing against the walls, or lying on
the floor, I found even a greater number of mummy cases of
stupendous size and weight. Their gold coverings and their
polished surfaces so plainly reflected my own excited visage
that it seemed as though I was looking into the faces of my
own ancestors."

Among the mummies discovered in this cache were those
of the most famous kings and queens of the New Empire:
Seqenen-Rē, Amenhotep I, Queen Nefertari, Thutmôsis II
and Thutmôsis III, Seti I, Rameses II (who was once identified as the Pharaoh of the Exodus), Rameses III, and many
others. It was a whole catacomb of ancient Egyptian royalty,
and nothing like it had ever before been known.

A special boat was sent from Cairo, and three hundred
Arabs laboured for six days, carrying the mummies of the
kings and queens aboard. As the boat sailed down the Nile
an extraordinary scene took place. The banks of the river
were lined by frantic crowds on both sides, from Luzor to
Quft, the women wailing, tearing their hair, and casting dust

on their faces, the men firing rifles into the air, in salute to
the dead pharaohs.

I learned from the sheik that 'Abd er-Rasûl Ahmad, like
many another who has presided for a while over unlimited
wealth, died in abject poverty, an old man of nearly a hundred. He was haunted for the rest of his life by the dream that
came true, only to vanish as his fingers were stretched out to
grasp it. He would never consent to approach the shaft after
the departure of the mummies, until, when ninety years of
age, a visiting archaeologist, Robert de Rustafjaell, persuaded
him to go there and be photographed at the entrance. But
when the old man reached the place, he was so overcome by
emotion that he fainted.

The sheik accompanied me in the polite Arab way to the
edge of his territory, and then left me to the heat that beat
upward from the rocks. As I passed down to the place where
I had left my hired Ford, a small group came racing towards
me with the usual collection of relics. It was led by an eager
child holding the hand of a mummy. I recoiled in horror
and passed on. A second group was waiting behind some
rocks. A young man ran up and drew from the pocket of
his *gallabia* another mummified hand. I waved the claw I
was carrying threateningly at him, but he followed, pestering
me, and I heard in the conversation of the crowd behind me
the words "Abu yadd." So they had given me a name. I was
"Father of the Hand." The news had gone round that at last
a man had come who was willing to pay good piastres for
the hands of mummies, and every person with such a relic
had produced it. There were many more, which I refused to
notice, as I strode indignantly to the car.

As I was stepping into the boat to cross the Nile, a youth
who had been sitting in the shade of a rush hut came racing
down to the water's edge, and, of course, I knew that he had
another hand for me. I left him standing on the sand, an

expression of bewildered disappointment upon his face, and, thrusting the mummy's hand into the folds of his garments, he walked slowly away.

With the feeling of futility which must occasionally come to all reformers, I managed to sink the hand in the depths of the Nile, in whose mud, I trust, it will find decent oblivion.

V

It is difficult to convey to any one who has not been there, the extraordinary beauty of the Nile at Luxor. The words "blue," "hot," "calm," and "yellow," no matter how you use them, do not really convey the true atmosphere of this place. By some fortunate accident of light and climate Luxor greets each sunrise with a hushed serenity which, although every morning is precisely the same as the one before, never becomes monotonous.

I would step out on my balcony in the early morning and find everything exactly as I knew it would be. The Nile, lying below, is untouched by any wind, and I can tell what time it is by the way the light is lying on the Libyan Hills opposite. The rising sun touches first the crests of the tall mountain behind the Valley of the Tombs, lighting its ridge in a slender bar of warm, pinkish light which, even as I look, begins to travel down the mountain as the sun mounts into the sky. This line of light pours downward over the hills, turning lower ridges and peaks from lifeless sulphur into glowing gold. Then a cascade of light pours itself over the trees in the garden like a warm shower; and I can feel it on my hands and face. A ship, with white sails lifted, moves slowly in a breeze that is just strong enough to fill the tall canvas without rippling the water; and it moves forward as if on blue oil, making a path in the smoothness and sending out two expanding lines on either side, which travel slowly to the banks. It is so still that I can hear an Arab boy singing far across the Nile in the sugar-cane near Qurna. I know that he is singing at the top of his voice, with his head flung back and his mouth wide open; but even so it is a long way for sound to travel. Hawks hang in the sky, hoopoes come and cock their heads, and bring their wives to look at me in the most impertinent way, and the old gardener walks out carrying a length of hose-pipe, which he directs at the flaming flowers and the burning earth.

In the evening, when the sun goes down behind the Libyan Hills, an enchanted hush repeats the spell of early morning. And there are evenings when the whole western sky turns to a sheet of orange flame shot with thin tongues of crimson, and behind the massed colour you can see the throbbing vitality of fire blazing in mid-air. The natives think nothing of these sunsets, indeed they hardly look at them, but a visitor arriving at Luxor in the middle of one might well fear that he had arrived during the opening moments of Judgment Day.

Minute by minute the fierceness of the colour fades from angry crimson into pink. Feathery wings of light ascend the sky like flocks of heavenly flamingos, and hang there glowing; then the fires fade in dull metallic bars of red and gold which lie upon a background of apple-green. There are perhaps ten minutes of stillness, in which, it seems, one should be able to hear the stars getting ready, and then darkness, like an overdue assassin, swoops down upon the world.

PALESTINE

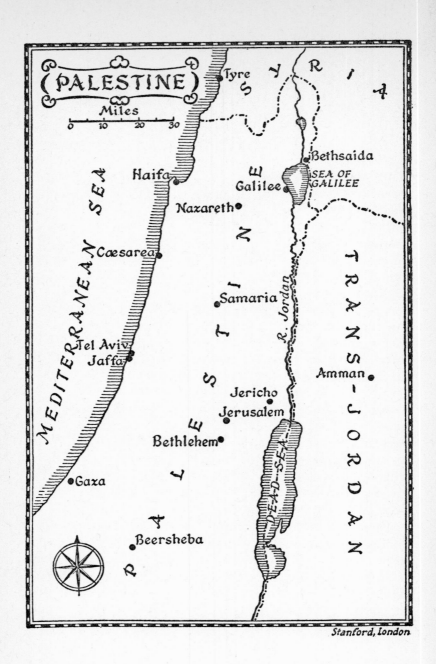

I

JERUSALEM

THE lanes of Jerusalem are striped like a tiger. You pass perpetually from strips of sunlight into bands of shadow. Some of the bazaars are vaulted. They exist in a stealthy twilight, the sun spurting down through cracks and holes in the roof as water spurts from a punctured water-skin. But most of them are open to the sky, the shadow of minaret, dome, and tower flinging darkness over the cobbles and the walls.

One could write a book about walls. There are walls in Andalusia, in the south of Spain, which seem built as a barrier against lovers. There are walls in Tuscany which have been erected to keep out the assassin: and there are walls in England, like the walls of Hampton Court Palace, which seem made to hide from common eyes the pleasures of the privileged. But the walls in the old city of Jerusalem are unlike any walls I know. They have a furtiveness born of fear and uncertainty. They are high and mildewed and sunk in age. The doors in them seem built for dwarfs, and if you ring a bell, or bang one of the rusty iron hammers, it is almost certain that a grid will shoot open and an aged eye will look out at you before the bolt is shot.

Centuries of suspicion and persecution, during which Christians, their armies disbanded and scattered, held their own by the feminine qualities of guile and diplomacy, have cast a virginal terror over the walls of Jerusalem, almost as though every ringer of the bell, or every knocker at the gate, might be a ravisher of altars. All the beauty is carefully hidden behind these walls. They seem, in fact, deliberately ugly, as

123

if to deceive the plunderer and, looking at them, one thinks
of those holy nuns who mutilated their faces and cut off their
noses in order to preserve their virtue when the barbarians
thundered down on the last of the Roman Empire.

Sometimes, when a postern gate is open, you see beyond
the stained wall to a cool, paved courtyard lined with the
stumps and pediments of old Roman columns. In the centre
of the courtyard there may be a lemon-tree, and beneath it
an old monk reading a book. Then the door closes; and you
wonder whether the brief glimpse of the peace on the other
side was true, or merely the vision of a sun-stricken brain.

As one plods over these narrow lanes in Jerusalem, the
confusion of centuries presses on the mind. There is an over-
powering solemnity in the memory of all the Jerusalems that
lie underfoot. The Jerusalem of the Gospels was itself rooted
in old bones. And the Jerusalems that have grown up and
have vanished since the time of Christ—the Roman city of
Hadrian, the early Christian city of Constantine, the Jerusalem of Omar, the Jerusalem of the Crusades, the Jerusalem
of Saladin, the Jerusalem of Sulieman and the many Turkish
Jerusalems—these, lying one upon another and thrusting
their relics through the soil, almost strike terror into the mind.
To walk through Jerusalem is to walk through history. Beneath one's feet and scattered around in every direction lie
the bones of the Past.

As I went on through the old city, I was conscious also of a
feeling of imprisonment. All the dark little lanes, the high,
blank walls, and the jumbled buildings erected to the glory
of God, are bound tightly together by a high city wall. The
wall of Jerusalem, her armour and shield in time of trouble,
exerts such a powerful influence on the mind that you are
sub-consciously aware of it every minute of the day. You are
either inside the wall, acutely aware of its encircling embrace,
or you are outside it, looking back at it, thinking that it clasps

the city in its brown stone arms as if trying to shield it from the modern world.

I came by way of narrow street and blank wall, by sunlight and by shadow, to the ancient Gate of St. Stephen. I saw, framed in the graceful Saracenic arch of its stones, a brilliant little picture of the world beyond the wall. I sighed with relief at the sight of so much air and openness, so much sky, and mountains with the sun over them. And the hill-side that rose up opposite was the Mount of Olives.

Climbing to the top of the hill I mounted to a dome near the Chapel of the Ascension, which now belongs to the Moslems. On the paved space round the dome an elderly little guide, wearing sun spectacles, a European suit, and a scarlet tarbush, was explaining Jerusalem to a crowd of English tourists, pointing here and there with an unrolled umbrella. I noticed that he talked to them about Jesus Christ as if he were a missionary explaining the rudimentary facts of Christianity to a crowd of rather feeble-minded Patagonians.

"You remember, please," he said, "that our Lord ascended into heaven."

Two or three of the tourists, who appeared to be worn-out with Scripture, turned away, while an elderly man, exactly like the caricature of a colonel in *Punch*, cleared his throat in an embarrassed way, as if it were not quite good form to mention such things in public.

"Well, please," continued the little guide, pointing with his umbrella, "the site of the Ascension is just there by the little round building, which we can enter in a moment. You will remember, please, that it was here that our Lord said good-bye to His disciples."

The group nodded. The little guide's high voice ploughed on through his deliberate recital:

"And He said, 'Go ye therefore, and teach all nations, baptizing them in the name of the Father, and of the Son, and of the Holy Ghost, teaching them to observe all things whatsoever I have commanded you: and lo, I am with you alway, even unto the end of the world.'"

There was silence for a few seconds. I like to think that all those people, who were touring Jerusalem as they would tour Cairo or Athens, felt, as I did, that a ridiculous situation had been lifted by those lovely, shining words into another world. "And lo, I am with you alway, even unto the end of the world." Even the little guide's high voice with its odd accent could not hurt those words. It seemed to me that something supremely beautiful had shone for a moment on all of us, and had gone. Then the colonel cleared his throat and asked his wife if she had remembered his sun glasses.

I came down from the Mount of Olives. The noonday sun burned above Jerusalem. I saw the city lying compactly within its wall, modern Jerusalem scattered round it in clumps of white stone buildings. And the colour of old Jerusalem is the colour of a lion-skin. There are tawny yellows and dark browns and pale golds. It must have looked like that when Jesus saw it in the time of Herod Antipas: a city like a lion crouched in the sun, watchful, vindictive, and ready to kill.

BRITISH WAR CEMETERY
OVERLOOKING JERUSALEM

II

THE CHURCH OF THE HOLY SEPULCHRE

THE afternoon sun was filling the courtyard of the Holy
Sepulchre when I made a second visit to that puzzling collection of churches.

It is, at first, difficult to understand its confusing topog-
raphy. It is, in essentials, a round church, with the tomb of
Christ in the centre of it. A large crusading choir leads from
it, round which cluster a series of chapels. Some distance
away, and fourteen feet higher than the rest of the church, is
a chapel built over the holy hill of Golgotha. There is another
church connected with, and behind, the choir, known as St.
Helena's Chapel, from which steps lead down into a rock
cistern where the mother of Constantine discovered the Cross.
But the two main sites on which the Church of the Holy
Sepulchre have been built are the hill of Golgotha, or Calvary,
and the garden tomb of St. Joseph of Arimathaea which was
"in the place where he was crucified."

The church gives one an overwhelming impression of
darkness and decay. There were passages so dark that I had
to strike matches to find my way. And the decay everywhere
of stone, of wood, and of iron was fantastic. I saw pictures
that were rotting on their canvases and I even saw canvases,
still framed, that were bleached white: the last fragments of
paint had peeled off, but they were still in position. There
were ominous cracks and fissures in stone and marble. I
thought how odd it is that extreme devotion can have exactly
the same effect as extreme neglect. The Church of the Holy
Sepulchre wears its air of shabby decay for the simple reason
that the rehanging of a picture, the repair of a stone, and

even the mending of a window, assume such gigantic importance in the eyes of the communities that they provoke a
situation capable of indefinite postponement.

What an incredible confusion of pillars and passages, of
underground caves and semi-underground tunnels, has descended to us over sixteen centuries of battle and burning!
It is an extraordinary muddle, and no one can understand
this church in one or two visits. It is a labyrinth of passages
and chapels embracing the three main shrines.

I ascended and descended steps and, led on by the light of
glimmering tapers, explored dark galleries and pitch-black
corridors. Once I was brought to a halt by kneeling Franciscans who were visiting the stations of the Cross, the light
from their tapers shining on devout bearded faces which
might have come from the walls of El Greco's house in Toledo.
The first impression of the church is of a series of treasure
caves. It is unlike the most ornate Roman Catholic church
in Italy or Spain. Its richness and flamboyance are those
of the Orient. It is as though the spoils of Asia Minor, of
Russia, and of Greece, accumulating for centuries, have been
heaped in candle-light on the overburdened altars. Art and
vulgarity stand side by side. A priceless chalice, the gift of
an emperor, stands next to something tawdry and tinselly that
might have been pulled from a Christmas tree. And hundreds
of ikons, glimmering in old gold, receive candle drippings on
the stiff Byzantine figures of saint and king.

The Greek monks swing their censers towards the blaze of
candle-light and the blue clouds of their incense spurt out to
hang about the ikons and the gilded screens. The worshippers, kneeling on the marble floors, seem to be prostrate before a series of exotic jewellers' shops. Only in the chapel of
the Franciscans is there that chastity of decoration which one
associates with a Western church. It is plain and rather chilly.
It strikes at once the note that divides the Western from the

Eastern Church in the Holy Land. Those who associate the
Church of Rome with outward gorgeousness of vestment and
ritual find in Jerusalem that the Latins are the staid and
dowdy "Protestants," in brown robes girded with a rope,
while the Greeks and the Armenians go garmented in scarlet
and gold, with crosses of crystal and precious stones carried
before them and incense in clouds about them.

Ascending a dim flight of steps, I found myself kneeling
on a marble floor with a crowd of hushed people, each one
of whom carried a lit candle. The person next to me sighed
as though his, or her, heart were breaking. I stole a look
and saw a black Nubian face, the white eyeballs shining in
the candle-light, but whether the person was man or woman
I could not tell because of the voluminous folds of drapery in
which he, or she, was concealed.

We knelt before an altar that shivered in yellow candle-
light and glittered with golden lamps and ikons. Divided
from this chapel by two pillars, was a similar chapel before
which the Franciscans were kneeling, the candle-light moving over their devout, uncomplicated faces. We formed two
congregations, kneeling together and facing the same way,
but worshipping before separate chapels.

This was the hill of the Crucifixion: Calvary, the holiest
place on earth. I looked round, hoping to be able to detect
some sign of its former aspect, but that has been obliterated
for ever beneath the suffocating trappings of piety. The
chapel before which I was kneeling was the Chapel of the
Raising of the Cross; the chapel next to it was the Chapel of
the Nailing to the Cross.

When the crowd thinned, I approached nearer to the altar.
There was a Greek priest there, watching the candles, snuffing
some and lighting others. He beckoned me to come near the
altar and pointed out a silver disk edged with candle-grease
and, below it, a hole in the rock in which, he whispered to

me, the Cross of our Lord was fixed. The pilgrims came up, weeping and praying, to touch the rock with trembling fingers; and I went away wishing that we might have known this place only in our hearts.

I followed a band of pilgrims down a fight of steps into the Church of the Holy Cross, which is also called the Church of St. Helena. More steps lead down to the grotto in which St. Helena, in the Fourth Century, is believed to have discovered the true Cross. This is the Chapel of the Finding of the Holy Cross, and its roof and sides are formed of the black unsmoothed rock.

I found myself, as every pilgrim does, drawn irresistibly back to the marble shrine in the centre of the round church. I sat in front of it for a long time, thinking how unworthy a shrine it is for the Tomb of Jesus. It was built by the Greeks in 1810 after the fire in the Church of the Holy Sepulchre, so that it is not even redeemed by antiquity.

And while I sat there the services of three different churches were in progress, all within earshot of each other. The Franciscans were holding a service in their chapel, and the Greeks, next door, so to speak, were intoning their long and unmusical prayers. Immediately behind the Tomb of Christ, where the Coptic Church has an altar, rose up a weird, raucous chanting. The sound of these three services, one in Latin, one in Greek, and the third in the ancient tongue of Egypt, mingled together round the Tomb of Christ.

One of the most difficult things for the average visitor from the West to appreciate, and some never attempt to do so, is the divided ownership of the Holy Sepulchre. The shrines within the church are split up between six churches: the Eastern Orthodox Church, the Armenian Church, the Coptic Church, the Syrian Church, and the Abyssinian Church.

The Western Church is represented by the Latins, who have entrusted the custody of the Holy Places to the Franciscans since the Crusades. The head of the Franciscans in the Holy Land is known as the "Custos"—the Father Custodian.

The divided ownership began to take shape after Saladin broke up the Christian Kingdom of Jerusalem in 1187. The Crusades were Western Christianity's bid for the ownership of the holy sites in Palestine, and, during the eighty-eight years of the Christian rule which was established by the swords of the Crusaders, the Western Church controlled the Holy Sepulchre. After the Moslem conquest, however, the Eastern Churches found it possible to enter into possession by payment of rent to the infidel; so they took over as tenants what the Crusaders had won at the point of the sword.

The fluctuating fortunes of the various communities within the Church of the Holy Sepulchre would make a large and fascinating book. Every inch of the holy space is engraved on a map of tradition. The frontier between the property of the Franciscans and the Greeks is as real as the frontier between Austria and Italy, and the space on which the Copts, the Syrians, and the Armenians may tread in the course of their daily offices has been laid down by centuries of tradition.

The Tomb of our Lord and the rotunda in which it stands are the common property of all the churches. They have certain established rights to hold processions there, or to celebrate mass on stated occasions. The choir of the Crusaders, leading from the Rotunda, belongs to the Greeks, while in the corresponding sanctuary to the north, the Chapel of the Apparition of Jesus to His Mother, the Franciscans have their choir. The Copts, as I have said, have a little chapel built on to the end of the holy Tomb itself. The Syrians have a pitch-dark chapel devoid of all decoration, which leads off from the central Rotunda and is entered by a low stone door like the entrance to a dungeon. The church of St. Helena and the Chapel of the Parting of the Raiment belong to the Armenians. Golgotha is divided between Latins and Greeks; one chapel, that of the Raising of the Cross, is Greek, and the adjacent chapel, that of the Nailing to the Cross, and also the altar of the Stabat Mater—the place on which the Blessed Virgin received into her arms the lifeless body of Jesus—belong to the Latins.

One could go on enumerating many other chapels and holy places, but I have named the most sacred. The Abyssinian Church, which in the Sixteenth Century possessed a valuable foothold within the church, has been gradually dislodged, until to-day the colony of dark-skinned monks has taken refuge on the roof, where, round the dome of St. Helena's Chapel, they have built their huts.

Other sects and churches have in the course of their history been obliged to give up their hold on sites within the Holy Sepulchre, such as the Georgians, who were forced to retire in 1644 because, owing to national misfortunes, they were unable to pay the exorbitant dues of the Turkish Government.

When people hold up to scorn the occasional squabbles that break out between the various communities in the Holy Sepulchre, they forget, or are unaware of, the extreme delicacy of the position. Such squabbles are undignified and regrettable, but human nature being as it is, they are understandable.

For instance, every inch of the territory is, as I have said, clearly marked out, and the boundaries, although invisible to the eye, are as clear in the eye of tradition as though they were outlined in electric light. But certain territories contain shrines that are common property, and the various sects have the right to light a lamp over them on specified occasions. In order to do this it is necessary for them to make a privileged

invasion of neighbouring church property. This is the time of
danger. When the Copts have the right to make a procession
through Greek or Armenian territory, or vice versa, the weakness of the flesh is sometimes too strong to be endured!

The late Bishop Gore was once shown round Jerusalem by
a friend of mine, who asked what he thought Jesus would say
about the sectarian disputes round His tomb.

"I believe He would say, with that wonderful smile of His,"
said the bishop, " 'My children must have toys. Do not all
children sometimes quarrel about their toys?' "

III

THE TOMB OF CHRIST

The Tomb of Jesus Christ is a small cell lined with marble, six and a half feet long, and six feet wide. Only two or, at the most, three people can enter at one time. On the right hand is a cracked slab of white marble, three feet in height, covering the rock on which He was placed after the Crucifixion.

From the marble roof of this tiny cell hang lamps which belong in various proportions to the Greek, Latin, Armenian, and Coptic Churches. The Roman Catholics are known in Palestine as the Latins. Standing at the head of the marble slab was an impassive Greek monk with a soft, spade-shaped black beard. He wore a black cassock and a high, black, rimless hat, beneath which his hair was pinned at the back in a round bun. He held a bunch of candles in his hand and, as the pilgrims entered, gave one to them, which they lit from others burning in the tomb.

I could see a pilgrim kneeling at the sepulchre, so I waited in the small, dark ante-chamber outside.

Becoming impatient, I bent down and, peeping through the low entrance, saw that the man inside was an old, bent peasant in ragged clothes, his feet in a pair of huge shoes made of felt. He was a Bulgarian who had come over in a pilgrim ship, as the Russians used to come, and he had probably been saving up all his life for that moment.

He was kneeling at the marble slab and kissing it repeatedly, while tears ran down the deep wrinkles of his face and fell on the stone. His large, rough hands, the nails split and

black with labour, touched the marble gently with a smooth-
ing motion; then he would clasp them in prayer and cross
himself.

He prayed aloud in a trembling voice, but I could not
understand what he was saying. Then, taking from his pocket
various pieces of dirty paper and a length of ribbon, he
rubbed them gently on the Tomb and put them back in his
pocket.

I thought there might perhaps be room for me, so I bent
my head and entered the Sepulchre. The Greek monk, the
kneeling peasant and myself quite filled the small space. And
it would have been all right if the old man had continued to
kneel, but, disturbed perhaps by my entrance, he rose up,
the tears still falling, and whispered something to me. We
were now standing, our chests touching, and, looking into his
eyes, I realized that I was looking at real happiness.

This was his life's dream. I had never seen such happiness
before. Never in all my life have I beheld peace and contentment written so clearly on a human face. I would have given
the world to have been able to speak to him, but we stood
there in the Tomb of Christ, he whispering something to me
which I did not understand, and I shaking my head.

He then turned from me towards the Greek monk and said
the same thing to him. But the monk could not understand,
and he also shook his head. The old man became frantic
with anxiety. He raised his voice slightly and then, casting a
swift glance towards the marble slab, lowered it, and pointed
to his forehead and to the lamps that hang over Christ's
Tomb. Then the monk understood. Nodding gravely, he
lowered one of the lamps on a chain and taking a piece of
cotton wool, he dipped it lightly in the oil of the lamp, and
with this made the sign of the Cross upon the peasant's face.

The old man sank down on his knees and turned again to
the Tomb, unwilling to leave, incoherent with faith and de-

votion, his big, scarred hands touching the marble lovingly as if stroking the hair of a child. Presently he backed out of the candle-light into the dim Chapel of the Angel.

IV

BETHLEHEM

I

THE white houses cluster on the hill like a group of startled nuns. They stand on the edge of the road and gaze down into a pit of heat. Where the striped terraces end and the bare rock begins, the last olive-trees seem to be struggling desperately to run back up the stony terraces away from the heat and the sterility of the rock. The white houses watch them with open mouths that are doors, and startled eyes that are windows. And sunlight beats down from a blue sky.

Above the flat, white roofs rise the bell-towers of convents, orphanages, and monasteries. There is always a bell ringing in the heat. If it is not the bell of the Salesian Fathers, it may be the bell of the Sisters of St. Vincent de Paul. At the bottom of the road that leads up to this white hill-town is a notice-board which absurdly pins this region to reality: "Bethlehem Municipal Boundary," it says. "Drive slowly."

The traveller, approaching Bethlehem with his mind on St. Luke and Botticelli, pauses in surprise before this board because it has never before occurred to him that Bethlehem could be confined by municipal boundaries. It seems to him, at first, almost sacrilege that Bethlehem should possess a mayor and a municipality. Then, when he ceases to feel and begins to think, it occurs to him that the Mayor of Bethlehem is a wonderful symbol. He is a sign of an almost terrifying continuity of human life. His predecessors in office extend back before the time of Christ into the days of the Old Testament, and probably into dim, distant regions of legend. Beth-

137

lehem is typical of the strange immutability of these Palestinian towns. Wave after wave of conquest has swept over them without, apparently, making much difference to them. Bethlehem has known the Jews, the Romans, the Arabs, the Crusaders, the Saracens, and the Turks. They have all erected their notice-boards on her boundaries. And now there is one in English at the bottom of the hill asking you to "drive slowly."

As you walk up the hill into Bethlehem, wishing only to be left alone, young Arabs in European clothes, red tarbushes above their eager faces, greet you and lead you against your will into strange little shops. There you are offered pious objects carved in mother of pearl, in olive wood, and in a black stone that comes from the Dead Sea. If these fail, they try to sell you the wedding-dress of a Bethlehem woman. When you ask what on earth you would do with such an embarrassing possession, they smile and thrust the garments towards you:

"You have no wife? Ah, young English ladies much like! Verry pretty. . . . Look, sir. . . ."

But they seem quite pleased if you buy a post-card.

The British passion for justice, which to the Arab is one of the many perplexing problems about his new master, is stamped clearly on the ancient face of Bethlehem in the form of a new building: the Bethlehem Police Station.

"Justice!" an Arab is reported to have said. "In the old days of the Turk we paid money to the judge and knew the result beforehand, but now we pay much more money to the solicitor and know nothing till the case is over. And you call that Justice!"

But the police station is like a new bookplate in a very old book. It is a sign of the latest owner. Its very newness accentuates the illusionary nature of possession. A few paces beyond it the narrow main street of Bethlehem begins, running now up and now down through the clustered warren of white

houses. Even in Rhodes and Malta and Cyprus, where, so I
believe, the Crusades have lingered in bastion and out-work,
there could be nothing so vividly crusading as the main street
of Bethlehem. Here the Crusaders are still alive! They look at
you with their blue European eyes. Although they call themselves Christian Arabs, their faces are Flemish and French,
and, perhaps, English. Old women sit in the shade of white
walls and lift towards you the lined face of an authentic Mem-
ling.

The dress of the Bethlehem woman is believed to be a relic
of the Crusades. The married women wear a high head-dress
covered with a flowing veil which is pinned under the chin
and falls down the back and over the shoulders. This is a
fashion that in Medieval Europe developed into the tall fools-
cap with its pendant veil, the head-dress worn by nearly all
princesses in fairy-tales. Whether the fashion was brought
to Palestine by European women during the Crusades, or
whether it was developed by them in the East—a version of
the silver horn head-dress that has only recently died out in
Syria—and carried back to Europe, I am not able to say. But
those who have studied this question, and that of Bethlehem's
crusading blood, agree that both the fashion and the face beneath it are a relic of the Latin Kingdom of Jerusalem.

Why should this not be so? Bethlehem is an entirely Chris-
tian town. In punishment for an insurrection the Moslems
were driven out about a century ago by the terrible Ibrahim
Pasha, whose memory lingers in Bethlehem much as that of
Judge Jeffreys lingers in Wiltshire. It is true that recently some
Moslems have come back, but there are few of them.

Throughout the centuries the Christian community, descendants, if you like, of the Crusaders, have lived in Bethlehem, keeping to themselves, marrying and intermarrying and
thus preserving the marked European strain.

II

The town itself is small and unspoilt. Shops and workshops line a part of the main street. They are merely arches open to the road, which is so narrow that the cobbler can sit at his last and without raising his voice talk to his friend, the grocer, on the opposite side of the road.

The impression I received in Bethlehem was one of peace and graciousness. Jerusalem is taut with mental conflict. Bethlehem is quiet and, I think, happy. For once the prevailing Mohammedanism is keyed down and almost inaudible. There is only one muezzin in Bethlehem, but there are many bells.

I thought at times that if the white houses had been bowered in trees, or if bougainvillaea had spilt itself from white walls, I might have imagined myself in some little town of Andalusia. But one is never quite permitted to imagine this. The hot highlands of Judæa are always visible through an archway or at the end of a street.

I once read a story, I think it was written by H. G. Wells, in which some one discovered a door in a very ordinary wall which led into the Garden of the Hesperides. The memory of it came to me in Bethlehem when I encountered a door in a massive wall. It was so low that even a dwarf would have to bend his head in order to pass through it. On the other side of it was the Church of the Nativity. They say in Bethlehem that all the doors into this church were walled up long ago, except this one, which was made low in order to prevent the infidel from riding into the building on horseback and slaying the worshippers.

But no sooner had I bent my head and stepped across than I straightened up—in Rome! It was the Rome of Constantine the Great, or, perhaps I should say, New Rome. It was the biggest surprise I had had in Palestine. I expected the usual ornate church, the dark, burdened altars, the confused stairs

and passages of a reconstructed building, and here I was in
a cold, austere Roman basilica. Massive Corinthian pillars
made of some dull red stone upheld the roof and divided the
church into a nave and aisles. I was in the church that Constantine the Great built long ago as a sign that he had become
a Christian. Surely one of the marvels of Palestine is the fact
that this church should have survived the dangers that have
swept the other buildings of its time to dust? Here it is, the
earliest Christian church in use to-day, and more or less as it
left the hands of its builders. On the walls are the remains of
dim gold mosaics.

I looked up to the roof. Is there, I wondered, anything left
of the English oaks with which Edward IV reconstructed the
roof of the Church of the Nativity? He cut down oaks and sent
tons of lead for this purpose, which the Republic of Venice
transported to Jaffa. There the Franciscans took charge of the
pious gift and conveyed it to Bethlehem. I believe the lead
was melted down by the Turks in the Seventeenth Century
and used as bullets against the very Republic that had conveyed it to Palestine; but somewhere, perhaps, high up above
the Roman nave, may linger a fragment of oak from the
forests of Fifteenth Century England.

The church is built above a cave which was recognized as
the birthplace of Jesus Christ two centuries before Rome became a Christian state. The grotto must have been sacred to
Christians in the time of Hadrian. In order to defame it, as he
tried to defame Golgotha, he built over it a temple to Adonis.
Constantine pulled down that temple and built this present
church in its place. There seems to me something so touch-
ingly formal about it, as if the Roman Empire did not yet quite
understand this new faith, but was making a first, puzzled
genuflection in its direction. One feels that these pillars are
really the pillars of a temple to Jupiter.

A service was in progress. I thought the choir was filled with nuns, but they were ordinary Bethlehem women wearing the tall veiled head-dress of the town. Beneath the high altar is the cave which tradition claims as the spot where Christ was born. It is entered by flights of steps set on each side of the choir. On the way down I had to press myself against the dark little staircase as two Greek monks, black of eye and beard, came up in a cloud of incense.

Fifty-three silver lamps hardly lighten the gloom of the underground cavern. It is a small cave about fourteen yards long and four yards wide. Its walls are covered with tapestry that reeks of stale incense. If you draw this tapestry aside, you see that the walls are the rough, smoke-blackened walls of a cave. Gold, silver, and tinsel ornaments gleam in the pale glow of the fifty-three lamps.

I thought I was alone in the cavern until some one moved in the darkness, and I noticed the policeman who is always on duty to prevent disputes between the Greek and the Armenian priests. This church, like the Church of the Holy Sepulchre, suffers from divided ownership. It is in the hands of the Latins, the Greeks, and the Armenians.

So jealous are the various churches of their rights that even the sweeping of the dust is sometimes a dangerous task, and there is a column in which are three nails, one on which the Latins may hang a picture, one on which the Greeks may do so, and a neutral nail on which no sect may hang anything.

In the floor there is a star, and round it a Latin inscription which says: "Here Jesus Christ was born of the Virgin Mary." The removal of this star years ago led to a quarrel between France and Russia which blazed into the Crimean War.

Such truths may seem terrible; but this, alas, is an imperfect world. It is therefore necessary, as you stand in the Church of the Nativity, or in the Holy Sepulchre, to try to forget the frailties of men and to look beyond them to the truth and the beauty which they seem to obscure.

As I stood in this dark, pungent cavern I forgot, I am afraid,
all the clever and learned things written about the Nativity by
German professors, and I seemed to hear English voices singing under a frosty sky:

> O come, all ye faithful,
> Joyful and triumphant,
> O come ye, O come ye to Bethlehem.

How different is this dark little cave under a church from
the manger and the stable of one's imagination! As a child,
I thought of it as a thatched English barn with wooden troughs
for oats and hay, and a great pile of fodder on which the Wise
Men knelt to adore "the new-born Child." Down the long
avenues of memory I seemed to hear the waits singing in the
white hush of Christmas night:

> While shepherds watched their flocks by night,
> All seated on the ground,
> The Angel of the Lord came down,
> And glory shone around.

There was a rhythmic chinking sound on the dark stairs.
A Greek priest, with a black beard curled like that of an Assyrian king, came slowly into the cavern swinging a censer.
The incense rolled out in clouds and hung about in the candle
flames. He censed the altar and the star. Then, in the most
matter-of-fact way, he genuflected and went up into the light
of the church.

Beneath the church is a warren of underground passages.
In one of them, a dark rock chamber, St. Jerome conducted a
number of his keen controversies and translated the Vulgate.

But I found my way back to the cavern where the incense
drifts in the lamp flames. The grotto was full of little children,
standing silently two by two on the stairs. They came forward,
knelt down, and quickly kissed the stone near the star. Their
little faces were very grave in the candle-light. Some of them

closed their eyes tightly and whispered a prayer.

No sooner had the last of them gone, than I heard the chink-chink of the censer; and into the gloom of the Grotto of the Nativity came again a Greek priest like an Assyrian king.

V

GALILEE

I

I WENT down to the little jetty one morning and arranged to go for a day's fishing on the Sea of Galilee.

The boat was a large, clumsy affair manned by four fishermen who took it in turns to row with oars as thick as cartshafts. There was a sail lying in the bottom of the boat, ready to go up in the unlikely event of a breeze. So we set off in burning sunlight over a still, blue lake.

About sixty men earn their living on the Sea of Galilee by following the trade of St. Peter. They are all Arabs and are mostly Moslems. The fishing nets used on the lake are of three kinds: the hand-net, or *shabakeh;* the draw-net, or *jarf;* and the floating-net, or *m'batten.* The first two are the most popular. The hand-net is used all over the lake, and the draw-net is employed chiefly in the Jordan estuary at the north end.

While two of the fishermen rowed, the other two sat in the boat preparing their nets. These were circular and of very fine mesh, weighed down on the outer edge with dozens of small leaden weights. They are flung by hand and are evidently the same kind as those mentioned in the Gospels. The disciples, when first called by Jesus, were "casting" their nets.

The youngest of the fishermen spoke quite fair English, and from him I learnt that fishing on the Lake of Galilee is not a very profitable business.

"We go out all night and catch our fish," he said, "but in the morning we get only a few piastres for them. But the merchant, he get many, many piastres. . . ."

145

And my mind sped northwards, far from the sunny waters of Galilee, to the cold North Sea and to the pilchard fleet of Cornwall, where so often I have heard the same complaint against the middle man; it is the eternal lay of the fisherman.

There was not a breath of wind. The sky was blue. But Abdul, the young fisherman, sniffed the air and, looking to the south, said that a storm was coming. This is, and always has been, one of the peculiarities of the Lake of Galilee. Sudden storms swoop swiftly over this low-lying sheet of water, whipping the surface of the lake with fury and covering it with waves that frequently swamp the small rowing-boats. The reason is that winds from the west passing over the highlands come swirling down through a hundred gorges and narrow valleys into the deep pit in which the lake lies. The water is smooth one moment and the next it is a raging sea in which men battle for life. Three men had recently been drowned in such a storm, said Abdul, and their bodies had not yet been recovered.

It was one of these storms that is described so vividly in the Gospels:

"And, behold, there arose a great tempest in the sea, insomuch that the ship was covered with the waves: but He was asleep.

"And His disciples came to Him, and awoke him, saying, Lord, save us: we perish.

"And He saith unto them, Why are ye fearful, O ye of little faith? Then He arose, and rebuked the winds and the sea; and there was a great calm."

How lovely it was on this hot morning, the shores receding, no sound but the creak of the huge oars, the splash of the water and the little Arab songs that one of the men would sing, softly humming a verse that would lead to a shouted chorus.

We made for the opposite bank, where the hills of Gergesa

seemed even more terrible and inhospitable as we drew nearer. They looked as they must have looked in the time of Christ: thirsty, burnt-up hills scored with thousands of thin slashes, the marks of dried-up torrents, and invaded by dark gullies in which no man would venture unarmed.

How faithfully the Gospels paint the characteristics of this country. Even to-day, after a lapse of nearly two thousand years, the country of the Gergesenes is the place in which one would expect to meet a madman.

It was from one of those fearful precipices that the Gadarene swine stampeded into the lake. Has it ever occurred to you to wonder why swine, an unholy beast to the Jew, should have been feeding round the Sea of Galilee? Tucked away in these hills are the ruins of Greek cities which flourished in the time of Jesus, the cities of the Greek-speaking Decapolis. And they had no prejudice against pork.

We jumped ashore and clambered over the hot rocks. There were three or four Bedouin tents pitched near by. The Bedouin were poor, hungry-looking people. The whole tribe turned to look at us, staring with the uncompromising intensity of animals.

A few minutes' walk from the encampment brought us to a wild little valley in which a few strips of barley were growing. Here we saw a Bedouin crouched on the ground, eating grass.

"He is hungry," commented Abdul, "and has nothing else to eat."

"But the lake is full of fish," I said. "Why doesn't he catch some?"

This seemed to puzzle Abdul. He shrugged his shoulders.

"The Bedouin do not catch fish," he said.

The sight of the man's poverty depressed me so much that I performed the usual act of a sympathetic European and gave him a shilling. But in order to buy anything with it he would have to cross the lake to Tiberias, or walk about thirty miles into the mountains!

Poor Nebuchadnezzar! He looked at the coin in his palm and thanked me; then, with the innate politeness of the desert Arab, he bent down and swiftly plucked some long blades of grass, which he pressed into my hands. It was all he had to offer.

We rowed off again and set our course for the supposed ruins of Capernaum. This town, like all the lakeside villages which were so well known to Jesus, has disappeared from the map. Many archaeologists, however, believe that its site is marked by a mound of black basalt ruins lying on the eastern bank of the lake; a fine synagogue was recently discovered here and has been as far as possible rebuilt.

There is a grove of eucalyptus-trees through which the synagogue shines like a small Roman temple. Many people believe that this is the ruin of the synagogue in which Jesus preached, but I think I am right in saying that the building is of a much later date, probably of the Second Century.

Within ten minutes by boat from Capernaum is a little bay which is said to mark the site of Bethsaida, and next to it is a squalid huddle of Arab houses called el Mejdel, the supposed site of Magdala, the town of Mary Magdalene.

We beached the boat in a desolate little bay. One of the fishermen girded his garments to the waist and waded into the lake with his nets draped over his left arm. He stood waiting, as if watching for a movement in the water. Then, with a swift over-arm motion, he cast the hand-net. It shot through the air and descended on the water like a ballet dancer's skirt when she sinks to the ground. The dozens of little lead weights carried the bell-shaped net through the water, imprisoning any fish within its area.

But time after time the net came up empty. It was a beautiful sight to see him casting. Each time the neatly folded net belled out in the air and fell so precisely on the water that the small lead weights hit the lake at the same moment, making a thin circular splash.

While he was waiting for another cast, Abdul shouted to him from the bank to fling to the left, which he instantly did. This time he was successful. He waded out and felt around with his feet. Then he drew up the net and we could see fish struggling in it. I was interested in this, because the fishermen were unconsciously repeating one of the most wonderful incidents in the Gospels.

Jesus appeared to seven disciples after the Resurrection. He stood on the shores of the lake at dawn and cried:

"Children, have ye any meat?"

They answered Him, "No."

"Cast the net on the right side of the ship, and ye shall find," He said.

They cast as Jesus had directed and "drew the net to land full of great fishes, an hundred and fifty and three: and for all there were so many, yet was not the net broken."

No one unfamiliar with the fishermen and the fishing customs of the Lake of Galilee could have written the twenty-first chapter of St. John's Gospel. It happens very often that the man with the hand-net must rely on the advice of some one on shore, who tells him to cast either to the left or right, because in the clear water he can often see a shoal of fish invisible to the man in the water.

Time and again these Galilean fishers are in the habit of casting and getting nothing; but a sudden cast may fall over a shoal and they will be forced to "draw the net to land"—as St. John says so exactly—and their first anxiety is always to discover if the net has been torn.

St. John, in describing the miracle, makes the amazingly matter-of-fact statement that "yet was not the net broken."

Who but a fisherman, or one intimately acquainted with them, would dream of mentioning this at such a moment?

The fish we caught were *musht*, or comb-fish. This is the characteristic fish of the Lake of Galilee. It is a flat fish about six inches long, with an enormous head and a comb-like spine that stands up along its back. It is also called St. Peter's Fish, for legend says that it was from the mouth of this fish that Peter took the tribute money.

I sat with a pile of these strange fish before me and remembered the incident as described by St. Matthew. Jesus and Peter arrived in Capernaum together after the Transfiguration on the slopes of Mount Hermon. One of the gatherers of the Temple Tribute came to demand payment of the half-shekel, levied on every male Jew of religious age, which was devoted to the enormous expenses of the daily sacrifice and other offices in the Temple at Jerusalem. Jesus and Peter were evidently without money, and Jesus said to Peter:

"Go thou to the sea, and cast an hook, and take up the fish that first cometh up; and when thou hast opened his mouth, thou shalt find a piece of money: that take and give unto them for me and thee."

Just out of curiosity I opened the mouth of a *musht* and placed a ten-piastre piece inside it. This is the same size as an English two-shilling piece. The coin went in easily, for the mouth of this fish is out of all proportion to its size. The male *musht* has the peculiar habit of carrying the spawn about in his huge mouth, and when the young fish hatch they use the parent's mouth as a nursery and a place of safety in time of danger. As the young fish grow, the mouth of the parent fish becomes so distended that it is difficult to understand how he can feed himself.

But to return to the fishermen. No sooner were the fish dead than one of the men built a little fire of twigs. Another made

three slashes with a knife on the backs of the fish and roasted
them on the fire. Abdul ran to the boat and brought back with
him two or three "loaves," or rather flat cakes of Arab bread,
thin, brittle stuff like an overdone pancake.

One of the fish was taken from the fire, placed on a cake of
bread and given to me. I pulled it apart with my fingers; and
it was very good.

Once again, these fishermen were re-enacting one of the
most solemn and beautiful episodes in the Gospel of St. John.
It was in this way—the way the Galilean fishermen always eat
when out fishing—that Christ, risen from the grave, commanded the seven disciples to cook the miraculous draught of
fishes.

He stood on the shore in the greyness of dawn. At first they
did not know Him. When He told them to cast their nets, they
obeyed, thinking that He was a fellow fisherman on the bank
who had seen a sudden shoal of *musht*. But when they came
nearer St. John whispered: "It is the Lord."

"Now when Simon Peter heard that it was the Lord, he
girt his fisher's coat unto him (for he was naked) and did cast
himself into the sea. And the other disciples came in a little
ship; (for they were not far from land, but as it were two
hundred cubits) dragging the net with fishes. As soon then
as they were come to land, they saw a fire of coals there, and
fish laid thereon, and bread. Jesus saith unto them, Bring of
the fish which ye have now caught."

I have seen many things in Palestine which have not
changed since Bible days, but nowhere else have I met modern
men acting quite unconsciously a sacred chapter of the Gospels. The fishermen of Galilee may be Arabs and Moslems,
but their habits, their method of work, and the tools of their
craft are the same as in the days of Peter, of Andrew, and of
Philip.

II

Throughout the month of March the cranes fly north over the Sea of Galilee. They migrate from Central Africa and journey up through Palestine to Russia. "The stork in the heaven knoweth her appointed times; and the turtle and the crane and the swallow observe the time of their coming: but my people know not the judgement of the Lord," said Jeremiah.

I shall always think of the flight of the cranes as one of the most characteristic sights of Galilee. They fly at a great height and you might not notice them until the sun, shining on their white feathers, turns them into a snowstorm against the blue sky. They move slowly, wheeling in the air, in great companies many thousands strong, sometimes seeming to stop and wheel above one particular spot as though contemplating a descent. But in half an hour, if you look for them again, they have vanished against the white head of Mount Hermon.

Everywhere round Tabgha you see black and white kingfishers, generally in pairs. They hover above the Sea of Galilee like hawks and plunge down to the water, rarely failing to rise with a small fish. These white and black kingfishers, so plain in plumage compared with the iridescent blue-green kingfishers of English streams, remind me of a curious legend about this species. The story goes that they were all originally grey or white and received their lovely colours when, released from the Ark, they flew straight into the light of a sunset. How the kingfishers of Galilee escaped the Flood I am not prepared to say!

There are several other birds very like our own brilliant kingfishers, but these are the Smyrna ice-birds and the bee-eaters.

The most homely sound on the Sea of Galilee is the chirping of sparrows. There is a tremendous colony of them in the eucalyptus wood at Tabgha and every evening they set up a shrill chirping that lasts until dusk, when they settle down and go to sleep.

This grove is the most exquisite spot on the Sea of Galilee. It is always cool under the tall trees, and the ground underfoot is soft and crackling with dead leaves, almost like a wood at home.

I can sit there for hours in the heat of the day, watching the kingfishers and the water-tortoises. The tortoises are timid, but the young and inexperienced sometimes lie on the edge of the stream instead of occupying stones in the centre. It is not difficult to catch them, and you are rewarded by the sight of a funny little snake's head popping back into its shell and the beady glance of two sharp, slanting black eyes. They swim with remarkable speed under water, and you can trace their journeys by the blunt noses thrust above the surface every so often as they come up for air. I am glad that the Arabs have not discovered any commercial possibilities in their shells, or they would very soon cease to exist. Although they venture out round the edges of the Sea of Galilee, they seem to like the warm rock pool best of all.

The Arabs tell a pretty story about the tortoise. They say that once upon a time a woman was busy baking bread at her oven when another woman passed by and asked for some of it. Although it is a terrible thing to refuse bread to any one, the woman said that she had nothing to spare. Then the Lady Fatma, for she it was, put a curse on the baker of the bread, and the curse was that she should go about the world for ever with the oven on her back. The poor woman became a tortoise, and the Arabs, picking a tortoise from the water, will point out to you the brown marks of burning on the oven, or shell.

Sometimes in the evening an Arab boat will slide in near the shore and Abdul the boatman, who has never recovered from the size of the first tip I gave him, will jump into the water and leap on land. He loves English cigarettes, which he inhales with his head thrown back.

I asked him if the Arabs on Galilee tell any stories of Jesus. "Oh, yes," he replied. "Jesus cured the daughter of the King of Gergesa, who had devils under her nails."

I have no idea what "devils under the nails" can be, and no one has been able to explain it to me.[1]

The Arabs know that Jesus walked on the waters of the lake, and they hold in great reverence a tree which grows on the top of a hill and stands on the place where, so the story goes, one of the miracles was performed. This tree is called the Tree of Blessing, and a branch of it burned in a fire is believed to cure all manner of diseases.

A number of Abdul's stories seem to have no point, or possibly his English is not adequate, or perhaps my wits go wandering in the heat of Galilee. I like to sit listening to the soft drone of his voice, watching the blue water of the lake, the tortoises sunning themselves on the stones, and the slow flight of the cranes on their way to the North.

III

The Lake of Galilee is, of all the places that I have seen, the one in which the Spirit of Christ is still present. There are no warring sects, no rival shrines; only lake water falling on black stones, a slow procession of crops, the ripening of fruit, the bright flight of kingfisher and bee-catcher, the sun by day and the stars by night.

Time has taken no revenge on the lakeside where Christianity was born. It is even lovelier than imagination paints it. There are no temples made by hands, no clash of creed, no

[1] Since this was written correspondents in many parts of the world have identified the "devils" as a tropical germ.

jealousy, and no hate.

In the silence of night the little fishing-boats set off under the stars as they used to do when a Voice called from the shore: "Come ye after me, and I will make you fishers of men."

VI

THE HOLY FIRE

I was given a seat in the Armenian Gallery in the Church of the Holy Sepulchre by courtesy of the Armenian Patriarch, and was told to be in my place four hours before the ceremony of the Holy Fire would begin. The approaches to the church were full of excited people, and it was with some difficulty that I struggled through crowds that had been waiting all night inside the church.

My seat looked directly down upon the Tomb and afforded a good view of the Rotunda, which was a tight press of people. The Eastern Christians, and many of them seemed to be Copts and Syrians, have little reverence in our sense of the word and therefore it is rather unkind to criticize them from our standpoint. They see nothing shocking in screaming, fighting, and shouting round the Tomb of Christ, of trampling each other to the ground in a frenzied dash for the fire which they believe comes straight from heaven: but their belief in the sacredness of this fire is so great, so terrible in its stark, fierce faith, that one hesitates to write the usual disgrace-to-Christianity kind of tirade. So I will just describe what happened.

Hundreds of people had slept all night in the church. Between the pillars that support the central dome, wooden scaffolding had been erected which formed a series of little boxes, exactly like boxes at an opera-house; and in each one of these was displayed an intimate picture of domestic life. Many of the boxes had been rented by rich Copts from Egypt. They sat cross-legged on cushions, surrounded by their families. Mothers, feeding their infants, sat on the bedding. The men sat in the front of the boxes, slowly telling rosaries of yellow

amber or excitedly arranging to lower a bunch of candles on a
string to be lit by some one in the crowd when the supreme
moment should arrive.

The crowd moved like an uneasy beast. Something was always happening in it; either some one was fighting madly to
escape from it or some one was struggling to enter the church.
From the Coptic chapel came a tuneless Eastern chanting,
and from the crowd came wild songs sung by Arabs mounted
on the shoulders of their friends. These leaders, swaying perilously over the heads of the crowd, beat time with their hands
or with sticks, and chanted in Arabic such verses as:

> The Fire has shone and we have feasted,[1]
> We have visited the Sepulchre of our Lord,
> Our Lord is Jesus Christ.
> Christ came to us, and with His blood He bought us.

And here is another one:

> We are rejoicing to-day,
> And the Jews are sad!
> O Jews, O Jews!
> Your feast is the feast of monkeys,
> Our feast is the feast of Christ!
> There is no religion but the religion of Christ!

The songs went on, mingled with the chanting, working up
a tense, excited atmosphere, so that I was reminded of the
Bedouin of Petra, who clapped their hands as they danced.
Once there was a serious dispute below me in one of the
densest patches of the crowd. It appeared that some man,
whether rightly or wrongly I cannot say, was believed to be a
Jew. The police were quickly on the scene and the man was
removed.

The crowds have been told time and again that the Holy
Fire is a piece of symbolism, but nothing will shake their belief

[1] From *When We Lived in Jerusalem*, by Estelle Blyth (John Murray).

that on this day it descends straightway from heaven into the Tomb. The ceremony is of unknown antiquity. I believe Bernard the monk mentioned it during his visit to Jersualem in A.D. 870. In early times the Pope forbade it and, of course, only the Eastern Church now takes part in it. It is a thoroughly Eastern, and probably fundamentally pagan, ceremony. Dean Stanley, for instance, wondered whether the Arabs and Greeks who fight their way round and round the Sepulchre, attempting to make the circuit a certain number of times, are reproducing without knowing it a dim memory of the funeral games round the tomb of a king.

When the excitement had reached its height, a number of banners were seen slanting perilously over the heads of the crowd. The police forced a way for the patriarchs and the clergy of the various communities.

On each side of the Tomb are two round openings set at a slant in the stone. The stone about them is blackened by the Holy Fire of other years, and at these holes stood runners, stripped for their ordeal, with bunches of candles shielded by caps of perforated tin. Instantly the fire springs from the openings in the Tomb these men have to fight their way outside, where others are waiting who leap into motor cars and take the sacred flame to churches all over the country. In the old days a ship with steam up was always ready at Jaffa to take the Holy Fire to Russia.

In a noisy and violent excitement, the acting Greek Patriarch and the Armenian Patriarch were conducted by priests and police to the entrance to the Tomb. On the steps, in full view of the shouting, gesticulating crowds, the Greek Patriarch was divested of his cope and other ornaments. His wrists were tied with linen bands. He looked round, pitifully feeble to face such a howling mob. I noticed that ten officers of the Seaforths surrounded him as a kind of bodyguard. They all looked like Rugby forwards. The old man then turned and entered the

Tomb, while the Armenian Patriarch waited in the vestibule.

There were three or four minutes in which nothing happened. The air was tight with suspense. Suddenly came a burst of flame from each of the Tomb openings, one torch being thrust out by the Greek Patriarch, and the other by the Armenian. The next instant the church was a shrieking, stamping madness. Tongues of flame swept over it. Men fought to escape with the fire. The crowds lit candle from candle, laughing with joy. Some moved the flames over their faces. Women passed it under their chins and over their breasts. The people in the galleries hauled up lit candles on strings, and in the inconceivable pandemonium the ancient figure of the Greek Patriarch emerged from the Tomb, grasping a lighted candle in each hand, and was swept onward like a piece of drift-wood on a flooded river, the Seaforth officers fighting a way for him to the altar of the Greek church.

While the crowds went mad with the fire, the bells of the church began to ring and the wooden gongs of the Armenians were beaten with strips of metal in the gallery. The whole church was a chaos of sound and movement. In the utter confusion of the moment all the lamps were rekindled in the Holy Sepulchre and hundreds of simple, but apparently mad, Christians believed that God had sent fire from heaven.

I sat there for an hour after the appearance of the fire, watching the excitement of the crowds. The fire did not appear to burn them as they licked the flames and ran them over their faces, neither did it singe their hair. I thought what an extraordinary thing it is that a frenzied ceremony that might have occurred in a grove of Adonis should have taken place at the Tomb of Christ.

VII

ABYSSINIANS SEARCH FOR THE BODY
OF CHRIST

A FRIEND who lives in Jerusalem offered to take me to the strangest of all the ceremonies of the Eastern Holy Week. It is held by the black monks of Abyssinia on the roof of the Holy Sepulchre.

As the moon was rising, a Greek monk let us into the church by a side door. It was pitch dark. We had to strike matches as we stumbled up over worn stairs to the roof of St. Helena's Chapel, where the black monks worship Christ under the stars. Long years ago the Abyssinians owned important shrines within the Sepulchre, but during centuries of struggle they were unable to hold out against more powerful Churches and so, bit by bit, they found themselves dislodged and driven from their sacred heritage. But, with a tenacity which has enabled these devout men to retain their faith since the Fourth Century, they sought refuge on the roof.

Lacking a church large enough to hold a big ceremony, they erect a tent in which once every year in Easter Week they celebrate a curious rite known as "Searching for the Body of Christ." This was the ceremony we had come to witness.

We found ourselves in bright starlight. The white domes gave to the roof the appropriate appearance of an African village. A long, brocade tent like a marquee had been set up in one corner, the flaps at one end looped up so that we could see inside, where, in a warm glow of candle-light, sat a barbaric assembly of Abyssinians dressed in gorgeous robes, with spiked gold crowns upon their heads. These were the cross-bearers.

A black monk led us to a row of cane-bottomed chairs at the end of the tent. Here we sat for a long time, watching the grave, dignified row of Abyssinians in their splendid vestments. They looked like pictures of the Magi.

After perhaps half an hour we heard the discordant African chanting, and into the tent came the monks, leading the Abouna, or abbot, to his place.

On the ground in front of him sat two monks with large silver-rimmed drums which they played with a quick hand-slapping motion, while the others shook sistra, filling the tent with an extraordinary shivering sound like the noise of shaken coins.

The sistrum is a metal frame with horizontal rods placed through it; these jingle when the frame is shaken. It was used in ancient Egypt in the temples of Isis to attract the attention of the worshippers and also to banish evil spirits. I did not know that there was a religious community in the world which still uses the sistrum in its services, and the shape of the instrument used by the black monks was exactly the same as the sistra of antiquity, which are discovered in the tombs of ancient Egypt.

The tapping of the drums, the shivering note of the sistra, and the raucous chanting of the monks, made it difficult to believe that one was attending a Christian ceremony on the roof of the Holy Sepulchre.

Nevertheless it was impressive to watch these black men worshipping Jesus Christ with a ritual so old that it has borrowed something from the ceremonies of ancient Israel and also from those of ancient Egypt.

Nothing could illustrate more vividly the many religious customs housed in the Holy Sepulchre. Beliefs and customs long obsolete in the Churches of the West persist round the Tomb of Christ. There is an echo of the language of the Pharaohs when the Copts say Mass, and the liturgical language of the Syrians is something like the Aramaic which Christ spoke: compared to these, the New Testament Greek used by the Orthodox Church is almost a modern tongue.

A plaintive note crept into the Abyssinian service. My friend whispered to me that the black monks were bewailing the death of Christ. The drum taps became slower and the notes of the sistra grew faint. The Gospels, printed in the ancient Gheez, the literary language of Ethiopia, were brought to the abbot and, while the monks swung a cloud of incense towards him, he intoned the story of the Lord's Passion.

Then the tom-toms, which had formed a low, throbbing background to the service, became quicker and louder and, with the gorgeous crowned cross-bearers leading, we formed up two by two, and, candles in hand, went out into the light of the full moon to search for the Body of Christ.

This rite is really a simple dramatization of the Resurrection. The abbot had read the Gospel story up to the point where the three Maries had gone to the rock-hewn tomb early in the morning with sweet spices to anoint the dead body of the Saviour. There they saw a young man sitting clothed in a white garment, and he told them that Christ was risen. . . .

And now the black monks took up the story and acted it. With a queer side-long, dancing shuffle they gyrated round the roof in the moonlight, crying that the tomb was empty, wailing because Jesus was dead and pretending to search for His Body in the shadows of the roof. Each monk held a lighted candle and the abbot walked under a green and gold umbrella.

The full moon was up, shining over Jerusalem, striking shivers of green and red light from the jewelled crowns of the cross-bearers. And so the fantastic assembly moved in a weird ritual dance to the sound of tom-toms and sistra.

Four times we circled the roof of St. Helena's Chapel. The plaintive chanting, dirge-like and inexpressibly mournful, went on, the African drums throbbed and the black abbot, surrounded by black monks, walked under his state umbrella making the sign of the cross in the moonlight.

When I looked behind me I saw the monks wailing in their sorrow, the moonlight turning them into grotesque figures from some savage African swamp, but in the nearer glow of the candles which they held, their mild black faces expressed every shade of devout emotion.

On the fourth time round the roof the tom-toms ceased, but the sistra continued to vibrate. The wailing went on and on. I remembered the words of the angels to Mary Magdalene:

"Woman, why weepest thou?"

"She saith unto them, Because they have taken away my Lord, and I know not where they have laid Him."

These black men, performing their ancient rite on the roof of Christ's tomb, were expressing in their own outwardly barbaric way the sorrow of all Christianity in the death of Jesus Christ.

Suddenly the wailing stopped. In silence the black monks re-entered the tent and grouped themselves round the abbot. We slipped quietly away.

"They will remain sad until the morning," whispered my friend. "Then they will celebrate the Resurrection and will become as happy as they are now miserable."

We descended the dark staircase and, traversing the silent Church of the Holy Sepulchre, passed into the sleeping streets of Jerusalem.

IRAQ

I

BY DESERT COACH TO BAGHDAD

i

THE air, already chilled at sunset, had a touch of ice in it. The winter, which I had seen spread whitely over the Taurus, was blowing upon the Syrian Desert. I piled every coat and available cloth on the bed. Glancing through the window, I saw Palmyra lying in the white light of the stars. It was silent and still. Columns rose over the ruins like marching ghosts. I thought of the men and women reclining beneath the ground at their last banquets, and it seemed to me that this city shared to the full the pathos of all silent places which have known the hopes and the desires of mankind.

Standing outside the hotel in the early morning was a long, experienced-looking motor coach. It was touched everywhere with brown dust. The words "Nairn Transport Co." were written on its side. It was a heavier, longer version of those coaches which roll so swiftly through the English countryside. It had made a special stop at Palmyra to take up passengers; for its normal route is straight from Damascus to Baghdad.

I went into the hotel lounge. A few cold passengers were drinking Turkish coffee, and looking rather like mail-coach travellers in a print by Alken. Instead, however, of the buxom wenches of those prints, a sleepy Arab boy in a striped *gallabia* slip-slopped round with trays of native bread and plates of crushed honeycomb, the colour of dark sherry. The stove filled the room with a blinding injection of wood smoke.

A broad-shouldered man over six feet in height sat filling in official forms at the manager's table. He wore a pair of old flannel trousers and a leather golf-jacket. When he looked up I saw that he was one of those large men who seem to have a schoolboy hiding somewhere inside him. He asked for my passport, and I gathered that he was the driver of the Baghdad coach, and everybody called him Long Jack.

While we were having a cup of coffee together, he told me that he had been born in Wellington, New Zealand, and had come to Syria as a boy of eleven. The Nairn brothers, Jerry and Norman, were also New Zealanders. They had served in Palestine during the War and then started their desert transport company. They gave him a job as driver—and how many times he'd driven the coach to Baghdad and back to Damascus, he really couldn't say! A Syrian came in and whispered to him.

"My mate," he explained. "We have two drivers in each desert car. One sleeps while the other drives, and so we keep it up all night."

He stood up and called out "All aboard!"; and we trooped out into the morning sunlight.

There was a mighty roar of the seventy-five horse power engine as the coach turned gently and rolled away through the ruins of Palmyra. It was not quite eight o'clock. We should be in Baghdad on the following morning.

II

The distance between Damascus and Baghdad is five hundred and twenty-seven miles, and the Nairn coaches accomplish the journey in twenty-four hours, with only two official stops: one, at Rutba Fort, half-way, and the other at Ramadi, the Iraq passport station. Before cars crossed the desert, the journey was possible only by camel caravan, and these sometimes took two months.

The desert which lay to the sky on each side was not sand,
but a gravelly plain, reddish in parts. It is firm in dry
weather, but becomes glutinous after rain. Ranges of low
brown hills relieved the monotony of the flat surface, and
there were occasional outcrops of volcanic-looking rock.
Long wadis, or water-courses, cut the plain, generally in a
north-easterly direction towards the Euphrates; but they
are bone dry except immediately after a storm. The road,
like that in most deserts, was merely the wheel-marks of
previous cars. When the plain became hard these tracks disappeared and Long Jack seemed to drive instinctively, but
I noticed that sooner or later he always picked up the trail
again on soft ground.

In the distance we saw herds of four or five hundred
camels grazing on thorn bushes, all facing the same way.
Whenever we saw camels or sheep we knew that a water-
hole or a well was somewhere about. How few and far between these were, we· could judge by the miles of lifeless
desolation. It was at a place called Helba Wells that we saw
our first sign of desert life. Men and women of the Ruwàlla
tribe were watering their sheep and camels. Two concrete
well-heads, made by the French military authorities, rose out
of the stony earth, and round these were grouped Bedouin
girls drawing up water. There were about two hundred
camels and several hundred sheep, and the picture they
made in that desert place might have come straight from
the Old Testament.

Long Jack stopped the car and told us that we could have
five minutes there. Walking with him to the wells, I found
that he was a voluble speaker of Bedouin Arabic. He had
the gift of making the Bedouin laugh, and soon those tall,
brown people were all rocking with merriment like a lot of
children. The Ruwàlla, who are frequently mentioned by
Doughty in *Arabia Deserta,* are among the best camel-

breeders in the Syrian Desert. Some of the women, I thought, had typical Mongolian faces, with high cheek-bones. They were impeded in their actions by long garments which looked far too big for them—some had tied cords round their waists and bunched their robes so that they exposed bright yellow heelless boots. All the time we were talking to the men, the women continued to work, and showed only by an occasional smile that they had heard the jokes that were flying around.

The wells were extraordinarily deep. The women sank a leather bucket at the end of a rope that seemed to descend into a bottomless pit. When the bucket was full, three girls would take the rope, and running back for at least forty yards over the desert, would draw the dripping bucket to the well-head. A man tipped the water into a trough, where a girl crouched, filling goatskins, and another girl would load these on the back of a donkey.

When the goatskins were filled, Long Jack said that they would take away buckets and ropes and depart with their flocks and herds, leaving the well without any apparatus for the drawing of water. The custom that each Bedouin shall bring his own tackle means, of course, that it would be possible for a traveller to die of thirst on the parapet of a well if no one were there with a bucket and rope.

There came to my mind the words of the Woman of Samaria when she saw Jesus sitting beside the well at Sychar. He asked her for water, obviously because she had brought with her the necessary bucket and rope. But before she lowered the bucket, Jesus spoke metaphorically of the "water of life," which she did not understand, thinking that He referred to the well-water. I thought that her words to Jesus are the first that would spring to the lips of any Bedouin girl if she came on a man sitting beside the wells of Helba without a rope and a bucket, yet promising apparently to

draw water. "Sir, thou hast nothing to draw with, and the
well is deep."

A heat haze trembled over the plain. Our eyes, seeking
for variety, seized eagerly on any rock or low hill, or even the
ragged line of a wadi, just as at sea one looks with pleasure
at a passing ship. At some point, where I believe there was
a post or some barbed wire, we passed into Iraq. There was
no customs-house or passport office—that happens near
Baghdad—nothing but the plain rising and falling, scattered
with stones and gravel like the dry bed of an enormous lake.

We crossed a plateau swarming with gazelle. These beautiful, swift creatures, alarmed by the desert car, always gal-
loped in herds straight across our path. It seemed as though
they were hypnotized by the line of our advance and had
to cross it, or perhaps we had caught them away from their
natural haunts and they instinctively made for them. Sometimes we saw them far away, visible only as a moving line
of dust on a dust-coloured plain, or against the sky-line as
a gliding black line which became invisible as the animals
left the horizon. Once only were we fortunate enough to see
them fairly close, straight ahead of us, galloping at about
fifty miles an hour, their white scuts shining through the
dust of their gallop.

The afternoon wore on. The sun was behind us to the
west. The shadows lengthened. We saw the swift twilight
go and darkness come to the desert. It grew colder and the
stars shone. With only a pale finger of light left in the sky,
we came to a gaunt square building standing in the treeless
desolation: a walled fort with stone towers at the four corners. The flag of Iraq flew over the gate; a wireless mast rose
from one of the towers; and two or three cars and some lor-
ries stood on the sand, while an armed sentry in a blue uni-

form marched up and down. This was Rutba Fort—the half-way house to Baghdad.

III

I went through the postern gate into a dark courtyard. Soldiers were lounging round the guard-house, gazing curiously, for the arrival of a desert coach is probably a great event in their lonely day. In contrast to the desert outside, this courtyard, with its bustle of life, was exciting. It also had the urgency and the drama of events that happen behind four closed walls: it was almost as if men were preparing for a siege. I could hear a dynamo throbbing, and when doors opened in the low buildings that ran round the four sides of the fort, I could see in the yellow oblongs of light dark men at desks, soldiers delivering a message, a wireless operator with ear-phones on his head.

An Arab came out and drew water from the well round which the fort is built. Two dark figures met in the centre of the courtyard. They greeted one another cheerfully in French—though I think one of them was English. They were air pilots. One spoke of a wind over Egypt; the other of rain over Mesopotamia. Then, as casually as they had met, they parted with an exchange of cigarettes. This, I thought, is a wonderful, romantic place: a modern version of the Roman caravan fort.

There was still a surprise for me. While I was blundering about in the dark, wondering where I should find something to eat, for though Rutba has plenty of light for its offices it spares none for its courtyard, a door opened and out came a little man like a brown monkey. He wore a white mess-jacket and looked like a Goanese steward from some P. and O. ship.

"A wash and brush-up, sir?" he asked in English. "There is hot water."

I followed him into a room where about twenty camp washstands were ready for travellers. Beside each was a white enamelled jug of hot water, with a spotless towel neatly folded and placed over the top. There was soap everywhere—English soap—and several clean hair-brushes. I felt pride and happiness rising in me, for this was undoubtedly English; but when I turned to ask the little man to explain it, he had gone.

On the veranda outside I saw a sign: "To the lounge." I followed it, pushed open a door, and saw a truly amazing sight. In a room dotted with little wickerwork tables, a number of men and women were sitting in basket-work chairs round a stove. Most of them were English. Some were smoking cigarettes and others drinking tea. I ventured in, and sat next to a woman in a tweed costume, who was reading an old copy of the *Bystander*.

This was the rest-house which the Nairn Company keeps at Rutba, and the people were passengers on their way east or west. Some were Britishers, some were French, a few were Iraqi, and one or two might have been Persians. It is amazing in these days to see phantom-like assemblies of this kind in out-of-the-way places. An aeroplane comes down from the sky. Men in town clothes and women in fur coats and Paris shoes walk on the desert sand, perhaps have something to eat, and vanish again into the air. The Arab accepts it all without wonder, having obviously heard of the magic carpet in his cradle. It was strange to find such people, some air travellers, some from desert cars, drawn together in the darkness in an atmosphere so strongly English that even the Iraqis, though on their native soil, appeared guest-like and faintly apprehensive.

Leading from this room was a little dining-room with tables set for dinner, all neat and clean and—English. There is a wonderful English way of setting a table which we don't notice at home because we see it so often. The cloth droops almost to the ground, decently covering the table's legs, and it generally has ironed creases in it. The knives and forks are set with precision, not with Gallic inconsequence or Latin fire, and the cruet is given a place of honour beside a bottle of sauce. Tumblers, the right size for half a pint of ale, stand to the right-hand, and inside each one is popped a little bishop's mitre—a folded table-napkin. No other nation sets a table like that, and when I saw all those tables looking so English, reminding me of country hotels in Hampshire and Yorkshire and Devonshire, of little restaurants run by tall, grey-haired gentlewomen in select seaside places, a feeling of love for this dear country of ours filled my heart, and I determined to pour Lea and Perrin's sauce over everything that night, out of sheer love for England.

Pinned to an announcements board in this fantastic room, next to an apology for the high price of bottled beer, was a notice which brought me back to reality.

NOTICE

Passengers are warned when leaving the fort always to keep the fort in sight. Cases have occurred of passengers becoming lost (through losing their bearings) when out for a stroll, owing to darkness falling suddenly and the fort not being in sight. The result of this causes danger to the passengers and trouble to the police.

By Order.
Administrative Commandant.

My eye lingered lovingly over "when out for a stroll," which brought memories of Eastbourne into Mesopotamia. No one but an Englishman could have talked about having "a stroll" at Rutba.

While I was wondering from whom all these blessings flowed, my curiosity was answered by the appearance of a short, stout man in a grey flannel suit, who passed rapidly through the dining-room, talking in sudden rapping bursts of fluent Arabic. Every waiter addressed by him seemed to have received an electric shock. Some fled into the kitchen, others attempted to hide, and several stumbled over chairs and upset the salt in a passion of obedience. He smoked a cigarette all the time, rapping out his orders between puffs of smoke and with a glance of pale blue eyes which had the fixed expression of expecting the worst; a look which men acquire from long contact with foreign troops. I put him down as an old soldier, and from the quick way he moved and the way he held himself, as a boxer or an athlete. And in none of these things was I far wide of the mark.

He was George Bryant, commandant of the rest-house. As I sat down to dinner, we attempted to talk, but this was difficult because he was interrupted every two seconds by one of his waiters. He would spring lightly to his feet and disappear with a gleam of frosty blue eyes, to return a minute later with the air of having quelled a rebellion. During his first absence I gazed incredulously at the card which was propped against the cruet.

Dinner.

Tomato Soup.
Fried Fish.
Tartar Sauce.
Roast Beef.
Horse-Radish Sauce.
Roast Potatoes.
Cauliflower.
Yorkshire Pudding.
Raisin Pudding, Lemon Syrup.
Fruit. Coffee.

I invite you to look at the map and, having found Rutba, to believe that this very night a meal of such superb English-ness is probably being eaten in that hut behind the fortress wall. In an age of half-belief, it is inspiring to meet that mood of stern faith which will recognize in no part of the earth a place that cannot be made a little like home; that must, in fact, be made like home before it can be called good. And although we may laugh at people who go about the world taking England wherever they may be, what finer thing is there to take about the world? For one brief hour, as we sat at the parting of the ways in that desert, some of us to travel towards the Mediterranean, others towards the Indian Ocean, we sat in peace, sharing the solid comfort of a tradition built up in generations of English families.

When George Bryant returned, I questioned him with re-newed interest. No; he had no woman to help him. He had trained the cooks and the waiters himself. Where did he come from? Born at Bath, played rugger for Bristol, entered the Palestine police force, stationed at Nazareth, left the force, and had been in the desert ever since. So much I got out of him in a quick-fire way between his jumpings-up and his sittings-down.

"Enjoy your dinner? Not too bad, is it?" And a frosty smile came into his eyes for a second. "Difficult? It's not too easy. You've got to keep them up to the scratch. That's the secret. You can't let one detail escape you. Excuse me a min-ute . . ." He came back. "Do you like the fish?"

"I was going to ask how you get fish in the middle of the desert."

"Comes from Baghdad. Tigris. Get it when the desert mail goes East. It's a bit coarse, naturally, but it's not too bad, is it?"

It was not, because the poor Tigris fish, entering into the spirit of the thing, had consented to look and taste like the "fried fish with sauce tartare" of more familiar places.

Long Jack came in to say the coach was ready, and I was given a pillow and two blankets. I walked across the dark courtyard with George Bryant, through the gate into the desert, enormously wide and silent under the stars. The car stood throbbing, and two beams of white light shone into the emptiness that was our way.

"Cheerio!" said George Bryant. "Look in again on your way back."

And he strode swiftly past the sentry into the fort.

There was no moon that night, and a blue wash of starlight lay over the desert in which stones almost achieved shadows. Our headlights sprang forward and became lost in the immensity of the space ahead. I was conscious of things moving in the light and escaping from it, for now the desert seemed to be livelier than by day. Sand-grouse rose in front of us and flashed off; a flock of desert pigeon flew in and out of our light, and all around us the desert moved with strange hopping creatures, propelled, it seemed, by springs: these were jerboas, little kangaroo-like desert rats. You had to watch carefully to see them, for they were the same colour as the earth and moved with the speed of birds, hopping in every possible direction.

I tilted my seat back, wrapped myself in blankets, and enjoyed those disconnected periods of unconsciousness which are usually accompanied by vivid and unlikely dreams. Awakening with a sense of bereavement, I would see Long Jack lying crumpled in the spare seat, his huge body sagging as if he had been shot, and the Syrian driver at the wheel, the smoke of an Iraqi cigarette streaming back.

So the night wore on; first crouched on the left side, then on the right; asleep for ten minutes, awake for half an hour;

and always the pale wash of starlight all round; the rising and falling headlights; the roar of the engine.

I was suddenly wide awake. The coach had stopped on a sandy road with buildings on each side. It was still dark, and looking at my watch I saw that it was only 2.30. Long Jack was standing outside talking to a policeman, holding in his hand the passports of passengers. We were at Ramadi, the Iraqi passport station, which is about ninety miles from Baghdad. I got out, and walking a few paces along the road, became conscious of something new and pleasant in the air. It was the sound of wind in acacia-trees; and I remembered that I had seen no real trees for many days.

Near the customs shed was a small building with a front garden. It was the Babylon Hotel, and there were lights in the windows. I entered a lounge where little brown waiters in white jackets, who might have been the waiters of Rutba Fort, were bustling about serving the sleepy passengers with pots of tea and trays of English biscuits. We had been offered tea and English biscuits at Rutba, and here they were again! This could not have happened in Syria. I drank four cups of strong tea, and smoked a cigarette. The hotel lounge was interesting. The walls were hung with Persian rugs so that the place looked like a carpet shop, and a picture of young King Ghazi of Iraq hung on the wall. But the waiters spoke English, and, from the way they served the tea, you could tell that whatever they knew of waiting was derived from English sources.

When I gave the waiter a ten-shilling note, he returned my change in the first Iraqi money I had handled. Since 1931 Iraq has had a currency of its own, based on the pound sterling. One *dinar*—which surely holds some vague memory of *Chu Chin Chow*—is worth an English pound, and this is divided into a thousand *fils*. Silver coins are of twenty, fifty, or a hundred *fils;* nickel coins of irregular shape, rather like our new threepenny pieces, are of four and ten *fils;* and copper coins are of one and two *fils,* but my tastes are evidently so expensive that I never discovered what I could buy with them, except the fleeting gratitude of small boys.

An insistent note from the klaxon sent us running to the coach. We crossed a wooden bridge. I saw the movement of swift water. This is the point where the Euphrates, after winding through Mesopotamia as if it were going to Baghdad, suddenly makes up its mind to turn south and leave Baghdad to its companion, the Tigris.

Awakening from a sound sleep, I found that we were running through flat country over a rough road of beaten brown earth, and ahead of us a cluster of mud-coloured buildings, minarets, and a few cupolas was spread out on a land as low, as wide, and as conscious of the sky, as Holland. And the sun was up.

II

BAGHDAD

I

THE irreproachable edition of Lane's *Arabian Nights,* which was once found in all Victorian libraries, probably explains why Baghdad is a magic name to most of us. To me it was one of those towers of romance which experience had not yet demolished, and I approached it with some apprehension, already aware that it was going to be—well, different.

As the car approached Baghdad through the sunrise of that morning, I took with me a certain proportion of juvenile dreams, and I told myself that the line of buildings, with a golden gleam of a distant mosque, was indeed the city of the Caliphs.

We crossed the river by a wooden pontoon bridge whose sections lift gently under heavy traffic. The Tigris at Baghdad is perhaps a little wider than the Thames at London Bridge: on the west bank, white-balconied houses stand amid the green fringes of date-palms; on the east bank modern Baghdad clusters, with its one main street and its incredible chaos of lesser streets and lanes. Blue skies, warm sunlight, a long, wide main street (called, I saw with a pang, Al Rashid Street) lined with little shops and animated by the movement of two-horse open carriages—these were my first impressions of Baghdad.

I entered a hotel in this street which is named after General Maude. The servant who answered the bell called me "sahib"; and in the breakfast-room the waiter, who gave me the best cooked bacon and eggs I have ever eaten, also called

180

me "sahib." It was the first time that any one had seriously
referred to me in this Kiplingesque manner; and it made me
think that there is a point in travel when the West fades out
and the East tunes in; when the Mediterranean is a far-off,
alien sea and the Indian Ocean is real and near. This point
is Iraq. India is only round the corner.

I remembered that men I knew who had served as administrators in Iraq had also been Indian civil servants, and suddenly many things were made clear: the bacon and eggs,
the tea and *petit buerre* biscuits at Ramadi; and goodness
knows what else.

Pleased with this deduction, I went out to see Baghdad.

II

For three centuries before the War, Iraq shared in the
living death of the Ottoman Empire. The War released it
from its torpor, and, after ten years of British mandated rule,
it is now an independent Arab state ruled by Feisal's son,
King Ghazi.

Baghdad, which may possess carefully concealed charms
visible only to the resident and the native, is, to the visitor,
a large, mud-coloured city on the banks of a mud-coloured
river. With the slightest wind, powdered mud as fine as talc
powder flies through its streets. In true Babylonian tradition,
the native building material is mud brick and, like the towers
and temples of Biblical times, the chief architectural decoration is the glazed tile, which in modern Baghdad is sparingly
applied to the cupolas of a few mosques.

The terrible poverty and inertia of the old Turkish rule are
still written on the face of Baghdad. It will take more than
ten years of Western influence to wipe out the memory and
tradition of three hundred years of mental and material corruption. It is true that a new spirit is fighting the old ways;

there are hospitals, public services, an excellent police force, schools, and a stirring feeling of national pride which may mean that the old tree, having been pruned and trained in the way it should grow, is putting out new wood. The long main street, with its ramshackle booths and shops, is still mainly Turkish in appearance, although an occasional ladies' hairdresser, or an up-to-date chemist's shop, seem to herald the dawn of a new day.

This main street is filled with activity. From morning until night earnest little *'arabîyât* drawn by two horses ply up and down. There are so many of these questing victorias, and their fares are so cheap, that there is no need to walk anywhere. In the absence of finer shades of social distinction the people in the street may be divided, like a hymn-book, into ancient and modern. The modern wear European clothes with the national head-dress, a forage cap of blue cloth rather like that worn by members of the Church Lads' Brigade; and the ancient wear anything from the green turban and robes of religious aristocracy to the squalid sacks which cover the limbs of the Khurdish porters.

In the capital of a land which resembles nothing so much as a billiard table, the presence of mountains is curiously proclaimed by fierce, ragged men who by their bearing would be recognized anywhere as highlanders. They are nomads from the mountains of Kurdistan or from the high country round Mosul. Then there are Persians, Arabs, Jews, Afghans, Indians, and Negroes; a curious mixture that rides, walks, or lies in the dust of Baghdad's main street.

The reason why nothing now survives of the cultured city of the Abbasid Caliphate is to be found in history. Baghdad has been plundered and destroyed, rebuilt and flooded, time and again, so that little remains to-day to remind the visitor of "the golden prime of good Hārun al-Rashid."

The bazaars are a confusing warren of twisting alleys

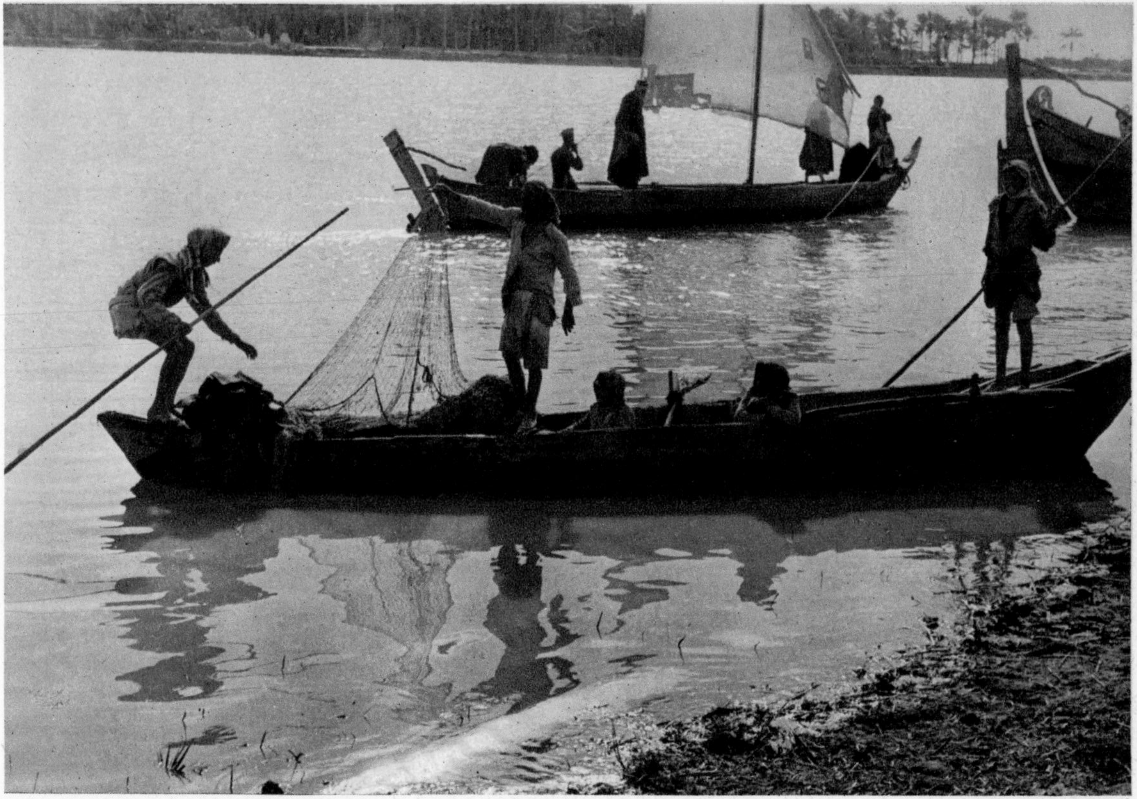

ON THE EUPHRATES

crammed with life, with cheap Japanese cotton prints, with copper work of infinite variety, and with trivial silver and gold work; they are dark, save for dusty stabs of sunlight that fall from rents in the cloth covering overhead. I looked in vain for ancient khans such as I have seen in Cairo, Damascus, Jerusalem, and Aleppo, for Baghdad is a city with a great but invisible past, and there are no architectural relics worth speaking about.

The Museum is Baghdad's greatest attraction. Here are to be seen the astonishing objects found at Ur, and much else besides. It is strange, perhaps, that while everybody knows something about the Tut-ankh-Amûn discoveries, which did not really increase the world's knowledge, the finds at Ur, which removed the dawn of history from Egypt to Babylonia and set it back another thousand years, seem to have made little impression, except on those people who happen to be interested in such matters.

It was in Baghdad's main street that I came on the only really surprising shop in the city. It is called Mackenzie's Book Shop. Although it might pass without comment in Oxford or Cambridge, it stands out from the Oriental booths on each side. It is packed from floor to ceiling with new and second-hand English books, and is, of course, a relic of the British Mandate. It is, however, more significant now that the Mandate has been surrendered than ever it was when the British patronized it; for the customers are chiefly modern young Iraqis. You will always find a group of young men wandering about there, dipping into the latest books, and it will occur to you that Mackenzie of Baghdad is proof that though England and France have made little cultural impression on Palestine, Trans-Jordan, or Syria, this is not so in Iraq.

Ten years of British rule have taught Iraq to speak our language and to read our books. And from the size of Mackenzie's shop and, still more, from the kind of books that fill it, you can confidently assume that Baghdad's literary appetite is critical and intelligent.

In the afternoon I hired a taxi and told the man to drive for a couple of hours anywhere outside Baghdad.

We bumped along a road of beaten mud with cultivated land on each side. Every passing horseman covered us in brown dust, and our wheels made a sand-storm for the unfortunate people behind. The cultivation soon began to thin out, and I had some idea of the difference between the country to-day and in ancient times.

The modern habit of giving the name Mesopotamia to the lower reaches of the Tigris and the Euphrates probably originated during the War, when the Press and the Army always referred to these parts as Mespot. But the Mesopotamia of the ancient world was the country north of Baghdad—the wide, grassy plains between the two rivers—and the country south of Baghdad was known as Babylonia.

When you look at this land to-day, stretching brown and barren to the sky, a land green only on its river-banks and in irrigated areas, it is difficult to believe that such a desert could ever have been the home of great civilizations. But when Abraham lived at Ur, and when the Children of Israel were carried captive to Babylon, they saw a different country. If we can imagine the wheat-prairies of Canada varied by groves of date-palms and intersected in every direction by canals, we have some idea of the appearance of ancient Babylonia.

Agriculture has always been impossible in this land unless the flood-waters carried down in the spring by the two rivers are retained and used to water the land during the dry season. The Chaldeans, the Babylonians, and the Assyrians were irrigation experts who harnessed the Tigris and the Euphrates, and by a complicated system of control distributed the water as it was required. The system was taken over by the Persians and by the Arabs of the Caliphate, but when the Arab Government weakened it fell into disrepair, until, with the Mongol invasions of the Thirteenth Century, the magnificent series of waterways with their intricate dams and dikes fell into utter ruin, and a legacy from the world's first civilizations was lost.

At the present moment engineers are tackling the problem of irrigation, but it is not an easy one. The river-beds have been ruined by centuries of neglect. Water has been tapped to serve individual needs in a way which makes it impossible for the rivers to scour their beds properly, and canal-cutting, which has gone on without plan, has diverted the flow of water and helped to cause floods. Thus the restoration of Babylonia to its former prosperity presents not one problem, but hundreds, and not the least important is the problem of population. Nevertheless, even a glance at the immense dry plains suggests that if Iraq, like ancient Babylonia, could once again become productive, she might influence the wheat markets of the world.

III

THE SHIA FLAGELLANTS

I

I FOUND myself forbidden, like any Seventeenth Century "Christian Dog," from entering the Shia mosques in Baghdad. It was the first week in Muharram, the opening month of the Moslem year, a time when Shias flagellate themselves, cut their heads with knives, and achieve a condition of religious ecstasy which culminates in the passion play commemorating the death of Mohammed's grandson.

I stood outside the mosques and watched the lowering crowds of men which passed in and out, each mosque like a hive about to swarm. A fanatical crowd devoid of humour is a terrible spectacle, especially when you are detached from the object of its obsession. These men were terrifying in their single-mindedness. They were men not humbled by grief, but made savage and revengeful. Looking at them, I realized how quickly a human sacrifice must have cleared the air in pagan times; for these Shias, whether they were aware of it or not, wanted blood.

I should perhaps explain that Islam falls into two divisions, the orthodox Sunnis and a rigid fanatical minority called the Shias. The schism that separates them dates from the extinction of the Prophet's family in the year 680 when Mohammed's kinsman, Husain, was slain at Karbala in Iraq. The Shias have always maintained that all the caliphs of Islam since that remote time have been usurpers and impostors. Such fanatical nonconformists are mostly to be found in India and Persia. They have their own mosques, their own religious

186

hierarchy, and their own interpretation of the Koran. While the orthodox Sunni Moslem turns to Mecca as his holy city, the Shias turn to Iraq, where the four holy cities of the Shia world, Najaf, Karbala, Kadhimain, and Samarra, welcome something like two hundred thousand pilgrims every year.

The great Shia festival takes place during the first ten days of Muharram, a time when the faithful celebrate the death of Husein at Karbala with all manner of morbid austerities. Baghdad at this time is full of pilgrims who, as they work up to the emotional climax of their pilgrimage, march through the streets at night whipping themselves. It would be as un-safe for a Sunni Moslem as it would be for a Christian to enter their mosques or to encounter their processions.

Having made friends with several local Christians, mem-bers of the ancient Chaldean Church, I told them of my desire to witness a procession of the flagellants, and one of them agreed to take me to the house of a friend in a back street of Baghdad from whose windows we could watch the Shias pass from one mosque to another. He promised to call for me at eight o'clock that evening and take me there.

It was dark when we set out, but crowds filled the main street, for Baghdad has contracted the Western habit of aim-less night sauntering, the result, probably, of electricity and of a new clerkly class unwearied by physical labour. Leaving the main street, we walked through narrow lanes in which our steps were hushed. Some alleys were like the Shambles in York. The houses leaned together, thrusting forward their top stories until only a knife-cut of sky lay overhead; and the lanes meandered so confusingly that they might have been designed by a flock of crazy sheep. After dark something of the mystery of old Baghdad returns to haunt the sleeping alleys of the old city. For the first time I felt that it would be possible to see the Caliph passing on some night adventure, or, glancing up, to see the dwarf, so dear to Eastern story, peeping from behind a lattice.

The men encountered in these lanes were not the capped and collared *effendis* of the main street: they were silent men who passed with a bat-like scrape of heelless slippers, giving a sidelong glance, as they went by, from the shelter of their head-coverings. Sometimes a long, yearning wail of Turkish gramophone music would sound from beyond a blank wall, and I went on with knowledge of life packed away there, of people sitting together as if in ambush.

My guide halted before one of the blank walls and knocked on a door. We heard the sound of feet descending a flight of stairs, and a voice on the other side asking who it was. At once the door was opened, to reveal not the eunuch which the street suggested, or the merchant in turban and silk caftan, but a young man in a black coat, a pair of striped trousers, and black patent-leather shoes.

Speaking good English, he led the way up a flight of stone stairs to a room leading off a galleried courtyard. Two divans, upholstered in Persian fabrics and fitted with white antimacassars, faced each other under the unshaded electric bulbs. A few Chinese pictures hung on the walls, and a number of knick-knacks were dotted about on bamboo tables. The most spectacular was a stuffed cobra strangling a mongoose; it stood on a side-table, very realistic and horrible, providing that touch of India which I was beginning to look for everywhere in Baghdad.

A smiling, dark girl of about eighteen, wearing a poppy-red dress, rose from the divan where she had been sitting in an attitude of formal expectancy, and shyly shook hands. She was our hostess. Although she had not left school for long, she was too timid to exercise her knowledge of English; but now and then she would contribute the words "yes" or "no" to the conversation, which we greeted with polite applause until she cast down her eyes and turned as red as her dress.

A servant brought in a tray of tea, English biscuits, oranges, and sweet limes.

We sat talking of the Shias whom they, as Christians, deplored as dangerous and fanatical persons, and they told me of the physical mortification endured by the sect every year during Muharram. The body-beaters, which we should see passing down the street that night, were the commonest of the flagellants. Every night for ten nights they would march from one mosque to another, beating themselves. There were others who scourged themselves on the back with chains. The most savage mortification was the head-cutting which takes place on the morning of the tenth day of Muharram.

My host had seen this at Najaf and also in Baghdad. He told me that all kinds of people took part in it, but the Turcomans were the most violent performers, sometimes slashing too hard and killing themselves. There were several men in the Government office in which he worked who occasionally got a day's leave to join the head-cutting procession.

I asked my host to tell me how the head-cutting is done. He said that a band of men, who for days have been dwelling on the gory emotionalism they are about to enjoy, would gather at the mosque.

"In Karbala or Najaf," he said, "you can see these men for days whispering to the swords which they carry about in their arms, polishing and sharpening them."

Arriving at the mosque, they form a circle and revolve round a leader, working themselves into a state of emotional excitement by uttering the names of Ali, Hasan, and Husein, until, suddenly, the leader gives a great cry and brings down his sword on his head. As soon as the others see the blood they go mad. With cries and shouts of "Husein!", "Ali!", "Hasan!", they cut their heads until their white robes are stained everywhere with blood.

They then go off together in twos and parade the town,

cutting and slashing until the blood falls in the gutter and spurts on the walls of the houses. Spectators, hearing the cries and the sound of the swords on skulls, and seeing the streaming blood, begin to cry and give the mourning wail, and sometimes people who have nothing to do with the orgy lose all control, and pulling out penknives or scissors begin to stab at their arms and wrists until the blood flows.

While he was describing this, we heard, far off, a dull, rhythmic sound.

"They are coming!" said my host. "We must go up."

He led the way up a flight of stairs to a little bedroom overlooking the street. Some one switched on the light, but he turned it off at once, asking if I minded sitting in the dark. It was better, he said, not to attract attention to ourselves. As the room protruded for a yard or so into the lane, sitting in the window was rather like being in a box at the opera. I could have touched with a cane the head of any one passing below. The buildings rose dark and mysterious, and the lane twisted away out of sight, merging itself into another as dark, as narrow, probably as serpentine. The only light came from a booth let into the opposite wall, where an old man sat cross-legged among a chaotic assembly of cigarettes and tobacco. I was aware of something pleasantly adventurous and exciting in sitting concealed in the dark, watching the shrouded figures in the lane below, the customers suddenly appearing in the glow of the booth and going off again into the darkness. At intervals came a queer sound, growing gradually nearer, as if a thousand nurses, taking their time from the matron, were delivering in rhythmic chastisement a thousand resounding smacks on the posteriors of a thousand children. But as it came nearer, we heard the fierce, grief-stricken background of this sound—the sound of men groaning, crying, and shouting. The noise then became horrible. There came into view, swaying down the lane, the strangest procession I have ever seen. Boys and young men came first, holding banners which, with true Eastern inconsequence, slanted this way and that. Behind them were men bearing on their shoulders the poles of palanquins on which rested boat-shaped clusters of lights. The dark lane now blazed with the moving orange glow of paraffin flares. Behind these lights, eight abreast, came rank after rank of men naked to the waist, the sweat of their austerities clammy on their faces and shining on their brown bodies. They were like a regiment of half-naked soldiers marching as captives to their doom. Each company was preceded by a leader, and above each company one of the strange, barbaric boats swayed in the smoke and yellow light. The companies halted every few yards and the leaders faced them, crying out: "Husein!" A deep, agonized wail immediately rose from hundreds of voices. "Hasan!" Another wail. Then, in a rhythmic Arabic chant, the whole company would shout:

> "Welcome, O Husein,
> When you enter Karbala."

At the beat of each word the men lifted their arms in unison and brought them smack against their naked chests. Some chests were bleeding, a revolting sight; others were swollen with weals which would soon become wounds; and as they beat themselves, their eyes gazed fixedly ahead from faces pale and terrible in the torchlight, like the faces of martyrs on their way to the stake.

Their soldierly bearing, the perfect rhythm of their arms, the timed responses, their implicit obedience to their leaders, were a contrast to the disorder of the dipping banners and swaying boats. Those breast-beaters were like men transfigured in some sorrowful dream, and in their fanatical eyes was something of the anguish of Husein, parched and wounded on the plain of Karbala.

As I looked at those hundreds of faces, men old and young, men with hairy chests of bulls, men smooth and slender, men with beards, and others with the clean-shaven faces of boys, I wondered why human beings should behave like that for the good of their souls, and from what dark jungle of antiquity such spectacles had their beginning.

Surely this beating of the body, and the cutting with knives, was the sight that Elisha saw on Carmel, when the priests of Baal "cried aloud, and cut themselves after their manner with knives and lancets, till the blood gushed out upon them." A writer of one of the books of the Old Testament might have called this strange, savage sorrow for the death of Husein one of the last sins of Babylon. As I looked at the faces and wounded bodies, and the sailing tabernacles of light, I felt that I was watching something which had happened long ago in this country, when the altars of Baal and Ashtoreth were smoking on the ziggurats.

About a thousand men passed by, and the sight of their reddened torsos and the sound of their chant became monotonous, for each group was in every way like its predecessor. Now and again an added vigour was given to the breast-beating when women, standing in the street or gazing from behind latticed windows, would set up the twittering funeral cry, and at the sound men would beat themselves with renewed frenzy.

The last group disappeared down the lane, and I felt that never in my life should I forget the "lil-hala, lil-hala" of their wailing chant, which had sung itself into my brain. I rose to go. My host switched on the light and said that it would not be wise to venture into the streets until the Shias had reached their mosque. Those kind people produced more tea, more biscuits and sweet limes; and, with the clock nearly at midnight, I went through the now silent lanes back to my bed.

IV

BABYLON

I

Among the most incongruous acts of my life is the journey I made in a taxi-cab to Babylon. The Baghdad owner-driver, unaware of a conflict in association between his cab and Babylon, often pulls up at the kerb and suggests that you might like to take a taxi there at a specially cut price.

The ruins are sixty miles south of Baghdad, and the journey takes three to four hours. The road begins well enough, but soon becomes rough and uneven. I knew we were drawing near when we crossed a single railway track running over the sand, and I saw a notice-board bearing, in English and Arabic, the words: "Babylon Halt."

I have read books which have described the humiliations visited by Time upon the once mightiest city in the world, but this notice-board translated them into the idiom of our own civilization. That "the glory of kingdoms, the beauty of the Chaldee's excellency" should be known as a "halt," a place which even local trains pass with a derisive whistle, seemed to me as bitter as anything prophesied by Isaiah.

On every side I saw sandy mounds lying in the sunlight: some large enough to be called hills, others low ridges, and still more the merest uneasy risings and fallings of the earth. But for miles around the earth was blasted and unhappy with the memory of Babylon. So this was the city whose Hanging Gardens were among the Seven Wonders of the World. Four-horse chariots could pass on its walls; on one altar alone a thousand talents' worth of incense was burned every year.

I climbed a sandy hill in which are embedded the impressive remains discovered by German archaeologists from 1899 to 1917. I found it difficult to understand them, for I saw acre upon acre of brown mud brick walls, broken vaulting, and the lower stories and cellars of buildings lying in such confusion that only a trained architect could sort them out with any certainty. Palace and hovel, wall and roadway, are equally humbled in this post mortem. But one section of the ruins still stands in unmistakable splendour: the great Ishtar Gate of Babylon built by Nebuchadnezzar. Its towers rise to a height of forty feet, and its mud bricks bear the impression in high relief of a hundred and fifty-two animals, almost life size, alternate rows of bulls and dragons, once brilliantly enamelled, but now bared to the mud from which they were moulded.

What a fortunate discovery this was! Nothing looks drearier than mud bricks all the same shape, dull in colour, crumbling and already returning to the dust whence they came. Even uncarved stone has a quality and a beauty which are absent from mud. And as I looked at those acres covered with Babylonian bricks, I wondered if the buildings in this land were really as beautiful as we have been told they were. But the survival of the bulls and the dragons on the Ishtar Gate leave no doubt. The bulls stride forward with the grace and spirit of young horses, clipped like French poodles. Their hair from head to tail along the back, round the jaw, under the belly, down the chest, and curving round the haunches, was arranged in fringes of tight little curls, in which jewels or beads may have been tied. What superb animals they are; not massive and heavy like the Egyptian Apis, nor fantastic and half-human like the Assyrian bull, but proud, vigorous young creatures, striding forward into the morning and capable of taking a five-barred gate.

Their companions, the dragons of "sirrush," are equally

well done, but they are not so appealing because they represent no known animal. They may have been put there to frighten Medes and Persians. The "sirrush" is really a compromise between a serpent, a lynx, and an eagle: the head, body, and tail are those of a scaly snake, the forelegs are those of a lynx, and the hind legs, which end in talons, might be those of any large bird of prey.

The "sirrush" is pictured on many other Babylonian works of art. Professor Koldewey, who discovered the Ishtar Gate, thinks it possible that the priests kept some strange reptilian creature in the darkness of a temple and exhibited it as a living "sirrush." If this is so, it lends colour to the story of Daniel and the Dragon, which appears in many forms but is not printed in the *Book of Daniel*. The story is that Daniel refused to worship a dragon in Babylon and offered to slay the creature single-handed. He was therefore placed in the animal's den, presumably in the belief that he would never emerge from it; but he took with him a potent pill, composed chiefly of hair and bitumen, which he persuaded the dragon to swallow. The poor "sirrush" then died; some accounts say that it blew up.

From the top of the mound you look down over the basements and the brick vaulting of Nebuchadnezzar's Palace. And how hard it is to realize that those incoherent masses of building material near by are all that remain of the Hanging Gardens, or that the mark like the shadow of a broad road losing itself round Babylon is the line of the mighty walls which once astonished all who saw them.

The flat country stretches to the sky, featureless, bare, and arid, except to the west, where the Euphrates flows in a narrow belt of palm-trees. You see no river, but you see this line of foliage running for miles, like a green snake on the sand. Even the "waters of Babylon" have deserted the city, for in ancient times the river ran along the west side of the

Kasr, bringing with it the happy sound of water and the
scent of flowers. As if obeying a command that no touch of
life should remain anywhere near Babylon, the Euphrates
has carved a new channel for itself and has departed, taking
all life with it.

While I stood on the summit of the ruins, an Arab approached and told me that he had worked there with Professor Koldewey. His name was Umran Hamed, "the guide
of Babylon." He was a good fellow, and he had absorbed a
quantity of accurate information from the German archaeologists, which he was tireless in imparting. We walked about
the ruins and he pointed out many things which I should
have missed without him.

He showed me the vestiges of three wells in the foundations of the Hanging Gardens and a chamber which he said
was a "refrigerator." As he had just confused the word par-
tridge with cartridge, I wondered whether he had got this
right.

"Yes; where food was kept cold in snow," he said earnestly.

"Have you ever seen a refrigerator?"

"No, sir," he replied, "but I have heard the Germans talking."

So if Umran overheard correctly, perhaps the lower stages
of the Hanging Gardens were stored with cold foods, iced
sherbets, and other cool things for the Median princess for
whose pleasure Nebuchadnezzar made those gardens. It is
believed that in the flatness of Babylonia she became home-
sick for her native mountains, just as the Jews must have
done, and to please her the King ordered the construction
of an artificial mountain terraced with gardens. The word
"hanging" is not a good description of these gardens. The
Greek word is *kremastos*, which was used in ancient Greek
for a man hanged, and is used in modern Greek for a suspension bridge.

It is certain that the Hanging Gardens were as solidly anchored to the earth as a pyramid. Like everything else in
Babylonia, they were built of mud brick and constructed like
a pyramid, or ziggurat, rather like the Mappin Terraces at
the Zoo. Water was pumped up from the wells in the foundations to irrigate the gardens. Each series of terraces was
planted with trees and flowers, and artificial water-courses
may have run musically here and there. In this lovely botani-
cal garden the princess wandered—longing, perhaps, for a
piece of real rock. One hopes that Nebuchadnezzar's manly
attempt to compensate a lady for a change of scenery was a
success. No man, certainly, could have done more; but history, and even the lives of humble men, suggest that such
gigantic gestures are not always the most acceptable. Perhaps
beneath the troubled bones of Babylon there lies a tablet
which records how the maid of the mountains received this
proof of the King's affection, when, after many months of
laborious rock-gardening, Nebuchadnezzar led her forth.

"Do you call that a garden? Why, it isn't even a hill!"

I asked Umran what he thought the Hanging Gardens
were like. He smiled rapturously and replied:

"Like the gardens of Paradise."

He led me to a convulsion in the earth such as you see behind a scaffolding in the City of London when a large building
has been pulled down. It was the site of the great ziggurat
of Babylon, the temple tower called E-temen-an-ki, which
archaeologists say was the traditional Tower of Babel. It was
evidently a ziggurat of typical Babylonian form, rising by a
series of stages sufficiently high above the dusty plain to give
astronomers an uninterrupted view of the sky. On the topmost stage was a temple, which Herodotus said contained
only a table and a couch which was occupied at night by a
single woman chosen by the deity out of all the women in the
land. It has been proved by inscriptions that this temple and

its high tower go back to the first age of Babylon, and that it was reconstructed from time to time by various kings.

We came to a series of broken arches which once supported the banqueting-hall of Nebuchadnezzar. This was the hall where, according to the *Book of Daniel,* Belshazzar saw the writing on the wall.

And as we wandered over the lonely mounds, silent except for the hum of the wild bee and the hornet, I thought how literally Isaiah's prophecy of the fall of Babylon has been fulfilled. It is, indeed, overthrown as God overthrew Sodom and Gomorrah.

"It shall never be inhabited, neither shall it be dwelt in from generation to generation: neither shall the Arabian pitch tent there; neither shall the shepherds make their fold there. But wild beasts of the desert shall lie there; and their houses shall be full of doleful creatures: and owls shall dwell there, and satyrs shall dance there. And the wild beasts of the islands shall cry in their desolate houses, and dragons in their pleasant palaces. . . ."

The "broad walls" of Babylon have been "utterly broken," as Jeremiah prophesied; her gates have been "burned with fire"; the city has indeed become "an astonishment" and "an hissing without an inhabitant." The words of Jeremiah have become literally true; the city is in "heaps." What word better describes this awful desolation: "And Babylon shall become heaps."

Isaiah prophesied that among the haunters of the ruins would be the *kippôd,* a Hebrew word which has puzzled translators of the Bible. In the Authorized Version it is translated as "bittern"; in the Revised Version it has been altered to "porcupine." I drew an admirable porcupine in my notebook and asked Umran if he had seen anything like it in the ruins.

His face lit up with recognition at once.

"AND BABYLON SHALL BECOME HEAPS"

"Ah, yes," he said, "it is the *kunfudh*. It is shy and comes in the night."

I saw no porcupines, jackals, serpents, owls, or any of the prophet's fauna, but I saw a creature that was not mentioned —a hare. He was the only living creature we disturbed all the time we were walking about the ruins. We put him up not far from Nebuchadnezzar's banqueting-hall.

"Look," cried Umran, " *'Arnabeh!*"

And a big hare sprang up and went off across the centre of the city.

When we returned to the Ishtar Gate, Umran pointed out the site of the "den" in which Daniel is said to have survived his ordeal with the lions. It is probable that lions were kept in the moat round the Ishtar Gate, and when Professor Koldewey began his excavations, he discovered thousands of coloured tiles at this place. When put together, they formed lions, some with white bodies and yellow manes, and others with yellow bodies and red manes. He thought that about a hundred and twenty lions must have guarded the main gate of Babylon.

Among the most interesting things to be seen in Babylon are bricks which are still stuck together with asphalt instead of mortar, exactly as Herodotus described them. He was in Babylon about a century after its fall, when it was still the greatest city in the world, although some of the buildings had been torn down. Possibly the punishment it had received from Xerxes gave the builders plenty to do, so that Herodotus may often have watched the asphalt gangs at work with their trolleys of boiling pitch.

The method of building was to lay a thin film of hot asphalt between each row of bricks; and bricks cemented in this way are so firm that they have to be broken apart with a pick-ax. Every now and then a layer of reeds would be inserted, and you can see their clear impression in the asphalt, in places where the reeds have rotted away. Supplies of asphalt were available, says Herodotus, at Hit, about seventy miles west-north-west of Baghdad, a town which even to-day smells horribly of sulphurated hydrogen, and has two asphalt wells, one hot and the other cold, within thirty feet of one another. Asphalt is, of course, found all over the Persian oilfields, and also round Mosul.

II

What happened to the Jews during their exile in Babylon? How did they employ themselves? Were they all weeping on the river banks, or was there another side to the picture? That a brighter side existed is proved by the reluctance shown by the Jews to return when the captivity was over, and re-build Zion. They were not poor slaves as their ancestors had been in Egypt. No one compelled them to make bricks, although they were in the greatest brick-making country on earth. We can be sure that had they been oppressed we should have been told about it by the prophets. That there was hardship, and that the various groups of exiles received different treatment, some good and some bad, goes without saying. The prophet known as the Second Isaiah, who detested Babylon, mentions that the Babylonians showed no mercy, and that upon the aged the yoke was heavy, which suggests that perhaps some were forced, regardless of age, to labour on the canals and dikes, or to engage in the hard work that is always going on in an artificially irrigated country. On the other hand, there is no hint of oppression in Ezekiel's description of the land of exile as "a land of traffick," "a city of merchants," "a fruitful field" into which a colony was transplanted like a willow beside many waters. And Jeremiah, who was a realist, would not have written from Jerusalem to tell the exiles to settle down, plant gardens, and eat

the fruit thereof unless this comfortable life had been possible.

The immense city of Babylon, with its fertile country, its
hordes of officials, its bankers, its markets, its quays, and its
countless industries, offered the quick-witted Jews thousands
of opportunities for getting on in the world. It was no doubt
in Babylon that the Jew first went into business.

Was the wealthy and old-fashioned firm of Egibi, which
for generations handled the financial business of the Babylonian court, a Hebrew firm, one wonders? Hundreds of clay
tablets recording their banking and mercantile transactions
have been found in the ruins of Babylon, and are now in the
British Museum. It has been pointed out that Egibi is Babylonian for Jacob, and it has been suggested that the founder
of the firm may have been a member of one of the lost Ten
Tribes who, having found his way to Babylon from Assyria,
set up in business and prospered. Many of the tablets record
the lending of money at 20 per cent interest, so that Egibi and
Company had obviously cast over any old-fashioned Hebrew
prejudice against usury. It is interesting, too, that although
the name of the firm remained Egibi (Jacob and Company),
all the members of the family had taken Babylonian names
such as Itti-Marduk-balâtu and Marduk-nasir-aplu, which in-
corporate the name of the local deity in an encouraging and
disarming manner, much in the same way, perhaps, as many
a Jew has been known to consider Mackintosh a better trade
name than Cohen.

The house of Egibi was evidently an organization that
managed estates, sold land and house-property, dealt in slaves
and palm groves, and was ready to lend anything from onions
to shekels of silver. Even if the firm observed a chilling attitude to their brethren from Judah, which as members of Israel
they well may have done, there can be little doubt that their
success must have fired the exiles with ambition and have

opened up new and glorious horizons.

But for the presence of a small group of religious men whose splendid vision and high faith in the future shone bright in exile, the Jews might have been lost among their conquerors. First among the teachers was Ezekiel, whose house at Tel-Abib, "the Cornhill," was the meeting-place of those who were building a new Judah. Ezekiel, while he welcomed the Exile as his nation's second chance, lived in the future, with a complete program for the new state in his mind: a theocratic state with the Temple of the Lord, and not the King's palace, as its centre and core. Ezekiel is interesting also because, as he went from house to house preaching, prophesying, and laying down the rough draft of the New Jerusalem, he not only for the first time developed the conception of the Good Shepherd who tenderly cares for his fold, but for the first time in the history of religion exhibited a care of souls which almost reminds one of St. Paul.

"As a shepherd seeketh out his flock in the day that he is among his sheep that are scattered, so will I seek out my sheep, and will deliver them out of all places where they have been scattered in the cloudy and dark day. . . . I will feed my flock, and I will cause them to lie down, saith the Lord God."

With these words of Ezekiel, written in Babylon, we seem to have entered the New Testament.

At the end of their sixty-years' nominal captivity, the Jews were to witness an event which is often misinterpreted and is always known misleadingly as the "Fall of Babylon." After Nebuchadnezzar's death the crown passed swiftly from head to head, coming at last to Nabonid or Nabunahid, who was a devout antiquary. He spent his time digging up ruined temples and inquiring into ancient cults. There is something pathetic in the thought of this monarch attempting to bring

the past of his country to light, while all the time the future
was rising to overwhelm him. He made the fatal mistake of
introducing into Babylon another band of exiles, the gods of
Babylonia. He gathered them from all parts and centralized
worship in Babylon. They were expensive guests, and funds
had to be diverted from the normal ecclesiastical endowments
for their upkeep. Thus the priests of Babylon were angry, and
the people from whom the exiled gods had been wrenched
considered themselves unrepresented in heaven. So the reign
of Nabonid holds a warning to all antiquaries and archaeologists who may feel inclined to introduce their harmless passions into public life. This King eventually locked himself up
with his studies in a palace at Teima, and may even have
abdicated in favour of his son, Belshazzar, whose hands, it
seems, held the government of Babylon.

The great power now rising in the world, Persia, was hailed
by Babylonians and Jews alike as their deliverer from archaeological monarchy. Cyrus the king was only too ready to act
the part, and he marched on Babylon. It will probably never
be known how Babylon fell. The *Book of Daniel,* which describes the last night in Babylon and the Writing on the
Wall, is now generally admitted to have been written two
centuries after to encourage the Maccabees against the Selu-
cids, and to have had more religious significance than historical accuracy. It is not counted among the prophetic books in
the Hebrew scriptures, neither do its facts agree with those
in the genuine literature of the Exile.

What is clear from history is that when Babylon fell, all the
horrible details of its fall, as prophesied by the Second Isaiah
and Jeremiah, were unrealized. The capture of Babylon by
Cyrus was as calm as Mussolini's march on Rome. Thus the
"Fall of Babylon," which sometimes creates in the mind a
vision of burning houses, falling ramparts, and dead bodies,

was merely a peaceful change of dynasty.

The prophets had sung of children dashed to pieces before their parents' eyes, of houses sacked, of men cut down like animals in a shambles, of fountains dried up in the heat of the conflagration. Even the most lovely of the exilic psalms, which begins "By the rivers of Babylon," concludes with the horrible words:

"Happy shall he be that taketh and dasheth thy little ones against the stones."

But the sack of Babylon, so eagerly anticipated by the Jewish prophets, never took place. Instead, the Persian armies entered the city in the year 539 B.C. without striking a blow and with orders to respect property and to do nothing to offend the populace. "Babylon is fallen and destroyed, howl for her!" Jeremiah had shrieked before the event, but there was nothing to howl about, because Babylon seemed delighted with her fall. The nations were indeed astonished, as the prophets had said, but not by the fall of Babylon, but because Babylon, with the finest defences and the greatest city walls in the world, had fallen without striking a blow.

Entering the city a fortnight after his army, Cyrus presented that sight rare in history, the conqueror turned philanthropist. Instead of knocking down the walls, he rebuilt them, and made necessary improvements and restorations to temples and public buildings. He sent the exiled gods back to their empty shrines and told the Jews, to their surprise and consternation, that they were free to go home. A close reading of the Second Isaiah, and of the books of *Haggai* and *Nehemiah*, combined with the irrefutable evidence of the great strength of Babylonian Jewry in Hellenistic and later times, proves that only a small number of exiles were willing to uproot themselves from Babylon in order to rebuild the National Home.

"Now that they were free to go, they discovered that they were well off in Babylon," wrote Maspero in *The Passing of the Empires*. "They would have to give up their houses, their fields, their business, their habits of indifference to politics, and brave the dangers of a caravan journey of three or four months' duration, finally encamping in the midst of ruins in an impoverished country, surrounded by hostile and jealous neighbours—such a prospect was not likely to find favour with many, and indeed it was only the priests, the Levites, and the more ardent of the lower classes, who welcomed the idea of a return with a touching fervour."

It was therefore a pathetically small contingent that set out with Sheshbazzar two years after the end of the Exile, and something like twenty years were to pass before the Temple was again built on Zion. Meanwhile the Babylonian Jews increased in numbers, in power, and in wealth. Though they had declined to go home, still, with a genius for having it both ways, they regarded the Temple in Jerusalem as their spiritual home, and never failed to contribute to its upkeep. At the head of the Jewish community in Babylon there lived a shadowy king of the Jews, a prince of the house of David, whose title was "Prince of the Captivity"—the Resch-Glutha. This potentate kept his own bodyguard, his ministers, his court officials, and appeared in public clothed in gold tissue and accompanied by the officers of his guard. He was noted for his hospitality and the splendour of his entertainments. When Babylon died, Seleucia inherited her fame, and from Seleucia it passed to Baghdad. There in the time of the Caliphs the Prince of the Captivity still held his court, and he, in whom we see the last reflection of Solomon's glory, was still reigning over Babylonian Jewry in the twelfth century A.D.

I left Babylon, its lonely, silent mounds, its cavernous ruins,

and its dusty, chocolate bricks, with the thought that though
the prophets may not have seen the expected desolation of
this city, still their words came true; for time is always on the
side of prophets.

TURKEY

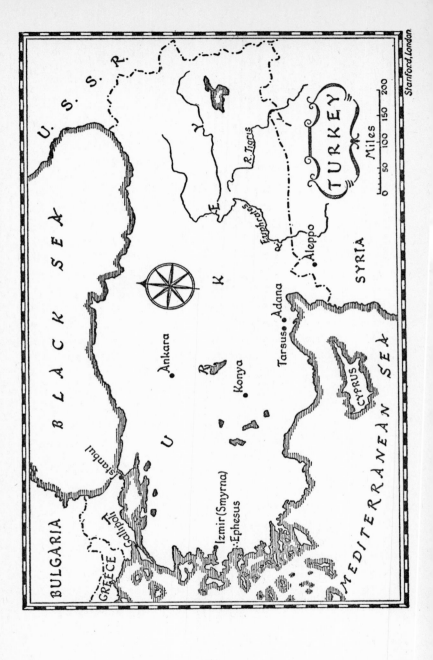

I

THE TRAIN TO ADANA

I

I FELL asleep for an hour or two, to awaken in the greyness before dawn. The train was standing in the station at Aleppo. Lying, like Damascus, on the edge of a desert, that big, mud-coloured city with its domes, its minarets, its thousands of flat-roofed houses, was fast asleep. The snores of the rich Syrian in the next compartment shook the frail partition. I wondered why he was going to Turkey.

Then into the silence of Aleppo clanked a weary, dusty train with the stain and grime of long travel on it; and I saw that this other wanderer in the dawn was our companion, the Taurus Express from Constantinople, or Istanbul as we must now call it.

So those trains met at Aleppo, one on the last lap of its journey to the south, the other on the first lap of its journey to the north. And as we rested together for a few moments in Aleppo, with the sun rising over the domes and minarets and the mud-coloured houses, those remarkable men in chocolate-coloured uniforms, the sleeping-car attendants, stepped down from their coaches and exchanged a few words in French.

Similar coaches were running into Berlin, into Paris, into Rome, Vienna, Budapest, and Athens. Men in chocolate-coloured uniforms made the beds at night, roused the traveller in the morning. The thought came to me that perhaps those international sleeping-cars are the only features of modern travel which link us with the Asia Minor of St. Paul.

209

In Roman times internationalism existed from Britain on the west to the Caspian Sea on the east. In St. Paul's day you could travel on a Roman road from Jerusalem to Boulogne, and Greek or Latin would see you through all the way. If you got into trouble anywhere on this long journey, you had only to proclaim Roman citizenship, as Paul did, to receive the same police assistance in Ephesus that you would get in Antioch, in Alexandria, or in Rome itself. But think how many different and unsympathetic authorities you encounter to-day on the same journey: French, Swiss, Italian, Yugo-Slav, Serbian, Bulgarian, Greek, Turkish, Syrian, and Palestinian. What was once an open road is now a series of frontiers, with customs men and passport officials lying in wait behind barriers ready to treat the traveller as if he were a spy or a smuggler.

Only the international sleeping-cars, whose beds, sheets, and blankets are similar in Paris and Istanbul, who serve food on the same thick blue plates in Belgrade as in Barcelona, reproduce in their uniformity something similar to the magnificent standardization of the Roman road.

As dawn came up behind Aleppo, we moved north into flat, hot country. I looked out of the window and admired the wild, unchanging East; the strings of camels crossing the ridges, the horsemen riding to some remote domed village of baked mud with rifles slung on their backs; and it pleased me to think that, in spite of all appearances to the contrary, the restaurant car was really the successor of the Via Egnatia.

The Syrian, shaved and scented, sat in the opposite seat and toyed with a cup of coffee. He wore his tarbush at an arrogant angle. He was going to Istanbul, he told me. It was, he said, a dying city. Kemal, the Dictator of Turkey, or Ataturk, "Father of the Turk," to give him his official title, had decided to let the old city die while Ankara grew up to be the capital of republican Turkey.

"But how can you kill Istanbul?" asked the Syrian with a wave of his manicured hand. "Nature has made it the bridge between East and West. It has always been a fortress and a bazaar. How can you kill it?"

I longed to ask him what mission took him to Istanbul, but refrained from doing so. With the tall red tarbush on his head, his scented hair, his flashy suit, and his soft, manicured hands, he looked, against the imaginary background of Istanbul, too like the wrapper of a mystery novel to bear investigation.

In a few hours the train climbed out of Syria into the mountains of the Amanus Range.

The flat country, the palm-trees, the mud villages and camel caravans were left behind. We mounted into a bleak land of towering peaks, fir and pine woods, and of dark valleys full of rushing water. The mountains dividing the country of St. Paul from the country of Christ reminded me now of Switzerland and now of Scotland. There were moments during that long climb into Turkey when I could have believed that we were approaching St. Moritz, and there were moments when I could have imagined that the train would run into Fort William.

We pulled up at the frontier station of Fevzipasa. A red flag with a white crescent and a star on it proclaimed that we were in Turkey. The Ghazi's [1] decree that all Turks must wear European clothes was pathetically evident. A crowd of men hung about the station, wearing cloth caps and incredibly old Western garments. An Arab in rags can achieve a certain dignity, but there is only squalor in a blue European suit patched with the remains of a brown one.

Police with red bands round their peaked caps, red cuffs to their grey, German-looking overcoats, brown belts from whose holsters shone black revolver-butts, entered the train

[1] The late Mustapha Kemal Ataturk.

and demanded passports. Customs men came along, prodding earnestly into luggage and even shaking the curtains of the carriages in search of contraband.

Meanwhile the silent, impassive crowd of men in cloth caps walked mournfully up and down the platform, gazing into the compartments. Soldiers with rifles on their shoulders patrolled the line. At last the train set off, and I looked out on a landscape that I shall never forget.

On his many journeys from Antioch to Asia Minor, St. Paul must have seen this country as I saw it in the morning sunshine. It is a land of immense, flat plains stretching to foothills and snow-topped mountains, no dwelling for miles, only flocks of sheep in charge of shepherds who wear square-shouldered cloaks. Those felt cloaks, called *kepenikler*, are impervious to wind or water. They are so stiff that the owner can step out of them and leave them standing upright. They are made of the tough Cilician goat's hair from which to-day, as in the day of St. Paul, tents, sails, and ropes are made.

As I looked at the shepherds standing like scarecrows in their stiff Cilician armour, I thought that in the course of his long journeys Paul must have wrapped himself in a *kepenik*. When he was in a Roman prison, did he not write, in his *Second Epistle to Timothy*, begging his "dearly beloved son" to bring "the cloak that I left at Troas with Carpus?" Surely Paul's cloak was a Cilician *kepenik* which, as no man knew better, would keep out the damp of any Roman cell.

The train sped downwards to a fair plain. At Adana I had to change for Tarsus, which lies about twenty miles to the west on a branch line. As I descended, I saw the Syrian from Tripoli leaning out of a window, but no longer wearing his native tarbush. His head was covered with a black beret. What a queer compromise, yet what a skilful one! The beret was European and would therefore find favour in Turkey, but as it had no brim, the Prophet himself could not have objected to it.

I stood for some moments on the platform at Adana, wondering what was the Turkish word for porter. The station was new and made of pressed concrete. Boys were wheeling trolleys full of chocolate, oranges, *semit*—rings of bread covered with sesame seeds—and also fox and marten furs. More mobile salesmen rushed about holding towards the travel-stained faces peering from the high windows sticks of sugar-cane.

My indecision was solved by a tap on the shoulder, and I turned to find myself under the puzzled scrutiny of two policemen. I had been told that a stranger cannot move two yards in Turkey without attention from the police, but I did not believe it. I showed them my passport, but this only seemed to make them more suspicious. I was taken to an office in the station, where a superior officer sat behind a desk, with a revolver at his waist. I began to feel like a character in a spy film. From the suspicion with which this officer glanced at my passport, and from his air of disapproval, his whispered remarks to his companions and his side-glances at me, I realized that I was up against the iron wall of a bureaucracy based on fear and on a complete ignorance of the outside world. To a German, a Frenchman, or an Italian, a thousand little things about me and my luggage would have told their harmless story, but to these men I was a profound mystery. The police officer could speak no English and I did not know what was going to happen, when a policeman appeared accompanied by a young American. I felt a happy sense of delivery. The young man explained that he was attached to the American Mission at Adana.

"They want to know what you are doing here," he said.

"I have come to see Tarsus."

"They want to know why."

"Because I am writing a book about St. Paul."

I could see that this shattered the morale of the police

force. The officer got up and, lighting a cigarette, he turned and asked, earnestly:

"Are there politics in your book?"

"No."

After grave deliberation, they decided that I must leave my passport in their charge. They told me politely, but in a manner which left no doubt that I was under police supervision, that I might travel to Tarsus on the daily train at seven o'clock on the following morning.

That first ten minutes in Turkey taught me that in addition to my passport, I should have possessed letters from the Ghazi himself vouching for my harmlessness.

I am still not sure what would have happened to me had the American Mission not given me a faint status by accepting me as a guest. Owing to the regulations of the republican Government, the work of the Mission has dwindled to that of a clinic in charge of one earnest American doctor, who gave me a bed in what was once the maternity ward of his now disused hospital.

The contrast between this room and the view on the other side of the mosquito-netted window was remarkable. Below my window a tribe of Kurdish refugees was encamped in mud and pools of water. They had built pile dwellings with old wood and had made walls of rusty kerosene tins. Hens strolled in and out of their dwellings. The encampment echoed with every kind of cough, from the asthmatic to the genuine whoop. I was startled to hear a cough of a super-human calibre. I wondered what human frame could stand the shattering effect of it, and was relieved to see that it came from a group of camels crouched in the mud.

The American Mission did wonderful work in old Turkey. It was established in 1819 with the object of giving free medical treatment and education. Colleges, high schools for boys and girls, hospitals and churches, sprang up all over the country; for over a century this Mission kept alight the lamp of Christian endeavour which St. Paul lit there so long ago. But now that republican Turkey has taken for its motto "Turkey for the Turks," the American Mission has found its powers curtailed.

II

Adana is the third largest town in Turkey. Lying on the rich Cilician plain, it is a centre of the cotton trade. One of two large mills produce cotton-thread for export.

It is a typical old Turkish town, a huddle of ramshackle wooden shops and of narrow streets with a surface of hard earth that becomes a quagmire of sticky mud in the wet season.

Strings of camels come softly through the lanes, laden with bales of cotton. Fat men sitting on donkeys thread their way through the crowds. Loud-speakers bellow Turkish music from cafés. Wild countrymen from the plains, and shaggy mountaineers from the Taurus, stand looking at humble little shops as if they were in a grand metropolis.

There is one wide new street which leads from the station to the town. It expresses the European urge of the Republic. Pretty villas, which might have been picked up from a suburb of Hamburg, dot its length, and in a park stands one of those statues of the Ghazi which are rising in every town.

Statues are a revolutionary break with old Turkey. Graven images are not permitted by the Moslem religion, and the first statue ever erected in Turkey is only a few years old. It must have caused a tremendous sensation. It stands in Istanbul and symbolizes the birth of the Republic. As if to challenge Moslem opinion, or to make up for lost time, the sculptor has created a crowd of bronze men, so that rarely have so many figures stood on one plinth. The group is almost a "Who's Who" of the Republic. Since that creative moment statues of Ataturk have gone up all over the land, so that they no longer horrify even the most conservative.

I was surprised to see a plaster cast of the Venus de Milo standing at the door of the little museum at Adana, in strange contrast to the Hittite monuments that surround her. I was told that she is a regulation "issue" to all museums, and must be placed on view to educate the people. How strange that a race which has ground down the work of Praxiteles for mortar, and has built statues by Pheidias into the walls of its stables, should now be asked to admire the art it has done so much to destroy.

Yet how significant this is of modern Turkey's break with Islam. The present rulers realize that the Mohammedan ban on graven images has warped the mind and closed the windows of the soul. Century after century the beauty of the human face and form has been a forbidden thing in this country, so that the artist and the architect have been obliged to confine themselves to the tracing of mathematical spirals. What a world of irony there is in the gentle body of the Venus de Milo standing at the door of a Turkish museum to teach the beauty of Greece to people whose ancestors built a mosque inside the Parthenon.

One of the most interesting things in Adana is a fine bridge about three hundred yards in length, spanning the river Si-hun, the Sarus of antiquity. There is one arch among the many arches of this structure which is said to have been part of a bridge built by the Empress Helena, when she was on her way from Constantinople to Jerusalem to discover the Holy Cross.

While I was walking in the streets of Adana I heard the call to prayer, and looking up towards the minaret of a mosque I saw the muezzin, not in his flowing robes and

turban, but dressed in a blue reach-me-down suit and a cap.
The old high-pitched, resonant call was there just the same,
but the general effect was rather ridiculous. The man might
have been selling fish.

The Ghazi's reforms in Turkey are astonishing. He is the
greatest iconoclast in modern history. Just as the Soviet has
obliterated the Tsarist regime, so Kemal Ataturk is obliterat-
ing all memory of the Sultanate and the Caliphate and building a barrier between modern republican Turkey and the
static Turkey of the past.

He has carried his reforms into the strongholds of Islam
and no man has dared to object. The great mosque of St.
Sophia in Istanbul is a museum. The dervish and other religious orders have been disbanded and their mosques turned
into show places. The Moslem holy day, Friday, has been
abolished in favour of the Christian Sunday. Religious schools
have been closed and no religious instruction is permitted in
elementary schools.

Some Europeans smiled when they read that all Turks are
compelled by law to wear hats instead of the fez, thinking it
to be merely a childish imitation of dress in Europe. It is more
than that. It strikes at the root of social and religious custom
and is an even more sweeping change than the unveiling of
women.

Headgear has always had a profound significance in the
East. One glance at a man's head and you know his religion
and also his social position. The fez is not really Turkish, but
is Greek in origin. Two centuries ago, when the Turks still
wore turbans, the social and religious significance of turbans
was carried to fantastic extremes. There was a different kind
of turban for every official and dignitary in the Sultan's palace.
When these turbans were abolished and the fez was adopted
as the national headgear, old-fashioned Turks thought the
end of the world had come. Similar feelings were expressed

when Kemal abolished the fez. But the hat with its brim—
for centuries the sign of the Christian dog—was an astonishing substitute, and in no way has the Ghazi proclaimed his
power more surely than by compelling his countrymen to
conquer their prejudice against it.

No Moslem hat may have a brim, for a devout Moslem
cannot bend forward and touch the earth with his forehead
if there is a brim to his hat. Therefore it would be easy to
make prayers in a mosque both ridiculous and impossible by
decreeing the wearing of bowler hats. Turkey's Dictator has
not done that. The faithful are still allowed to pray—in cloth
caps.

When you go into a mosque in modern Turkey, you realize
at once why this most hideous of Western head-coverings is
popular with the devout. By reversing the cap so that the
peak is at the back of the head, a smooth, brimless surface
lies above the forehead and the ground can be touched with
ease. Museum curators, Customs officials, and even policemen who obey the call to prayer, can perform the same act
by reversing their peaked service caps.

That evening members of the small Christian community
in Adana, a few Syrians, Armenians, and one Greek girl, came
to the Mission and, sitting round the stove, we talked, as all
people talk to-day, of peace and the need for peace in the
world.

I walked out on the flat roof before I went to bed. The
stars were enormous in a velvet-blue sky. To the north I could
see the dark ridge of the Taurus Mountains, and all round was
a gigantic emptiness under the stars. There were no sounds
but the pitiful coughing of Khurdish refugees and, far off, the
barking of dogs.

II

TARSUS

I

WE took a carriage and drove for some way down a long, straight road and into a shabby little town where rows of wooden shacks faced each other across roadways of hard mud. And this dusty malarial little town crouched in a swamp was Tarsus.

I looked for something that might have lingered from the time of its pride, but there was nothing. Invasion, war, and centuries of inertia have obliterated every vestige of the past. I was told that remains of the ancient city lie fifteen and twenty feet beneath the surface of modern Tarsus. People digging in their cellars and back-yards have felt their spades strike hard against the crowns of arches and the capitals of columns buried in the earth.

I was shown an arch called St. Paul's Arch, but it has nothing to do with the Apostle. It is probably a Byzantine arch to which the Greek Orthodox clergy, who were driven out in 1922, had given a picturesque and obvious name.

The modern town occupies only a small portion of the land once covered with the marble temples, colonnades, baths, and public squares of Roman Tarsus. Miles away in open country, bits of the city wall stand like old teeth in the cotton fields. No longer does the ice-clear Cydnus, the pride of ancient Tarsus, flow through the centre of the town. The Emperor Justinian had made a flood channel to the east of the city to carry off surplus water in the spring, but in the days of decadence, the people of Tarsus neglected to clean the river-

219

bed, with the result that many centuries ago the Cydnus flowed into the canal of Justinian instead of traversing the city.

The same terrible ignorance and sloth have caused the once magnificent inland lake and harbour of Rhegma to silt up. It is now a marsh thirty miles wide, a nesting-place for wild duck and a breeding-place for the malarial mosquito.

The ancient Tarsians loved to sit chattering like water-fowl beneath the marble colonnades on the Cydnus bank, and could they see the downfall of the city whose splendour and beauty once rejoiced their hearts, there is probably no word in Greek or Hebrew that could adequately express their sorrow or their incredulity.

I had expected streets of squalid wooden shanties, unmade roads, and patches of waste land where groups of unshaven men stood among shaggy horses, but the contrast between the fair Hellenistic city mentioned by Cicero, Strabo, Apollonius, and St. Paul, was so great that I felt a sense of shock. Had it not been Tarsus, I should perhaps have felt only the traveller's interest in strange sights and sounds. But the thought that Tarsus could have sunk to this seemed to me so tragic that I should have been glad to have escaped from the place.

There is, however, one relic in Tarsus which may have been there in the time of Paul. It is a piece of ground about two hundred and eight feet long and one hundred and thirty feet wide, which is enclosed within a wall of Roman concrete about twenty-four feet high and twenty feet thick. In the centre of the enclosure are two huge concrete platforms of the same height as the wall. The enclosure and the wall are overgrown with grass and asphodels.

The Turks call this structure the *Dunuk Tash*, or the "overturned stone." They say that the building was once the palace of an ancient prince of Tarsus with whom Mohammed was offended. Therefore the Prophet overturned his palace and buried the offender beneath it. A less elaborate but equally erroneous theory is that it is the tomb of Sardanapalus.

There is an easy way to the top of the wall, and I think that any one who examines this structure will agree that it is the *podium,* or platform, of a Roman Temple. It is evident that the concrete now exposed to view was once hidden by stonework which was probably covered with marble.

The wall and the concrete platforms within it have been penetrated in many directions by tunnels made by treasure-seekers, but their spades soon became blunted against the steel-hard Roman cement. William Burckhardt Barker, who was resident in Tarsus in the middle of the last century, gave an account of some of the determined assaults on this Roman wall in a book called *Lares and Penates,* published in 1853. The one or two educated Europeans in the town at that time were convinced that the platform was some kind of tomb, and that if they once found a way into it they would discover rich treasures. One of the most energetic excavators was the French consul, who, after many a bitter disappointment, was rewarded by the discovery of "the first and second fingers of a man in marble, of gigantic size, joined together, but not as if they had belonged to the hand of a statue, but a finished work in itself."

The modern traveller appreciates this ruin because the top of the wall is one of the few places in Tarsus which affords a good view over the low-lying country. But even from its height the Mediterranean Sea is not visible. One can, however, follow the course of the river Cydnus as it winds its way southward through the level plain towards the great marsh of Rhegma, five miles away. When one looks to the north, the ground is seen gradually rising towards foothills which become higher until, thirty miles off, they lie against the tremendous wall of the Taurus.

When Paul was born, Tarsus was already one of the ancient cities of the Hellenistic world. The city owed its importance to its geographical position and to the enterprise and the energy of its people. Like the citizens of Glasgow, who for centuries have dredged and deepened the Clyde, making it one of the great shipbuilding rivers of the world, the citizens of Tarsus dredged and deepened the inland lake of Rhegma into which their river emptied itself before meandering to the sea.

They cut a channel for ships and deepened the lagoon. Great docks, arsenals, and warehouses were built, and their foundations still lie in the marsh. As long as the engineers drained and deepened the channel and maintained the harbour works, this splendid sheltered stretch of water remained one of the great ports and anchorages of the ancient world.

The engineers of Tarsus cut a road through the Cilician Gates and thus created one of the historic mountain passes on the main road from the Euphrates to Ephesus and Rome. So, by sea and by land, Tarsus became not only a famous port and a rich caravan city, but it became also the buckle which bound East to West. There is a certain inevitability in the fact that the man who was chosen to interpret Christianity to the West should have come from the city which, above all others in the Hellenistic world, was a perfect amalgamation of Orient and Occident.

Tarsus is also interesting in the history of municipal experiments because it realized, for a time at any rate, the Platonic ideal of government by philosophers. The famous University of Tarsus was known all over the world. In its zeal for learning, Strabo placed it above the universities of Athens and Alexandria. Thus the same persistent energy which drove the sons of Tarsus to reform Nature in the service of commerce, inspired them when they approached the intellectual life. Among the many qualities which every one must appreciate in St. Paul are his tremendous energy, his single-mindedness, and what to-day we should call "drive." He was a true son of the city that hewed the Cilician Gates out of the rock, and it is important to realize that Paul was not born in the lassitude of an Oriental city, but in the proud and virile atmosphere of mental and physical achievement.

The students of Tarsus University were all drawn from Cilicia. Unlike Alexandria and Athens, Tarsus did not attract visitors. But the Tarsians loved to study in order to be able to visit other universities to complete their education, and few such, Strabo says, ever returned home: their zeal and enthusiasm found professional posts for them wherever they settled. If the physical achievements of Tarsus reminds us of Glasgow, the mental attitude may possible suggest a resemblance to Aberdeen.

It was to Tarsus that Cleopatra sailed when Antony was resting there after his victory at Philippi. He had sent for the Queen of Egypt to punish her for the aid she gave to Cassius. Cleopatra, knowing well how sternly he punished and fined his enemies, decided to make the sensational appearance which Plutarch and Shakspere have immortalized. When the Egyptian fleet came in from the sea and entered the lake of Rhegma, Antony, sitting on his throne in the marble streets of Tarsus, noticed that the crowds had melted away, leaving him alone. They had gone to watch the approaching pageant. They saw a vessel with a gilded stern, sails of purple outspread and silver oars moving in time to the sound of flutes, pipes, and harps. Dressed like Aphrodite, the Goddess of Love, Cleopatra lay beneath an awning bespangled with gold, while boys like painted Cupids stood on each side, fanning her. At the helm and at the rigging stood her most beautiful slave women in the guise of Nereids and Graces. The crowds on the river bank could smell the perfumes burning on the ship.

How often must Paul have heard this story told by old men who had seen Cleopatra.

II

I walked down a side street in Tarsus where a number of humble little workshops are open to the gaze of any passer-by. In the darkness of these sheds men spin thread from goat's hair and weave it into coarse cloth.

This street of weavers is the only link with the Tarsus in which St. Paul was born, for I saw with a start of surprise and delight that these men were making tent cloth for the nomads of the Taurus.

My interest was so obvious that the weavers invited me to go inside, where, with gentleness and kindliness and a sense of humour which made me feel that I was home in England again, they showed me the whole process of their work.

I learnt that the goat's hair comes from the herds which live on the Taurus Mountains, where snow lies until May. In this cold atmosphere the animals grow magnificent coats, and for centuries the hair has been famous for its strength and durability.

In the East a tent-maker is a weaver of tough fabric. In antiquity the Apostle's birthplace was famed for tent cloth, or *cilicium,* as it was called, after the province of Cilicia; an interesting memory of this survives in the modern French word for hair-cloth—*cilice.*

The method of weaving and spinning is primitive. The spinner, with a bag of goat's hair over his shoulder, advances and retreats from the wheel as he feeds the yarn with pinches of hair. In an adjoining shed the weavers sit at ground-level, with their legs in a pit. Their looms are upright, warp-weighted looms of a type that has been used since the dawn of history. The warp threads hang down from the roller and as the cloth is made, it is wound round this roller. Such clumsy, but efficient and picturesque, structures were the only type of loom used in ancient Greece and Rome, and I recalled a painting on a Greek vase in the British Museum which shows Penelope sitting beside a loom of the same design.

As I watched the weavers at work, I knew that I was watching something that St. Paul had seen. If he returned to Tarsus to-day, he would look in vain for the temples, the baths, the statues, the market-place, even the river; but in these little workshops he would recognize the trade that had supported him in Thessalonica, Corinth, and Ephesus.

How remarkable it is that such a humble trade can survive empires. The explanation is that it fulfils a common human need, and that no matter what race of barbarians pulled down marble statues or destroyed aqueducts, and no matter how savage the war, the siege, or the massacre, the time would always come when life became peaceful again and some one would come to Tarsus anxious to buy a length of tent cloth.

III

KONYA

I

ALL that day the train pounded across Turkey.

There was an unforgettable three-quarters of an hour leaving Adana, when we climbed at a snail's pace into the after Taurus Mountains. We passed in and out of rock tunnels and cuttings, with a view to our left of savage gorges which, although the sun was shining brilliantly, lay below in partial darkness. We gazed down into desolate ravines reminding me of the Pass of Killiecrankie on a gigantic scale. Far below a small stream tumbled from rock-shelf to rock-shelf, winding its way through a crack in the mountains. Fir-trees and pines climbed the heights.

We emerged on a high plateau where the air was colder than in Tarsus or Mersin; where spring was at least a month later than in Cyprus and on the Cilician Plain; where clouds over the vast slopes of the Sultan Dagh threatened rain. I felt that in climbing up through the Cilician Gates we had climbed in less than an hour out of the East into the West.

I wearied of looking out of the window on the featureless, greenish-brown plains, enlivened only by an occasional horseman or enormous flocks of sheep. The shepherds in their square-shouldered, felt cloaks, would pause to watch the train go past, sometimes waving their sticks. The big white dogs would bare their teeth and stand on the defensive. As they lifted their necks, I could see the massive collars, worn by all sheep-dogs in Asia Minor as a protection against wolves.

They are ringed by sharp iron spikes about three inches in length.

Hour succeeded hour, and there was nothing but the same vista receding to distant hills, here and there a poverty-stricken village, but usually only desolate uplands, bleak and wild, on whose unfriendly expanse a band of wandering *yuruks* had the air of explorers.

The sign that we were approaching a town was generally a clumsy four-wheeled cart bumping along a rough track beside the train. Where there was a cart, there must be a track; and all tracks lead to towns. Sure enough in a few minutes we would come to feathery poplar-trees, the white finger of a minaret rising above them; and so we would rest with a weary sigh in a station full of ragged loungers who walked two by two along the track, gazing with dull, silent curiosity into the carriages.

Soldiers in loose-fitting, putty-coloured uniforms would patrol the line, rifles slung on their backs. The ubiquitous police, with red tabs on their tunics and red bands round their caps, would come out of the station office and look about with searching eyes.

There is, however, a lighter side to travelling in Turkey. Every journey is a prolonged picnic. It is only on the trains running from the new capital at Ankara that such luxuries as *wagons lits* and restaurant cars are to be found. On ordinary trains the passenger forages for himself, and the provision of food seems to be the main occupation at some of the poor little wayside halts. Some stations specialize in *kebab*, which is meat cut into slices and grilled on a skewer. Small boys come along selling this, shouting down the corridor. They come into the carriage, put their fingers at the top of the skewer and, withdrawing it, shoot the pieces of roast meat on to a piece of newspaper.

Sometimes there are oranges or apples, or bags of roast

chestnuts; and always there are delicious rings of bread covered with sesame seed, called *simit*, and little cups of hot, sweet coffee, carried rapidly through the corridors by small boys.

But on this journey to Konya I did not need to buy food. My companion, Hassan, had brought with him a large basket containing a roast chicken, slabs of cheese, and a quantity of bread.

The other occupant of our carriage was also a model of courtesy and hospitality. He was a young infantry officer returning to his regiment from leave. His luggage was redeemed from the commonplace by a woman's silver fox fur and a bowl containing five gold-fish.

Every now and then he would plunge a tumbler into the bowl and empty out water, which he would throw through the window. Then he would rush to the lavatory at the end of the coach and return with fresh water, which he would pour into the bowl.

His mother had given him enough food to feed the regiment. He had a large tin packed with every kind of Turkish delicacy, including excellent *dolmas* of savoury rice wrapped about with vine leaves. These he handed round to us. We offered him some of our chicken, but he opened another tin and showed us that he also had a cold roast chicken.

He unpacked his bag and brought out a bottle of scented water called "Kemal Lotion," with which he refreshed his hands and his face. He then produced a bottle of the excellent white wine which is now made in Turkey.

So the hours wore on, and the endless brown plains slipped past the window. The sun crossed the sky. . . . The officer removed his tunic and, placing his gold-fish out of the sun, went to sleep. Hassan pillowed his head on an overcoat and also slept.

I looked out of the window at country which was rather like Salisbury Plain on a large scale.

II

Hassan had been in Konya some years before, in command of a squadron of republican cavalry. He was eager, as the train approached the town, to see again the scenes of his exploits.

"Look!" he cried excitedly, pointing towards a belt of trees, "that is where I burnt a farm to the ground! Rebels were hiding in it. I burnt it over their heads, and they ran out in the smoke right into the arms of my men."

He looked again, and seemed disappointed to find that the place had been rebuilt.

I looked with curiosity at the town, once the Iconium of the New Testament, which I had come so far to see.

The train approached miles of feathery trees and bright green gardens, a welcome contrast to the brown, stone-scattered Lycaonian Plain which we had endured since morning. Wherever I looked, there were blue mountains rising on the horizon like islands from a sea; only to the north did the flat plain vanish in brown distance.

Above the tops of trees I saw the roofs of single-story buildings, with here and there the minaret of a mosque. I saw a file of camels slowly padding along a track on the outskirts of the town. I saw an old Ford car, full of Turks, trying to race the train on a fairly good road that had sprung up from somewhere and went beside the track for a few miles. As I looked at Konya and tried to imagine what Roman Iconium once looked like, I realized that Paul must inevitably have compared it with Damascus.

Both cities lie in a sudden burst of green due to the presence of water. Just as the Abana, gushing through the limestone rocks of the Anti-Lebanon, has created Damascus, so water flowing from the mountains of Pisidia irrigates the plain of Konya. Both Konya and Damascus are high above sea-level, and in Paul's time both towns were commercial stations on the great caravan routes of the world.

When the train stopped, we jumped down to the track and found ourselves in the motley crowd which gathers at Turkish stations. Weary-looking men in shirt-sleeves leaned down from the windows of the coaches and bought skewers of *kebab,* bottles of water, and oranges. Turkish officers gazed out from the windows of first-class carriages, looking rather British in their khaki tunics, but German when they were wearing their high-waisted coats of field-grey.

In the station yard were waiting about thirty shaky old carriages, each one drawn by two lively, well-matched little horses. The box-seats were occupied by whip-waving and whip-cracking drivers, who in pre-Republican days would have worn Turkish dress, but are now obliged to wear the European reach-me-down. Their caps were so old and their suits so ancient and patched that they would create despair in the Flea Market of Paris.

"I know they look shabby," said Hassan, "but that matters not. These clothes represent a change of mind and a break with tradition."

We selected an *araba* and set off with much whip-cracking for the town, which is some distance from the station. On the outskirts I saw a newly erected statue of the President in military uniform, standing on a decorative plinth in the middle of a small public garden. There is probably no other military statue quite like it, for the sculptor, wishing to express Kemal's policy of peaceful reconstruction has placed the Conqueror's hand, not on the hilt of his sword, but upon a stalk of ripe barley.

STREET IN KONYA, TURKEY

We clattered over a paved road into Konya, which, as befits the largest town between Smyrna and the Taurus, has a spaciousness about its new streets in strange contrast to the narrow, winding labyrinth of the old bazaars.

Side by side with the new houses and shops of Konya are ruined Seljuk buildings which date from the Eleventh Century, crumbling town walls of the same period, and miles of narrow shops, open to the street, where traders make and sell their goods.

Above this strange confusion of old and new rise the minarets of many a fine mosque and the stumpy candle-snuffer cone, covered with sage-green tiles, that marks the ancient headquarters of the now expelled Order of the Mevlevi Dancing Dervishes.

We caused great interest in Konya, where visitors—one of them obviously a foreigner—are not seen every day. Whenever I saw a policeman's eye on me, I thought with contentment of Hassan, ready always to present my credentials.

We had some difficulty about an hotel. The first one we tried had a gramophone which blared out Turkish dance music incessantly and did not look at all inviting. Eventually we discovered a modest-looking hotel, the *Seljuk Palace,* standing some way from the road in a little garden. I was told that it was owned by Russians.

The people were charming. They hastened to carry our bags up the uncarpeted staircase. They rushed to take possession of my passport, and no doubt they rushed it to the police.

I was given a small bedroom containing a wardrobe, a chair, and a bed. Two worn rugs covered the scrupulously clean floor-boards. The window-curtains had shrunk at both top and bottom so that complete privacy was impossible. The most important object, as I was to learn later, was a stove standing almost in the middle of the room, with a big black pipe that spouted up to the ceiling and traversed the room on its way to a chimney outside. Konya, lying over half the height of Ben Nevis above sea-level, can experience hot days, but during the night the temperature may be a little above freezing-point. When a wood-fire is lit in these Russian stoves, a room hitherto near freezing-point is warm in about ten minutes.

At dinner that night a smiling, collarless waiter placed before me a roughly hewn scrap of meat, and potatoes which had been painfully cut into thin slices and then subjected, before a slight heating, to a bath in one of the more revolting oils. From the expression of eager expectancy on the faces of waiter, proprietor, and proprietor's wife, I gathered that this was either a speciality or a death verdict. Sawing off a portion, I took an apprehensive mouthful, whereupon the waiter bowed, grinning all over his face, and the proprietor came forward and, also bowing, pointed to my plate, and said with some difficulty:

"Beef-roast!"

Then I realized that in this far-off place the pathetic sweetness of the human heart, that transcends all barriers of race, had devised a little compliment to England. I rose and told them in sign language that the meat was superb. They laughed and bowed with delight. And when the room was empty for a moment, a little hungry dog that had slipped beneath the table was a friend in need and—in deed!

Silence had descended on Konya when I went to bed. Then, suddenly, the quiet night was cut by a mournful whistle, and another, farther off, and another. It was as though many owls had chosen the same minute to hoot all over Konya. There came a whistle almost beneath my window. I tiptoed over and looked out. I saw a bulky figure emerge from the shadow of a wall opposite and walk slowly away in the star-light.

He was wearing a fur cap and a huge sheepskin coat with the fleece outside. He carried a thick staff, a revolver was belted to his fleecy waist, and every now and then he would pause and lift a whistle to his lips, uttering a long, melancholy call. There would come an answering whistle; and he would move on, a queer, barbaric figure who might have come from the camp-fires of Gengis Khan.

That was my first sight of the whistling watchmen who come out at nightfall in Konya.

III

Any one who knew Turkey in the old days would be as-tonished by modern Konya. Women who used to be veiled from head to foot now wear Western clothes, and even stop in the street to talk to their men acquaintances. They read fashion papers and do their best to copy the modes of Paris.

The old-fashioned, monumental woman, stuffed fat on sweets and idleness, is now merely a survival. The modern Turk claims to admire slim women, and I notice that his ad-vertisements for cigarettes, and any other product which of-fers an excuse for the picture of a pretty girl, show a slender figure dressed in the latest fashion, often smoking a cigarette with a self-conscious air of emancipation.

The most significant sight, as I look out of my window, is the large elementary school opposite, the finest new building in the town. About half an hour before the janitor unlocks the school gate a hundred noisy little boys and girls gather there with books under their arms, eagerly waiting to be let in. As soon as the gates open, I see children running from every corner, tearing across the playground and disappearing into the building. At the same time groups of young Turkish girls, aged about eighteen, walk sedately past, carrying port-folios or attaché-cases. They wear dark blue coats and skirts and rakish peaked caps bound with gold braid. They are pupil-teachers on their way to an academy. In days before the Republic they would have been veiled in a harem.

The more I see of Turkey the greater is my admiration for the achievements of the Ghazi and his band of staff officers at Ankara. Given ten years of peace, the world will see a new and remarkable Turkey.

The present rulers of Turkey took over a country that was riddled with inefficiency and nepotism, bound by tradition and custom, bankrupt and apparently hopeless. They have modernized it, flung over tradition, turned out the foreigner, and got the wheels to work again.

Kemal Ataturk is not unlike Alfred the Great. He has driven the Danes out of his kingdom and now, his sword cast aside, he is making new laws for his people.

The soul of Kemalist Turkey is, like all movements these days, intensely national. The Turk has for centuries been sub-merged by Greeks, Armenians, Jews, and other foreigners, in whose hands the whole commerce of the country was gath-ered. His language and religion have been invaded by Arabic words and beliefs. The Ghazi is creating a Turkish Turkey and, in order to do so, he has had to smash a thousand idols. Everything foreign had to go.

It is amazing to observe with what placidity the nation has seen the overthrow of tradition, the disappearance of Sultan and Caliph, the change in social custom, the freedom of women, the abolition of national dress, and the virtual aboli-tion of religion.

Even those who view with cynical amusement the model he has taken of cocktail-drinking, fox-trotting, bowler-hatted Europe, cannot fail to admire the tremendous drive and cour-age of the Ghazi in his determination to give Turkey a European status. He is even rewriting the history of the Turk in order to give his people a European outlook.

Of all his achievements perhaps the most interesting is the new system of education.

When I told Hassan that I wanted to see the big elementary school in Konya, he said, to my astonishment:

"I think I shall let you go alone; if I come with you, I may disgrace myself and cry."

I looked at him in amazement. Was this the man who boasted of burning down farms, slaying rebels, and charging with drawn sword on Greeks and royalists?

"You don't understand," he cried. "You come from a country where education is easy, where there is nothing remarkable about a school. But think! When I was a boy, I sat on the floor in a grimy building outside a mosque while an old man, who did not care whether we listened or not, read the Koran to us. That was Turkey in my youth. But now it is different. Every young Turk, boy and girl, can get knowledge free. Learning is like water in your country. It is free. Everywhere —free! I tell you, you cannot understand. When I see these children—I, I feel it here. . . ."

And Hassan, the cavalry officer, gave himself a great blow over the heart.

However, we went together to the school, a light, airy building constructed on modern lines. There was a bust of Ataturk in the entrance hall.

The head master told me that all classes are mixed. The teachers are men and women. The old Arabic alphabet is taboo. Every word written or spoken in the school is the new Turkish language, written in Latin characters. Religion is not allowed to be taught.

We went into a classroom. The fifty little Turkish boys and girls stood to attention. The classroom might have been that of any London County Council school. Each child had a desk of his own. There was a blackboard on which a young woman teacher had been writing. At the back of the room was a large tray of sand, perhaps six by three feet in size. The smaller children are taught the alphabet in a pleasant and original manner. They fill small funnels with sand and, rather as a cook ices a cake, spell letters in sand, controlling the flow by placing a finger across the hole in the funnel.

When the master asked the class if any boy or girl would like to stand forward and write a sentence on the board, every hand shot out. A small boy with a close-cropped head was chosen. He walked out without the slightest embarrassment and took the chalk. In a sure and efficient way he wrote a sentence on the board, bowed to the head master, and went back to his desk.

"What has he written?" I asked.

"He has written," said the head master, " 'When I grow up, I shall be of service to my country.' "

Looking round to say something to Hassan, I was just in time to see him disappearing through the door with his handkerchief to his eyes.

I was taken into classroom after classroom. I was impressed by two things: the solemn intelligence of the children and the fact that girls and boys worked together in perfect equality. For centuries the Turk has been brought up to regard woman as an inferior being. A son is the god of a house, but a daughter is the servant. One might think that this feeling, existing century after century, would have had some effect on the atmosphere of a mixed class of girls and boys. But no; the atmosphere of the harem and the subjection of woman has had no effect on this generation.

Suddenly the play-time bell rang through the school. There was a crash of feet all over the building as children stood to attention. They marched out two by two, singing a patriotic song.

Hassan wiped his eyes again and coughed, blowing his nose violently.

"You see the new Turkey," he whispered. "Is it not wonderful?"

The head master stood beaming in the hall as the long files of singing children marched into the sunlight.

"These are the teachers, the doctors, the architects of new Turkey!" cried Hassan, his voice charged with emotion as little dark-eyed and blue-eyed Turks passed singing under the bust of Kemal Ataturk.

IV

As I talked to Hassan in the evenings, I began to share his enthusiasm for the Ghazi. This man has not merely rallied his people and given them a focus for self-esteem: he has given them a new spiritual life. He has turned their backs on the past and has set their feet on a new road that may lead—who knows?—to a great and splendid future.

Hassan described to me one of the most important moves in the national regeneration of Turkey.

"When I told you that we Turks should set up a monument to Lloyd George, you smiled," he said. "I said this to you at Soli. You remember? But it is true, and I say it again. The statesmen of Europe who permitted Venizelos to have his way in 1920 and 1921, when we were weakened and smashed after the War, roused our courage, put new blood into our veins, made us a nation again, more truly a nation that we have been since we captured Constantinople in the Middle Ages. Beaten as we were, we combined to fight the Greeks and we won our fight under the Ghazi. It was at the conference table at Lausanne that the new Turkey was born. From that moment, Turkey was to be Turkish. Foreigners must go.

"How many Greeks and Armenians do you see in Turkey to-day? Not many. There are fewer Greeks in Turkey than there have been since the days of Alexander the Great. It was arranged at Lausanne that Greeks in Turkey should go, and that Turks in Macedonia and Greece should come here in exchange. Between 1921 and 1927 more than one million three hundred and fifty thousand Greeks left Turkey, and nearly five hundred thousand Turks came here from Greece. The economists in Europe laughed at us. They said, 'How is it possible for this foolish country to progress if it turns out its commercial men?' But they did not know that the Greeks and the Armenians were the middlemen. They sold us goods from Europe which we can buy just as well ourselves. We have not suffered.

"The next move of the Ghazi was to expel the Khalif. 'What is this,' asked Europe. 'Has this country, which once dreamed of Pan-Islamism, gone mad?' For just that reason we expelled the Khalif. Islam is static. No progress can take place within its boundaries. Republican Turkey knew that if she wished to become a modern state she must throw off those traditions which bound her to the past."

Hassan took out a paper and a pencil and sketched for me a brief outline of Turkey's economic regeneration. Railway construction is going on at great speed year by year. New coal-mines are being opened up. By-products such as benzol, tar, and gas are to be produced. Copper-mining is soon to be started. Sulphur beds are being worked at Keciburly. A silk factory has opened at Broussa; a factory for woollen goods at Ankara; a glass factory at Pasabahce, on the Bosphorus, will soon turn out five thousand tons of moulded glass annually; a sugar refinery has been opened at Alpullu, and others are being built at Usak, Eskisehir, and Turhal.

"Is this progress, or is it not?" asked Hassan, his eyes sparkling.

"And all the money left over from these developments goes into the army and in state education?" I asked.

"Naturally," said Hassan. "We must keep our country safe, and we must educate our children to inherit the new Turkey."

"Has it ever occurred to you, Hassan, that the new Turkey which you are so proud of is the result of Christianity?"

He looked astonished, and told me that religion in Turkey was a matter of personal opinion.

"You don't quite understand. Europe is the result of centuries of Christianity. All the things you are striving for to-day are the result of Christian culture. You even observe the Christian Sunday and not the Moslem Friday. Perhaps some day you will become logical and accept Christmas."

v

We were invited to dinner in Konya. The house was that of a municipal official with whom I had had some dealings, a quiet, agreeable man who always wore a black jacket and striped trousers, like any London clerk.

The house stood in a dark, narrow street where the pavements were still unmade. It rose up with a sinister air that, in spite of its present occupants, spoke of harems and old Turkey. Once inside, however, we were definitely in the Republic.

The wife, a woman of about thirty, greeted us in the hall, and in the background—after the usual European custom—was the husband! He came forward and shook hands, leading us into a room in which everything was self-consciously Western. The walls had been distempered grey and were decorated with framed pictures of our host in military uniform. A suite of fumed oak, upholstered with snuff-coloured velvet, occupied the room, and a table was set for dinner.

A tremendous rebuff to the spirit of old Turkey was delivered by a small metal figure of a gilded and painted ballet-girl, such as one sees in the windows of French second-hand furniture shops. She stood pirouetting on the mantelpiece, a queer little household god suggestive of cabarets and dress-suits.

Our host offered us *raki* served in little glasses, and as we sipped it, his vivacious wife superintended the arrival of a lavish dinner.

It was all rather strange. I thought that had I come to this house in 1920, I should not have seen the wife, I should not have seen a dinner-table and a fumed oak suite: I might have been sitting cross-legged on a divan, exchanging courtesies with an outwardly different host.

How, I asked myself, do Turkish families in the middle of Asia Minor know how to furnish their houses in European fashion? If a London family had to turn their dining-room into a Turkish apartment, they would be hopelessly at sea. Then I realized that the French and German illustrated papers tell them all they wish to know. Those interiors of houses in Paris and Berlin, those pictures of women at Longchamps, have a destiny far beyond the dreams of their originators.

Our menu was composed of thick soup, red caviar, a *pilaf* made of wheat, ending with *baklava,* the sticky pastry made with honey that is a speciality of Tarsus. Eloquent of new Turkey was the bottle of white wine with a grey wolf on the label. It is an excellent wine and, could it be exported at a moderate price, might become popular in Europe.

I was interested in my hostess, who was typical of the modern emancipated Turkish woman. She spoke adequate English, learned at the American College in Tarsus, and her enthusiasm for the Republic and the new life it offered to the women of Turkey was apparent in everything she said.

Her maidservant, she told me, was a peasant girl from a neighbouring village, extremely old-fashioned and wrong-headed. It was difficult to make some of these ignorant people learn new ideas. It was all a matter of education. For instance, the girl's husband had just been called up to the army. When he had left to do his military training, the maid had come to live in, bringing also her newly born child.

"She has strange, wrong ideas from the old days," said my hostess with a frown. "For instance, she does not think it right to wash her baby until it is six months old. She thinks that water would kill it. But when she goes out, she does not know that I rush to her baby and wash it *all over*. Hygiene is one of the important things; do you not think so?"

After dinner my hostess gave me an ash-tray of lalique glass in the form of a flying nymph with trailing hair, an object that would have horrified her mother and would have had an effect on her grandmother which I find it difficult to imagine. While Hassan and the husband played a game of tric-trac, the wife sat beside me on the fumed oak settee, turning over the pages of a photograph album which revealed her husband in various stages of infancy. Strange as it may seem, it was an instructive social and political survey. I saw him first as a fat little Turk wearing the now forbidden fez, standing hand in hand with an ancient man in the costume of old Turkey.

"That is his grandfather," said the wife with a laugh; for it is the privilege of modern Turkey to laugh at its grandfathers.

As she turned the pages, I noticed that our host was becoming more and more European, his military *kalpak* of astrakhan merged into a peaked service cap, and then, as the years advanced towards the Republic, we saw him at last in the full glory of bowler hat, striped trousers, and black coat.

The game of tric-trac over, I listened to the two men discussing the question of inheritance in Moslem countries. Turkey has, among her many reforms, abolished the absurdities of this system. In the old days it was not possible for a man to will his possessions to any one individual: they were automatically split up among his immediate family. Thus it frequently happened that after a man's death, his house became the property of perhaps fifteen or more people, each of whom was entitled to move in with his wife and family. Even cattle and horses, and other indivisible objects, can have a plurality of owners in the East. It is no uncommon thing to hear of a man who has a tenth share in a cow or a fifth share in an olive-tree.

This, of course, explains in a great measure the horrible squalor of an Eastern town. Not only are many of its houses owned by twenty or thirty quarrelsome relatives, but property very naturally falls into ruin because these owners cannot come to an agreement about the sale of it.

Now that Turkey has adopted the Swiss Code, there will perhaps be greater incentive for a man to hand on to a single inheritor property which that descendant will keep in repair. Possibly that is why modern Turkey is building in stone, whereas old Turkey built in the cheapest kind of wood.

Two visitors arrived in the course of the evening. The husband was a shy young man who spoke only Turkish; his wife was a pleasant, chattering little creature who reminded me of a full-blown tuberose. Like so many girls of adequate dimensions, her manner was kittenish, and I watched with admiration how she bounced neatly among the knick-knacks with agility and success. This Turkish girl also had been educated at the American College, but she had not managed to absorb as much English as my hostess and I was soon to learn that her grasp of the language had not advanced beyond the kindergarten.

"Do you speak English, madam?" I asked. She nodded her head vigorously and, folding her hands, fixed her large dark eyes on me, saying, slowly and solemnly:

"Pusey-cart, pusey-cart, where haf you been? I haf been to Lon-don to see the Queen. Pusey-cart, pusey-cart, what saw you there? I saw a leetle mouse under the Queen's chair."

As I was applauding her, and, perhaps pedantically, correcting the last line, I noticed that the others had stopped talking and were listening with interest.

"But would such a thing be possible?" inquired Hassan, gravely. "Could there be a mouse under the throne?"

"It is unlikely," I replied.

He nodded his head, reassured.

"I thought so," he said, "but it is nice to know."

I had enriched the vocabulary of the tuberose with a rhyme, which she rendered with charming solemnity as: "Twankle-twankle, leetle stair," when the time came to say good night. Our host grasped a stout stick and said that he would escort us to the hotel. We begged him not to do so. He insisted, because, he said, the dogs were sometimes savage after dark. Bidding farewell to his wife, we followed him through the streets.

Konya looked very lovely that night, with moonlight spilling itself over old walls, half the narrow streets washed in green light and half in darkness. As we turned a corner, there was a piercing whistle and one of the burly guardians of the night moved out of the shadows in his sheepskin coat, his hand on the butt of his revolver.

IV

A TURKISH KNIFE DANCE

SOME three miles from the desolate site of Derbe Hassan and I came to a Turkish village called Zosta. From the hill above we looked down on the usual ragged mass of low roofs, stone and mud walls; in the centre was a domed mosque which I discovered later to be Seljuk.

The villagers came out to drive off the dogs and to greet us. One of them told us that the name of the village had recently been changed to Akar Kuey, which means "white village." As we went towards it, a crowd of men strolled out, full of curiosity; women peeped from behind stone walls, and children ran inquisitively all round us. In the middle of the crowd I saw an astonishing sight.

A group of men were leading a suspicious and indignant-looking ram. A wreath of hill flowers was set round his horns. There were coins hanging in the fleece. Across his back was a strip of vivid cloth.

"Ah, it is a wedding!" cried Hassan. "They are going to sacrifice the animal to bring good luck to the bride and bridegroom."

Although I knew that in remote places in Turkey peasants still observe all kinds of strange customs and superstitions dating from Greek and Roman times, I was surprised suddenly to encounter an animal garlanded for sacrifice. It was only a few miles away, at Lystra, that Paul and Barnabas had looked on a similar sight.

And here I was, in the year 1936, watching the descendants of the people mentioned in the New Testament bringing a ram and garlands unto the gates. We joined the crowd

244

that poured between the stone walls. A peasant approached and invited us to follow him up a flight of steps to the room of a house.

"Will you please enter?" said Hassan. "They wish to invite you to the wedding celebrations."

I saw a small door leading into a room. Bending down, I took off my shoes and stepped inside. Striped camel rugs were set against the walls, leaving a vacant space in the center. The room was about five yards long and four yards wide, and there must have been at least fifty men squatting on the rugs.

With the reserved temperament of the Turk, which is so different from that of the excitable Arab, the elders of the village stood with outstretched hands, bidding us welcome. We managed to insinuate ourselves into the assembly, and, squatting down, plunged into the usual polite greetings.

"Of what nationality is the pasha?" Hassan was asked.

"Of England," he replied.

The grave old men, who probably could neither read nor write and had never before, I imagine, come into contact with any one English, nodded their heads solemnly as if the arrival of guests from England were an everyday occurrence in the village.

The Turk has many qualities that remind me of the Englishman. One is his placid acceptance of the unusual and his reluctance to admit that he is, or could be, surprised. And as I looked round at this picturesque gathering in a mud hut in the middle of Asia Minor, I was struck by a remarkable thing. Half the men in the room were fair-haired and blue-eyed, and, except for their pitiful rags and tatters and their wild air, might have been Englishmen.

A young Turk entered, bearing the little cups of coffee that appear, as if by magic, even in the desert. As we sipped the coffee, three musicians, squatting in a corner, began to thrum on a guitar, a one-stringed fiddle, and a drum. Those sitting in the middle of the room edged away to the side as a remarkable figure bounded into the vacant circle.

At first I thought it was a woman, but a second glance at the flat flanks and the hollow chest revealed a young Turk dressed in a woman's red silk dress. His eyes had been blacked with *kohl* and his cheeks brightened with rouge. He was as fierce as a wild cat.

He began to posture to the sound of the tom-tom and the thin, discordant wail of the violin. He shook and shivered and stamped his feet, slowly turning, his eyes half shut, and tossing back a hank of black hair that kept falling over his forehead. Yet he was not ridiculous. I could not smile at him. He was too fierce and primitive, like some wild animal dressed up for a circus.

As he quickened his steps, his eyes blazed, his colour heightened, and his breath came in gasps. Every time he twirled round, his·skirt flew out and exposed a pair of knee-high Russian boots splashed with dry mud. Grey knitted stockings were folded down over the tops of his boots and into them were tucked the ends of his trousers. As he continued to turn and stamp, I thought that in just this manner the wild horsemen of Gengis Khan must have amused themselves in the light of camp-fires.

Oriental audiences are always interesting. They have the unblinking, uncompromising scrutiny of a cat. They rarely show approval or disapproval: they just stare. The men in the room gazed at this savage young dancer in a cold, aloof manner, tapping the ash of their cigarettes on the floor, almost over his feet. When he had finished, some one shouted out a request.

"They are asking for the knife-dance," whispered Hassan. "If he comes at you with knives, show no surprise."

I soon discovered that the first dance had been merely an

introduction to the knife-dance. The dancer, flourishing two thin daggers about a foot in length, began clashing the blades together, crouching and leaping, stabbing the air, and, in the intensity of the drama he was acting, muttering guttural words as the steel flashed in the uncomfortably small room.

The musicians thrummed a monotonous, rather hypnotic rhythm—the same theme repeated over and over again— and as they played, the dancer stamped until dust was breast-high in the room. His muddy boots and his whirling red skirt moved in a cloud like smoke; but his head, his grotesque face with its parted lips, and the moving flash of the knives, were in the clear air above the dust. It was a savage sight, for he now began to act the part of a man stabbing a victim.

He would single out some member of the audience and springing at him suddenly, and crouching before him, would slash the knives together within an inch of his throat and draw them with terrifying closeness before his eyes. The man selected for this ordeal would show no fear, gazing back at the dancer as if unconscious that the knives had nearly carried off his nose or his eyebrows.

I understood why Hassan had warned me. I expected to be put to the test and was ready. I thought they would be interested to see how the stranger would behave. But with the innate politeness of these people, he left me out of it, feeling, perhaps, that he ought not to subject a guest to such an ordeal.

When the dancer had finished, he flung the knives to a man in the crowd and made a clumsy exit.

"Who on earth is he?" I asked Hassan.

"Only a man of the village, who is a good dancer."

The appearance of the bridegroom brought the proceedings to an end. He was a shy young fellow who might have been a Norfolk farm labourer. He shook hands with me and, when I wished him happiness and many sons, blushed and said it was all in the competent hands of Allah.

We then rose and put on our shoes at the door. It was good to breathe fresh air again. The head man said that as the pasha was from Europe, he was doubtless interested in all ancient stones. Would he, therefore, care to see the old stones built into the wall of the mosque and into various houses in the village?

I replied that nothing would delight me more, and so we set off, a motley throng, through the muddy little lanes, between stone walls, and into backyards where children lined the roofs to watch us. They showed Greek stones to me with weathered inscriptions, fragments of Greek altars and such-like relics of the great city that had once stood on the hill near by, stones which had perhaps stood in the streets when Paul preached the Faith in Derbe.

The whole village saw us off. The women stood afar and gazed curiously. Somewhere was the house on whose door-step the blood of the ram had been sprinkled in deference to the old gods of Anatolia, the gods who were worshipped when Paul passed by, who are still alive in the hearts of these people.

I returned to Konya over the wide, featureless plain, thinking that nowhere could a stranger have received greater kindness, nowhere could he have met with better manners.

V

EPHESUS

THE ruins of Ephesus are forty miles south of Izmir, or Smyrna, near a village called Seljuk. The Temple of Diana is about one mile away, and the site of the city itself is another mile or so to the south-west.

I walked along a dusty road. Before this road leaves the village, there is a railed-in garden peopled by about twenty headless figures. They are a ghostly company of statues from the ruins of Ephesus, carefully mounted on plinths and standing with their headless bodies facing the road.

The road was lined on either side with bean-fields and with fields in which the wheat was already three feet high. Peasants bent over root-crops. Oxen came swaying across the dark earth, drawing ploughs as primitive as any in the tomb-reliefs of Egypt. The country bore that well-washed, brilliant air which follows a week of rain in Asia Minor. The sun seemed to say that it would never rain again, and the earth luxuriated in the heat. Poppies waved in the corn. Yellow pea-flowers, wild mustard, anemones, small marguerites and forget-me-nots, grew beside the road and on every space of unturned ground. Wherever I looked, I saw little chips of white marble. There is hardly a wall within miles of Ephesus in which you will not find marble that once formed part of a column or a pavement.

I turned off to the right and followed a narrow path that edged a field of wheat. I came to a big, stagnant pond covered so thickly with a snowy water-weed that at first sight it looked like white marble. As I stood still, the frogs, which haunt this pond by the million, set up their *brekekekex co-äx* until the air rang as if a hundred invisible rattles were being whirled. The croaking shaped itself in my mind. . . .

"Great is Diana . . . great is Diana . . . great is Diana . . . great is Diana . . . great is Diana of the Ephesians . . ."

That was the phrase which seemed to beat itself into the sunny air of that quiet forenoon: for this stagnant pond is the site of the Great Temple of Artemis—Diana of the Ephesians—once one of the Seven Wonders of the World.

Nothing in all my wandering filled me with a deeper sense of the pathos of decay than this water-logged ruin at Ephesus. The temple which once rose here, whose ground-plan is to-day so clearly outlined in stagnant water, was larger and more famous than the Parthenon. Pausanias said that it "surpassed every structure raised by human hands." Another ancient writer said: "I have seen the walls and hanging gardens of Old Babylon, the statue of Olympian Jove, the Colossus of Rhodes, the great labour of the lofty Pyramids, and the ancient tomb of Mausolus. But when I beheld the Temple at Ephesus towering to the clouds, all these other marvels were eclipsed."

I sat there listening to the chorus of the frogs, wondering if in two thousand years' time some student of England, wandering among marshes and brambles on Ludgate Hill, would look in vain for a relic of St. Paul's. Two thousand years ago Ephesus appeared permanent and invincible. It would have seemed impossible to any one of that time that the Temple of Diana should become a stagnant pond.

When Paul came to Ephesus, this temple and the powerful organization connected with it were at the height of their fame. Diana of the Ephesians was known the world over. She was not the lovely, graceful Artemis of the Greeks, the swift sister of Apollo: she was a goddess from remote antiquity, a dark, Asiatic being like some ogre from the past

of Man. Like the Aphrodite of Paphos, she was believed to
have fallen from heaven, and she may, therefore, have originally been a meteorite invested with miraculous quality
by the superstitious mind of early man. There is a statue of
the Ephesian Diana in the Naples Museum. It shows a
queer, barbaric figure, the lower part swaddled like an
Egyptian mummy, the hands and face those of a woman.
The upper portion is studded with a number of objects
which, in the opinion of Sir William Ramsay, are really the
ova of bees. These eggs indicate her function as the goddess
of fertility.

The bee was the symbol of Ephesus. It is found on most
of the coins and is one of the most beautifully modelled bees
in ancient art. The goddess was the Queen Bee, and the
temple organization included a crowd of priests or drones,
who dressed like women, and a crowd of priestesses known
as *melissai,* who represented the worker bees. This extraordinary organization developed in Anatolia from the primitive belief that in the life of the bee was seen the divine
intention.

Although the Greeks believed that the Queen Bee was a
male, the Asiatics, who evolved the worship of the Ephesian
bee-goddess, founded their cult on a true knowledge of the
sex of these insects.

The drone-priests and the worker-priestesses were assisted
by an immense concourse of flute-players, heralds, trumpet-
ers, sceptre-bearers, thurifers, sweepers of the sanctuary,
dancers, acrobats, and robers of the divinity. A special
mounted force of temple police patrolled the temple area and
maintained order within the territory of the goddess. Among
the signs of Hellenization were the annual games in honour
of Artemis—the Artemisia—which attracted thousands of
pilgrims from all parts of the world. At this time, the harbour of Ephesus was filled with pilgrim ships. No work was

done for a month, while the great throng of Ephesians and strangers enjoyed a daily program of athletic contests, plays, and solemn sacrifices. Thousands of silver shrines were purchased by the visitors to take home with them as souvenirs of their pilgrimage.

The temple was visited by awestruck strangers. An effigy of the goddess rose before the altar, but was usually concealed by a veil which had the peculiarity of being raised towards the ceiling, unlike that of Jupiter at Olympia, which was let down by ropes to the pavement, or the veil in the Temple of Isis, described by Apuleius, which was drawn aside at break of day. Why, I wonder, was Diana's veil drawn upward? There must have been a reason for the undignified procedure of first revealing the feet of the goddess, and then her body, before the head and face came into view.

The statue of Diana was wooden, but the writers of antiquity differ widely on the kind of wood which was used. Some say the image was of beech or elm, some of cedar, while others say that it was made of vine-stock. On most of the coins on which the goddess appears, two lines run from her hands to the ground. They represent rods, probably of gold, which were necessary to keep her in an erect position because of her top-heavy shape. On great festival days a statue of Diana was taken through Ephesus on a car drawn sometimes by mules and sometimes by stags or fawns.

And on those solemn occasions hymns to Diana were sung by day and night, and the streets of Ephesus resounded with the city's cry: "Great is Diana of the Ephesians."

Over sixty years ago, the weed-covered pond revealed its secret to an English architect, J. T. Wood, whose researches were financed by the British Museum. The Temple had

been lost for centuries, and Wood sunk experimental pits
all over the site for six years without a sign of success. Many
a man would have given up in despair; but this was the
passion of Wood's life, and he was convinced that he was
fated to discover the site. He had been inspired by Edward
Falkener's book on the lost temple and by that author's
conjectural reconstruction of it. In the face of such faith
and such stubborn determination, difficulties were as nothing.

Wood suffered from malaria, from Turkish interference,
from shortage of funds, and from distinguished visitors.
Still he persisted year after year, conducting his researches
in a stove-pipe hat and a tightly buttoned frock coat, like
the hardy Victorian he was. Sir John Forsdyke has shown
me a faded photograph of the explorer in this garb, the
property of the British Museum, posed and exposed at the
bottom of a deep pit after his triumph. Wood, bearded and
tightly buttoned, stands with an air of victory, one hand
resting on a drum of the discovered Temple. Alas, poor
Wood! If only he had known that when the photograph was
taken, he was standing immediately above the spectacular
foundation deposit of thousands of gold and electrum objects and statues of Artemis in bronze and ivory, now in the
museum at Istanbul, which D. G. Hogarth was to discover
beneath the altar thirty years later.

Wood's discovery was, however, one of the romances of
archaeology. After sinking pits all over Ephesus and finding
himself no nearer to the Temple, he dug one day in the
theatre, the same building in which the riot described in
Acts occurred, and there he unearthed a Roman inscription.
This said that a certain Roman, C. Vibius Salutarius, who
had lived in Ephesus about fifty years after Paul had been
there, had given to the Temple of Diana many silver and
gold images weighing six to seven pounds each. He had also

left a sum in trust for the repair of the images and the cleaning of them, decreeing, in addition, that when they were carried in procession from the Temple to the theatre, during the birthday feast of Diana, they were to enter the city by the Magnesian Gate and to leave it, on their return journey, by the Coressian Gate. This wide circuit of the city was doubtless prompted by his vanity: he wanted as many people as possible to see his munificent gift. Wood grasped at once the importance of this inscription. Thanks to the vanity of a man who had been dead for over eighteen centuries, he was given an almost certain clue. If he could find those two gates and the roads leading from them, they would take him to the Temple.

He set to work with redoubled energy, and discovered first the Magnesian Gate, and then the Coressian Gate. Following the roads, he was led on the last day of the year 1869, and at a moment when funds had expired, to the site of the Temple, lying twenty feet beneath the modern ground-level. What a moment that was for Wood! He had suffered from fever every night for three weeks, and the excitement was almost too much for him. But he rallied and carried on. He discovered columns, the pavement of the Temple, and the sculptured drums, an architectural feature which distinguished the Temple of Diana from every other temple of the Greek world. The story of that triumph is told by Wood in a discursive but readable book called *Discoveries at Ephesus*.

Among his visitors was Dr. Schliemann, who at that time had not discovered Troy. He was drawn to Ephesus by a desire to feel his feet on the pavement of Diana's Temple, and as he looked around him, he remarked, a little wistfully, that Wood had won immortality. It must have been an interesting meeting: Wood, who had realized his ambitions, and Schliemann, who was about to win greater fame by

TURKISH SHEPHERD, EPHESUS

establishing the site of Troy and by putting into operation
his uncanny gift of forcing the earth to stand and deliver
whatever gold treasure it happened to conceal.

Wood's weighty discoveries were transported to England
in a man-of-war. Thanks to him, and the British Navy, the
superb artistry of the sculptured drums of Ephesus may be
admired to-day in the British Museum.[1]

[1] When war broke out in 1939 they were found to be too heavy to be removed to safety, and they remain in an empty gallery surrounded by sand-
bags.

VI

ISTANBUL

I

As a thin rain was falling over the Bosphorus on the morning of November 17, 1922, a British ambulance drew up outside one of the back entrances to the Sultan's Palace in Constantinople. Sitting beside the driver was a young subaltern who, as soon as the ambulance drew to a standstill, went round and unlocked the doors, releasing as he did so a strong smell of disinfectant.

Presently a door in the palace wall was unlocked and three figures hastily emerged: a stout and agitated Turkish gentleman in the sixties, who was sheltering from the rain beneath an umbrella, a pale boy of ten, and a smooth, high-voiced person who carried a black bag. In his haste and agitation, the elderly Turk attempted to enter the vehicle while his umbrella was still open, and there followed a brief, undignified struggle. It was ended by the subaltern, who took the umbrella from the soft, white hands of its owner and, hustling his passengers into the antiseptic gloom, ordered the driver to go to the naval base. As the ambulance ran down the rough road, neither subaltern nor driver knew that with it was passing for ever from Constantinople the last shadow of the Byzantine Emperors.

The elderly Turk was the sultan Mehmid VI, Vahydu'd-Din Effendi, Khalif and Commander of the Faithful; the boy was the heir to the imperial throne, the Prince Ertoghrul Effendi; and the man with the black bag was a palace eunuch in whose care had been placed the Sultan's gold

256

coffee-cups and some hastily assembled jewellery.

Arriving at the naval base, the fugitives stepped into an admiral's barge and were soon speeding across the water to H.M.S. *Malaya*, which steamed off for Malta. Four years later the last Sultan of Turkey died unregretted and unsung in the improbable surroundings of San Remo.

Of all the disassociations which history brought about by the War of 1914–18, the end of the Sultanate was perhaps the most notable, certainly the most drastic. It was the final surgical operation in a series of partial cures and expedients which go back to the middle of the last century. Until the Kemalists seized power in 1922, however, no reformers in Turkey had had the courage or the vision to go to the root of the disease and, in their determination to stamp out Byzantinism, expel that strange and preposterous survival of the Emperor of Constantinople—the Sultan of Turkey.

It is not well known in the West that all the things which we think of as essentially Turkish are really Byzantine: the fez, the Turkish bath, the harem, even the crescent itself, which, against a red ground, was the flag of the Byzantine Empire. The mystery and the ceremony surrounding the Sultan, the intrigues of his women and his court, the power, until recent times, of his Janissaries—a shadow of the old Imperial Guard—the tortuous legal processes, even the ingenious spiced food of Turkey, were all borrowed from Byzantium when the Turks captured and settled down in the capital of the Eastern Roman Empire.

It is said that when Constantinople had fallen to the Turks in 1453, the victorious Sultan, Mohammed II, rode through the silent streets of the great city and explored the deserted courts of the royal palace, whispering under his breath the verses of a Persian poem which tell how the spider may weave his web in the hall of kings. If it be true that Mohammed did recall such a poem, we have a revealing glimpse into the mind of a warrior who was surprised, and maybe humbled, to find himself master of the greatest, the richest, and the most sophisticated city in the world. Although Constantinople was conquered physically by the Turks, it was never conquered in any other way, and, indeed, the time soon came when it began to conquer its conquerors. The Greeks and the Levantines continued to administer the city and the Empire, and to profit from their administration, just as they had done in the Byzantine Age. The Turks, however, controlled the army. And that state of affairs remained in existence from the Turkish Conquest, in 1453, until Kemal Ataturk swept away the last vestige of Byzantinism in 1922, in his determination to strip the Levantine ivy from the Turkish oak. As drastic and as logical as his expulsion of the Sultan, was his removal of the capital of New Turkey from the Greek embrace of Constantinople to Ankara, in the hard, Anatolian uplands.

It would be interesting if some student of Byzantine history, that most neglected of our studies, would take as his subject the projection into Turkish Constantinople of the customs and habits of New Rome. Now and then a writer familiar with Turkey briefly mentions this fascinating subject, as Sir George Young does when, mentioning the elaborate dress of the Turkish court officials a century ago, he says that such costumes were deliberately copied from those in vogue in Byzantine Constantinople.

In the elaborate and ancient ceremony which surrounded the Sultan in his palace, in the grovelling respect shown to him, in the multiplication of fantastic and extravagant court functionaries, each one with a high-flown name and an exact position in an involved hierarchy, in the plots and counterplots of the harem, we seem to see, as through the wrong end of a telescope, the brilliant, dissolute, and artificial life of the Greek Emperors in their Forbidden City.

Sir George Young believes that the famous Friday Selamlik, when the Sultan made a weekly appearance in public, was a travesty of a similar ceremony in Byzantine times; and, if so, no doubt the palace dwarfs, who stood on the steps of the mosque and were supposed to greet their master with the words: "O Padishah, be not proud—for there is One above!", were echoing in their cracked voices the formula used when the Basileus and his Empress passed in shimmering vestments of gold brocade to attend mass in the Church of the Holy Wisdom.

"They were all Byzantium in modern guise," writes Sir George Young, "the priests, the dwarfs, the eunuchs, the pages, the astrologers, the intriguing women, the Circassian odalisques, the imprisoned Prince, the shimmer of hidden treasure, the shadow of imminent death; and, most Byzantine of all, the 'Great Assassin' himself (Abdul-Hamid) reading *djornals*, signing death warrants, and playing 'La Fille de Madame Angot' on a cottage piano to his little girls."

II

Such were the thoughts that ran through my mind as the ship in which I was travelling steamed slowly up the Sea of Marmora towards Istanbul. I should like to have been going there in the Eighteenth Century, for it was then still possible to see the last Byzantine twilight falling upon the domes and minarets. As it was, I knew that I was to see a city which was no longer even a capital city, but a city degraded by Act of Parliament.

It was a bitterly cold morning in February, and perhaps because I had read of Constantinople lying in blazing heat, and had seen only those pictures and photographs made in summer, I was surprised by this. I was soon to hear that the inhabitants deny that they have any such thing as a climate, but only north and south winds. Although the city lies in the same latitude as Naples and Madrid, its closeness to the Balkan mountains on one side, and the Black Sea on the other, means that a mild Mediterranean winter, which its latitude would seem to suggest and to deserve, is a thing unknown.

As we neared the city, we ran into a storm of blinding sleet that stung my face like bits of flying steel, and the wind had that extra bite which causes you to turn your back to it. A Turkish official, who had come aboard at Chanak, told me that winter can be so cold that sometimes the Bosphorus and the Golden Horn have been frozen, and on rare occasions ice blocks have been known to form even at the entrance to the Dardanelles, so that men and cattle have been able to walk over from Asia into Europe.

It was through this moving white veil of sleet, and against a sky as grey as any above Manchester or Aberdeen, that I saw for the first time the dark domes and white minarets of Constantinople, grouped beautifully on gently rising hills.

There was a sound of traffic and tramcars from the bridge that links Stamboul with Galata, and from the quay below came the impatient hooting of high-pitched motor horns. Standing with a map which the icy wind tried to tear from my hands, I looked towards the lovely outline which lay behind the falling sleet, silent and smokeless in the early morning. I identified Seraglio Point and the great dome of St. Sophia. The outline of Constantinople stood up a little sadly in the grey light, like an unusual Christmas card.

On the quay below, with thin overcoats buttoned tightly and with upturned collars, faces blue with cold, but voices unimpaired, stood a group of determined touts, already seizing the passengers as they descended the gangway. As I set off with the gallant but foolish idea of walking across the Galata Bridge, I was followed by a young man in a cloth

cap who kept whispering to me in words which bore some
relation to English and some to French. He held an object
under his coat which he was anxious for me to see, but I,
suspecting the worst of him, was determined not to see it
and strode forward firmly and priggishly, with jaw set, saying at intervals "go away" in as many languages as I could
recollect.

None of this had any effect upon the young man who, as
he drew level with me, nudged me and begged me to look
at whatever he was concealing in the breast of his overcoat.
All the time he kept saying urgently: "Five pounds, sir, give
me five pounds for it!" At last, exasperated, and, I must admit, overcome with curiosity, wondering whether this furtive creature might not hold beneath his coat some Byzantine missal encrusted with jewels, I turned and saw that he
was trying to sell me a little plaster cast of John Wesley.
When I made it clear beyond all doubt that I had no intention of buying it, he reduced it to five shillings and then,
lifting his cap politely, hurried away in the crowds.

I went to St. Sophia, which is even more beautiful and
imposing than pictures had led me to expect, and I saw the
ladders and the scaffolding behind which the superb mosaics, placed there by Justinian, are emerging from the white-
wash that has covered them since the Fifteenth Century. I
tried to discover whether the curators and guides resented
the fact that the most celebrated mosque in Turkey had
been turned by the Republic into a museum and was now
regarded by most visitors, not as a mosque, but as a church.
But not one of them would admit to any regret or resentment; to do so might have savoured of high treason.

I forget whether it was on the site of the Hippodrome or
outside the Cistern of Philoxenus—what an eerie place this
is, with its tall Byzantine columns going down into still
water and a boatman, like Charon, rowing up to take you

into the dark—but at one or other of those places, I was
accosted by a young man in a shabby coat. Gazing down,
I saw once again the features of John Wesley. The price
now fluctuated between four pounds and seven and six-
pence. Why should I, I wondered, be dogged across Constantinople by John Wesley; and by what queer adventures
had that nonconformist saint found his way inside a shabby
overcoat in the city of the Sultans!

I went, as every one does, to the Seraglio or, as the Turks
call it, Topkapu Saray, the old palace and harem of the
Sultans, once the seat of the government and the site of
the famous Divan. It remained so until 1839, when Abdul-
Medjid removed to another palace on the Bosphorus; and a
fire in 1865, to say nothing of the invasion of the railway at
a later date along its seaward wall, caused the Seraglio to
be deserted save now and again for an occasional annual
ceremony.

I thought it was squalid, interesting, instructive, but also
depressing, rather like the White City or Wembley seen
several years after the end of the exhibitions they had
housed. In no way was it like the gorgeous surroundings of
the Grand Signor, as described in travel books of the Seventeenth and Eighteenth Centuries. But on a fine, warm day,
and given a coat of paint and peopled with fierce Janissaries, black and white eunuchs, dwarfs and palace officials in
vast turbans and robes of the finest silk, the Old Seraglio
might possibly have justified the wonder it aroused in the
minds of those who saw it in its prime. As it is, it illustrates
clearly and simply the fact that Turkish history can be divided into two periods: one in which the Sultan, in a huge
turban, sat cross-legged on a divan with a scimitar by his
side; and the other in which he sat uncomfortably in a
Louis Quinze chair, wearing a uniform between that of an
admiral and a general. The Old Seraglio belongs to the first

period, and is therefore more interesting than the later palaces in Istanbul, which look like wedding cakes that have been lost for a long time in Austria or in French provincial cities.

The curious and interesting thing about the Seraglio is that it is, in form, not a palace as we understand it, but an encampment of kiosks and outbuildings erected with no clear plan, but dotted about the gardens here, there, and everywhere. Some of these kiosks are large and others are as small as summer-houses, some stand by themselves, others are linked together by long, rambling passages. And it occurred to me that this place, which was first laid out by Mohammed II, in 1453, on the site of the Forum of Theodosius, immediately after he had stormed and captured Constantinople, reflected the nomad character of the ancient Turk, and was merely a military camp with its tents and pavilions translated into wood and stone.

I have since read somewhere that the palaces of the Byzantine emperors were the same series of rambling buildings and courtyards, and, if this is so, of course Mohammed took as the model for his imperial residence the Byzantine palaces which had been ruined or burned down during the siege of the city. Just as every mosque in Istanbul and in many an Islamic country is in some way a copy of the Christian church of St. Sophia, so the Sultan's Palace is probably a copy in a minor way of the great imperial palaces of the capital.

The guides who take visitors through what was so recently forbidden territory, even to Turks, are men in blue uniforms and peaked caps. They do not share the fiery enjoyment with which politically saturated guides in some parts of Europe take you through the silent palaces of exiled or departed monarchs, but they march about, giving a little information here and there, rather like bored English vergers.

Now and then they are stung out of their natural reserve by the sight of a camera, which the wretched tourist should have surrendered at the gate, for the modern Turk seems to have inherited from the old days a fear and hatred of photography that amounts to a mania. Whether it is inspired by the belief that a Byzantine column or the lodgings of the black eunuchs might have some military significance, or whether it is considered that private photography may injure the sale of official post-cards, I was never able to discover. All I can tell you is that, if you wish to create in the deserted courts where Jamshid gloried the same fury and commotion which might once have been caused by an attempt to invade the harem, produce a camera and try to take a photograph!

A tour of the decayed dwellings, the little summer-houses with their cracked paint, the domed halls with their rugs and their Arabic decorations, the long stone passages, the little barred windows, giving a glimpse of a garden path and a cypress-tree, the series of bare rooms, each with its fireplace like a *mirab* in a mosque, and the opportunity which such a rambling place gives for creeping and peeping and prying, fill one with a sense of the utter dreariness of the Sultan's harem. The Princes' School, a room in which surely no learning could ever have been imparted, stands next door to the bedroom of the Chief Eunuch, and struck me as a singularly depressing apartment. Amid an elaborate hotchpotch of decoration, rococo ornaments, gilded French stools and chairs, pallid little candidates for the bow-string or the throne were gathered for generations to receive that education which separated them from the rest of mankind.

The keynote of sumptuous discomfort is broken nowhere except perhaps in the Sultan's Bathroom, which is really a good bathroom, although, no doubt, many a Hollywood film actor would not think much of it. Like so many of the rooms

in the Seraglio, it is more ancient than it looks. Tiles are
dated "in the year 982 from the Hijara," which is 1574. It is
a luxurious apartment divided into three sections, two sets
of dressing-rooms and the bathroom itself, with its marble
basins and a marble bath with a fountain. I wonder what
kind of a bathroom Queen Elizabeth possessed in 1574, and
in this thought may perhaps lie the explanation of the impression which the luxury of the Sultan's court made upon
early travellers. In the Sixteenth Century the Sultan was no
doubt more sumptuously housed than many of his fellow
monarchs in Europe, but since then Europe has travelled a
long way upon the road of ease and luxury, while in the Old
Seraglio time has stood still.

I was wandering round the melancholy apartments which
housed the Sultan's "Byzantine" hierarchy, when, to my
surprise, I saw a figure like a ghost of other times pass from
one court to another. It was the figure of a dwarf, broad-
shouldered and long of arm, that waddled along a path between the cypress-trees, and, as he approached me, I looked
into a sad and wizened face in which I read the tragedy of
one whose world has vanished.

In the Treasury of the Sultans is an extraordinary collection of objects, some of interest and value, others ornate and
ugly, and nearly all of them the gifts of monarchs to the
reigning Sultan. The first prize for ugliness must be awarded
to the collection of porcelain with enormous stones, said to
be rubies and emeralds, inserted into the side of bowls and
dishes. Some of these stones are the size of pigeons' eggs.
Most interesting are the ancient turbans, some of gigantic
size, worn by various Sultans, which exhibit many intricate
tricks of folding and padding, and they remind us that, as
in Byzantine days, it was once possible in Turkish Constantinople to tell the exact rank and office of any great man
by observing the kind of turban he wore.

I passed out of the Seraglio by way of the ill-named Gate of Peace. The rooms on the left were fitted with everything necessary for executions, including an underground cistern in which men of rank were first drowned before they were decapitated. The rooms on the right are those in which it was sometimes the pleasure of the Sultan to keep foreign ambassadors waiting for days on end, until, wearying of the joke, he sent orders for "the dogs to be fed." In one of these rooms an attendant in a peaked cap sold me a guide-book in English.

III

Were the subject of ancient cookery better known, I think that the sophisticated food of Turkey might be traced to the Byzantine Age. The spiced *dolmas,* which are vine leaves ingeniously stuffed and folded over, the varied *pilafs,* the strange, dangerous-looking fish dishes served in gigantic mussel shells, and the sweets swimming in honey, are surely not the invention of the Turks, but are dishes which the Turks found in Constantinople when they captured that elegant Paris of the medieval world. Perhaps we may see in the attention which Republican Turks are paying to the outward forms of European life, and notably to its food and drink, a repetition of the ease with which their ancestors adopted Byzantine habits.

In Pera is a Turkish restaurant in whose window reposes a grand review of Turkish food. The menu is a long one, and the *plats du jour,* which are seen sizzling in large shallow pans, are remarkable for their colour, their highly spiced smell, and the intricacy of their composition. Indeed, looking at them, it occurred to me that it would be simple for any short-sighted Byzantinist, gazing through that window, to believe himself to be in a museum, looking, not at food, but at the work of Byzantine scribes, smiths, and enamellists.

In the short time I was in Istanbul, I found it difficult to
know what was truly Turkish in origin and what was Byzantine, so inextricably are they mixed.

As in Spain, where the food has an indescribably mediæval
taste, so in Istanbul the Turkish food touches not only the
palate but the imagination. There are flavours once common
to the ancient world which have disappeared from the food
of Europe, but they are to be met with in odd corners of
the globe, especially, I think, in the East. But so far as gas-
tronomic archaeology is concerned, Turkey holds first place;
for the herbs and flavours of this food, to say nothing of its
colour, rouse questions which could be answered satisfac-
torily only if the chef of the Empress Theodora had left us
his book of recipes. I felt that in eating a *plat du jour* in
that Pera restaurant, I had shared something with the
Palaeologi.

Then the sweets of Turkey are in themselves a study; and
no sweets are sweeter, as you might, of course, expect in a
country which was until recently, in theory, at any rate,
teetotal. But I was interested to see in Istanbul, in company
with the usual sweets encountered all over the Arabic-speak-
ing world, authentic bull's-eyes and sticks of Margate Rock.
I never remember having seen those old-fashioned sweets
anywhere else except in England, where their popularity has
of late years been so well eclipsed by chocolate that you
have to look for them now in village post offices. My first
thought was that English manufacturers, finding a declining
market for rock and bull's-eyes at home, had created a new
one in Turkey. And I should not have given the matter another thought had I not come across a reference to it in
The Sultan and His Subjects, a book written by Richard
Davey in 1907. This writer was impressed, as I was, by the
Englishness of many typically "Turkish" sweetmeats, having
met them nowhere else, he says, but in Norfolk villages. He

then asks the fascinating question: "Did our crusading forefathers bring the first bull's-eyes home with them, and did
the cunning fingers of English dames repeat and perpetuate
the triumph of the Eastern sweetmeat-seller's art?"

Tucked away at a street corner in Stamboul stands a sweet
shop which seemed to me infinitely more romantic than
many of the more famous sights of the city. It is the shop
of one, Hadji Baba, whose family used to be sweetmeat-
maker to His Divine Majesty, Abdul Hamid, and from that
shop came all the sweetmeats which, let us hope, in some
small way compensated the ladies of the Harem for such an
unpleasant master.

Behind a rampart of delicately tinted Turkish Delight
stands the proprietor himself, the son of Abdul Hamid's
Hadji, carving great slabs of his speciality, studded with
pistachio and walnuts, cutting huge hills of crystalline *halva*,
or weighing a delicious raspberry-coloured sweetmeat like
soft nougat, which is sliced and brewed with hot water,
making a sweet Byzantine potion into which almost any
kind of poison might be tastelessly introduced.

Hadji Baba is a great artist, and he rightly confines himself to the three or four kinds of sweetmeats which he makes
better than any one else in the world. As eaten by us in the
West in boxes and tins, Turkish Delight is a gluey sweetmeat that can be honestly enjoyed only by the young. If a
person of more critical years is persuaded to take a powdered cube, perhaps at Christmas, he wonders why this
glutinous tooth-aching confection has achieved so great a
fame. Well; the answer is to be found in Hadji Baba's shop
in Stamboul, where Turkish Delight, fresh from the oven,
scented with rose water and unobtrusively nutted, is the
king, as the Hadji's *halva* is the queen, of all sweetmeats.
Here again I would say that Turkish Delight, like the Turkish Bath, was never invented by a race of migratory war-

riors: it was the delight of the Byzantine palaces centuries
before Mohammed's archers appeared under the walls. Like
the cakes of St. Theresa at Avila, and the marzipan of Toledo
in Spain, and the resinated wine of Greece, it has the true
flavour of antiquity. It is as though the mosaics of Ravenna
had suddenly become eatable.

IV

No one will deny that Adolf Hitler is a psychologist, and
it would be interesting to know how much of his satanic
skill comes from his own brain and how much of it he owes
to a knowledge of history; for there have been other psy-
chologists. For instance, the political strategy of the Turks,
and the methods employed by them to capture Constantinople in 1453, provide some striking parallels to what is
known to-day as "the Nazi technique."

It may be said that the Sultans captured Constantinople
and sat upon the throne of the Caesars, because they were
opposing a divided Christian world; a world so torn by old
hates, jealousies, and religious dissensions, that it was in-
capable of unity. If the Latin and the Greek churches had
been able to sink their differences, and if the Christian nations of the West had been willing to combine, the Turk
would have been defeated; but no one knew better than
the Sultans that the crusading fire had burned itself out,
and that never again would the Christian princes of the
West ride out as they did against Saladin.

The Turks also possessed those qualifications necessary
to a successful military state: a strong rule, complete unity,
superior military organization, harder steel, and bigger cannon. In an age when standing armies were unknown and
most princes employed small, expensive bands of mercenary
troops, the Turks had created a military caste, and possessed

a huge standing army, recruited with diabolical cunning
from the ranks of their Christian subjects. They trained the
youth of these provinces from the ages of seven to twelve
in the arts of war, and in nothing else, vowing them to a life
of celibacy, hardship, and absolute obedience to their leaders. Such were the famous Janissaries, or "Yeni-Cheri," the
"new troops."

Long before the imperial city fell to the Sultans, the Moslem power had advanced in the Byzantine Empire by a deliberate policy of infiltration, seeking all the time to sow dis-
cord and moral confusion. A harsh autocracy appeared always in the guise of a tolerant democracy, always promising the Christian peasants in the conquered districts a
"New Order," setting them against their feudal lords and,
at the same time, binding those same lords in feudal service to the Sultan. Having spread disloyalty and dissension,
the Sultans went out of their way to welcome to their
court every kind of Christian malcontent, deserter, deposed
prince, pretender, and pure adventurer, whose grievances
they boldly organized. Thus they had at their disposal a
powerful Fifth Column that was always ready to stab its
compatriots in the back, and was also the best spy system
existing in the world.

Arrogant beyond belief, secure in its military superiority,
unbelievably skilful in capitalizing weakness, disloyalty, and
moral uncertainty, the Turkish power spun its web of intrigue throughout the Balkans, and bit by bit encircled the
victim of its ambition, whose last years form a pathetic
essay in the futility of appeasement.

In the National Library of Belgrade is a Serbian manu-
script of the Fifteenth Century which purports to give the
words of a speech made by the Sultan Mohammed II, the
Conqueror of Constantinople, on the subject of his *herren-*

volk. It is translated into English by Chedomil Mijatovich [1]
and it makes extraordinary reading to-day because, although
Hitler has probably never read this speech, he has made it
himself time and again.

"You have heard," said the Sultan, "that the Christians
have united against us. But fear not. Your heroism will be
above theirs. You know well the unwashed Gyaours, and
their ways and manners, which certainly are not fine. They
are indolent, sleepy, easily shocked, inactive; they like to
drink much and to eat much; in misfortunes they are impatient, and in times of good fortune proud and overbear-
ing. They are lovers of repose, and do not like to sleep
without soft feather beds; when they have no women with
them they are sad and gloomy; and without plenty of good
wine they are unable to keep counsel among themselves.
They are ignorant of any military stratagems. They keep
horses only to ride while hunting with their dogs; if one
of them wishes to have a good war horse, he sends to buy
it from us. They are unable to bear hunger, or cold or heat,
effort and menial work. They let women follow them in
their campaigns, and at their dinners give them the upper
places, and they want always to have warm dishes. In short,
there is no good in them.

"But you, my glorious fellows, you can show a great many
good qualities. You do not think much of your life or your
food. You sleep little, and for that you do not want beds;
the earth is your dining-table and any board your bed; there
is nothing you consider a hardship; there is nothing you
think it impossible to do.

"And then the Christians fight constantly among themselves, because every one desires to be a king, or a prince,

---

[1] *Constantine, the Last Emperor of the Greeks,* by Chedomil Mijatovich.
(Sampson Low, Marston & Co., London. 1892.)

or the first among them. One says to another: 'Brother, help thou me to-day against this Prince, and to-morrow I will help thee against that one!' Fear them not; there is no concord amongst them. Every one takes care of himself only; no one thinks of the common interest. They are quarrelsome, unruly, self-willed, and disobedient. Obedience to their superiors and discipline, they have none, and yet everything depends on that!

"When they lose a battle they always say, 'We were not well prepared!' or 'This or that traitor has betrayed us!' or 'We were too few in numbers, and the Turks were far more numerous!' or 'The Turks came upon us without previous declaration of war, by misleading representations and treachery! They have occupied our country by turning our internal difficulties to their own advantage!'

"Well, that is what they say, being not willing to confess truly and rightly: 'God is on the side of the Turks! It is God who helps them, and therefore they conquer us!' "

This glimpse into what is familiar to us to-day as the Nazi mind was provided by the Sultan in the year 1453, either before or during the siege of Constantinople, and it is chiefly interesting because of its echo in modern speeches from Germany, proving, even if the history of the Moslem Conquest did not do so, that the same psychological warfare now carried on by the Third Reich, and considered by many to be something new in war, was perfected nearly five hundred years ago by the Sultans of Turkey.

Constantinople fell on the 29th of May 1453, after a gallant but hopeless defence that lasted for nearly two months. Just before the siege began, the Sultan took the precaution of bribing the best cannon-maker in Constantinople to go over to him for more money, and this man, Urban, made a monster cannon, the largest calibre piece of its time, that

flung enormous cannon balls against the fortifications. Even
without this cannon, the Turks had better artillery than the
Greeks. While the largest Greek guns fired a stone ball not
exceeding 150 pounds in weight, the Turkish cannon could
fire balls that weighed 1,200 pounds.

It is a miserable commentary on the effect of years of
intrigue, and also on the lack of unity in Christendom, that
within the walls of Constantinople were not more than
10,000 Christians capable of bearing arms, while a con-
temporary observer estimated that no fewer than 30,000
Christians were fighting under the banners of Islam. It is
also a miserable commentary on the greed and indifference
of the Latins that it was from the merchants of Galata that
the Sultan bought the colossal quantities of lard and fats
with which to grease the slipway and the rollers on which,
in a single night, with the help of thousands of men and
buffaloes, he dragged his warships overland for five miles
and launched them in the waters of the Golden Horn.

The end came at last when the Turks swarmed over the
broken walls and came in by an unguarded gate. After the
city had been taken, a Turkish soldier appeared before
the Sultan bearing a severed head, the head of the Emperor
Constantine Caesar Augustus Palailogos, who had spurred
his horse into the carnage and had fallen in a last desperate
sortie. The Sultan's officers ordered the soldier to take them
to the body. They came upon a headless corpse which they
identified as that of the Emperor by the purple shoes embroidered with the double eagles of the Byzantine Empire.

Mohammed ordered that the Emperor's head should be
exposed upon a porphyry column in front of the imperial
palace, then, when all men knew that the last Caesar had
perished, the body was buried with the rites of the Greek
Church; and the Sultan himself paid for the oil that burned

in the lamps above the sepulchre. Constantine XII was the eightieth Roman Emperor since Constantine the Great, and the hundred and twelfth since Caesar Octavian.

v

I was privileged to be received at the Phanar in Istanbul by one of the most interesting historical dignitaries in the world, the Œcumenical Patriarch of Constantinople. He is an ecclesiastic whose Christian office survived the fall of Constantinople, and whose presence in the modern world is that of a faded ghost of the great days of old. His title perpetuates the only official use now permitted of the name of the imperial city. But before I describe the Phanar and its virtually imprisoned pontiff, I must sketch, as briefly as I can, the remarkable history of the Patriarchate.

When Constantine the Great removed the capital of the Empire from Rome to Byzantium in A.D. 330, the great Patriarchates of Rome, Alexandria, Antioch, and Jerusalem were already venerable. Byzantium was ruled by a bishop, who was not even a metropolitan. As Byzantium grew into Constantinople and became the greatest, the richest, the most splendid city in the Roman World and the seat of the Emperor and his court, it was natural that a fifth Patriarchate should have been created, founded, not upon apostolic authority, but upon the political supremacy of the Empire's new capital. Before long the Patriarch of Constantinople had become the first of all the Eastern prelates and he ranked in precedence first after the Pope. Indeed his conception of his own authority was such that he often contradicted and defied the Pope, from which came many of the troubles that afflicted Eastern and Western Christendom, and kept them apart.

When Mohammed conquered Constantinople in 1453, the

last Emperor had been slain, those Greeks who had not been massacred or sold into slavery were flying for their lives, and the Sultan saw a city whose normal life had ceased; he found himself the master of a deserted capital. A great manufacturing and commercial city had fallen to a warlike race that cared neither for manufacture nor commerce. Unless his rich prize was to stagnate and become a city of ruins he had to persuade the Greeks to go back to work. How was he to do that? The imperial power had been smashed, but the Byzantine Church still lived. It was his fear that, *in extremis*, the Byzantines might combine with the Pope to oppose and defeat him, therefore he decided to champion the Byzantine Church and, by supporting the office of Patriarch and promising religious freedom, to prevent any possible alliance with Rome and at the same time to encourage the Greeks to settle down again within the battered walls under a leader of their own race and faith.

The priests who remained in the stricken capital were accordingly ordered to appoint a new patriarch; for the office had been vacant for some time. With the appointment of a fanatical monk who was bitterly opposed to union with Rome, the ancient Patriarchate sponsored by the Moslem Sultan took on a new and surprising character. The Patriarch was made a Pasha of Three Tails and was solemnly invested by the Sultan himself with the insignia of his office, in imitation of the ceremony performed in Christian times by the Emperor. The result of this unnatural championship was indeed curious. Under Christian Emperors, the Patriarchs had occupied a secondary role and possessed no temporal authority: the Emperor, as the semi-divine head of the State, was also head of the Church. But the Moslem conqueror had no such priestly ambitions, with the result that the new Patriarchs were given civil and spiritual authority over all Greeks within the Empire; theoretically, at any rate, a great increase of power, lifting them, as it did, into the position of pontiffs.

It might be true to say that under this strange Moslem jurisdiction something of the power of the departed emperors was introduced into the office of Patriarch of Constantinople. In other words, like a shadow of Emperor and Prelate, the Patriarch lived on in the sadly changed world, the only great dignitary to descend through history from the imperial days of Constantinople. And, in order that this Christian "kingdom" within a Moslem kingdom might settle down immediately, a district on the shore of the Golden Horn, called the Phanar, from a pharos, or lighthouse, which stood there, was handed over to the Greeks.

The word "Phanar" at first denoted the Greek quarter, but it soon became applied to the Patriarch and his Synod, and is now used in that sense, much as we use the word "Vatican" in the West. The history of the Phanar is sometimes violent and often tragic, tragic because it is a frightful story of intolerance, ambition, and simony. It soon became the fashion to purchase the office, and sultan after sultan deposed patriarchs on the slightest pretext or on none at all in order to gather in the new fees. During the four hundred and eighty years since Christian Constantinople fell, the average reign of a Patriarch has been under four years! Only thirty-three Patriarchs, out of a hundred and seven, have died in office, and eight of these died violently.

So extraordinary have been the ups and downs of the Phanar, that many a Patriarch, recalled from exile time after time, has enjoyed three and four reigns! It is typical of Balkan politics, and also of the *Arabian Nights*, that a fall from power should many a time have been followed as swiftly by a return to favour. One singular result of this life of vicissitude was the establishment on the island of Prinkipo of a mansion and gardens, a kind of country club for

exiled Patriarchs, where the deposed dignitaries lived together, each one expecting to be recalled to occupy the
throne! Nowadays an exiled Patriarch generally retreats to
one of the monasteries on Mount Athos. But, to me, the
oddest thing about the Phanar is that a life so full of uncertainty, danger, and intrigue has exercised so great an attraction for the men of God. Princes have been known to
decline the uncertainty of a throne, but never has the See
of Constantinople been for long without its enthusiastic
victim.

The power of the Phanar, with that of the wealthy Greek
commercial aristocracy that was grouped round it, reached
its height in the Eighteenth Century, but since that time it
has rapidly declined, and to-day, under Republican Turkey,
it is hardly even a shadow of its former self. Nevertheless,
the outward forms are kept up, and something of the stately
etiquette derived from the Byzantine Empire still clings to
the lonely little band of Greek priests. The Patriarch's official
title is: "the Most Holy, the Most Divine, the Most Wise
Lord Archbishop of Constantinople, the New Rome, and
Œcumenical Patriarch." He is addressed in speech as "Your
Most Divine Holiness," or "Your All Holiness," and it was
until recently correct to address him in writing as: "All Holiest Lord, Glorious, God-crowned, God Uplifted and God-
favoured One! Servilely I cast myself before you and kiss
your sacred hands and venerable feet." This piece of Byzantine embroidery has been simplified within the past century.

The Patriarch, who is assisted by a synod of twelve bishops, is elected by Greek bishops in Turkey and he must be
a Turkish subject. The strange ceremony attending his election under the Sultans—his official visit to the Grand Vizier,
who presented him with a cloak and hat, a pastoral staff and
a white horse—has, of course, vanished with the Republic.
The Treaty of Lausanne modified the laws governing his

election but with the wholesale repatriation of Greek Christians in Turkey and the loss of territory to Turkey after the last War, his flock has dwindled to about 100,000, mostly Greek merchants still resident in Istanbul.

One and only one access of power came to the Phanar in recent times, and in an unusual and interesting direction. In 1922 the Orthodox Greeks in the United States were removed from the jurisdiction of the Church of Greece and placed under that of the Phanar. These Greeks number some 300,000. The Patriarch of the time, Meletios IV, organized an American Greek Church under the authority of Constantinople, but this did not please every óne and a rival policy to set up an independent holy synod for America has been put forward. Until this happens, if it does happen, the Patriarch of Constantinople is in the peculiar position of having most of his flock on the other side of the Atlantic, which is fully in accord with the complex and confused history of the Phanar.

A taxi-cab, threading the streets of Stamboul, took me to a part of the city where old houses cluster on ground that slopes towards the Golden Horn. We drew up on a rough road outside a tall shuttered building whose door was quickly opened by a Greek priest. He was evidently expecting me for, without questions, he led the way upstairs into one of those dead, unfeminine apartments that are to be found in monasteries. The walls were occupied by photographs from whose frames patriarchs, enlarged to life-size, gazed out with shrewd, but generally kindly, eyes, through a mass of venerable hair. There was a gold chair in the corner and, while I was waiting, I walked over to the window and saw the little narrow street below where a man walked selling bread from a basket, and through a gap in the opposite buildings

I could see a battered fragment of the sea wall and a patch
of the Golden Horn shining in the sun.

I sat on a cane chair gazing at a table covered with a
worn cloth fringed with wine-coloured tassels, some of which
were missing, and I thought how like this was to visiting
some great family worn out with living, reduced to a top-
floor flat, but retaining the memory of pomp and the manner of power. I was in the ante-room of the Patriarchs who
had crowned the Emperors of Byzantium; who had said
mass at the high altar of St. Sophia; who had crossed swords
with the Pope; who had moved through history in encrusted
vestments, like figures on an ikon, blessing the union of
Church and State and bending the knee only to the Basil-
ius himself. Shades of Emperors and Empresses, Constantine himself, Helena, Justinian and Theodora, Heraclius, the
Macedonian Basils and Michaels, the Commenian Johns, the
Palaeologi, move in the shades of that dark silent house in
the Phanar. Strange that the territory of the Byzantines,
whose cult was splendour, should have shrunk to a dark
room in Istanbul.

Two aged bishops entered, dignified old men, dark and
bearded, clothed in soot-black garments. Smilingly, they introduced themselves; and the trumpets sounded in Byzantium, for one was the *Great Logothete,* who keeps the Patriarchal seal, and his companion was the *Great Ekklesiarch,*
the Master of Ceremonies, two of the most important officials of the Patriarchal Court.

I asked after the health of His All-Holiness, Benjamin I,
and was assured that it was good. He is the sixth Patriarch
to reign at the Phanar since the Turkish Republic was proclaimed in 1923. Meletios IV fled for political reasons to
Mount Athos in 1923 and eventually abdicated, to be succeeded by Gregory VII, who died during the year of his
election. Constantine VI, who followed him, was expelled

by the Government for attempting to exert his ancient authority, to be followed by Basil III, who died after a reign of four years, to be succeeded by Photios II, who died in 1935; and so to the 'present occupant of the See.

I could sense in the very air of the Phanar that the disabilities under which this complex and difficult organization has always existed in a Moslem country have not been lessened by the laws of the Republic. The new Government insisted on the disestablishment of the Patriarchate, and that it should continue purely as a spiritual office with no political interests or temporal functions. Thus, having been subject for centuries to a power that was often hostile to the Christian religion, the Phanar now finds itself under a Republic that adopts a critical attitude to all religion. It is the rule in modern Turkey that no religious dress may be worn in public, with the exception of the dress of the Œcumenical Patriarch alone. All the other members of the Phanar, if they wish to leave the Patriarchate, must put on a suit of ordinary clothes; even so, it is a poor disguise for a spade-bearded Greek ecclesiastic!

While we were talking, a priest came to the door and announced that His All-Holiness was ready, so, with the *Great Ekklesiarch* leading together with the *Great Logothete*, we traversed a number of small rooms leading one out of the other until, at the end of the corridor, we entered a room full of bishops. As these dignitaries moved aside, I saw a frail old man sitting at a roll-top desk; and I knew that I was in the presence of Benjamin I, the last representative on earth of the Byzantine Emperors and the Patriarchs of New Rome. He wore a black robe with a fine pectoral cross on his breast and, upon his head, the tall brimless hat of the Orthodox priesthood, the *kalemaukion*. I bent over a thin ringed hand and was then presented to the members of the Synod. Once again I heard in imagination the trumpets

sounding in St. Sophia as, one after the other, the members
of the Patriarchal Court answered to sonorous titles that
have descended to them from the palaces of the last Caesars.
There was the *Great Khartophylax*, the archivist, the *Great
Economist*, the financial administrator, the *Rephendarios*, or
ambassador, the *Protekdicos*, or judge, the *Hypogonaton*,
who robes the Patriarch, the *Hypomimneskon*, a receiver of
petitions, the *Didaskalos*, who expounds the Gospels; and
many others.

It was the strangest thing to stand in that final contraction
of the Imperial Byzantine Court, with a man selling bread
down in the lane below, and the reigning potentate sitting
behind a roll-top desk. And this audience, I reflected, as an
historical experience, was equivalent to an audience with
the Pope in the presence of the Sacred College.

I marvelled at the vitality of human institutions that are
founded on faith, and at the determination of high-sounding
names and pomp to go down the ages, even when the world
from which they drew their majesty has vanished; for there,
as plain as anything, was a microcosm of the old Imperial
Court of Constantinople, that never ended, as most people
imagine, with the death of the last Caesar, but has been
meeting ever since: a strange shadow cabinet of the Palaeologi. No wonder the Sultans often deposed a patriarch
suddenly for no apparent reason! I can well imagine how,
startled maybe by a realization that the ghost of the old
imperial court still haunted his capital, he awakened from
an evil dream, in which he had seen all the minarets fall
down and had heard the church bells ringing out once again
over the City of God.

I found myself answering automatically those little ice-
breaking questions which His All-Holiness addressed to me
about England; and our conversation was made a good deal
easier than it might have been because I had just travelled

across Asia Minor, visiting the sites of St. Paul's missionary journeys; so, unlike most audiences of that kind, we really had something serious to talk about.

The interview over, I was taken by the members of the Synod to see the only two interesting places in the Phanar: the Treasury and the Church. I noted that the buildings which house the Patriarchate are larger than they appear from the street, being linked together by courtyards with outside staircases rather in the manner of one of the monasteries of Athos. Mounting a staircase, we came to a room which was heavily protected by fireproof and burglar-proof doors, and when the official who had the keys had been found, we entered. A bishop switched on strip lights that shone upon a dazzling array of vestments, mitres, pastoral staffs, Gospel cases, many of them of great beauty and antiquity, and all of them set out in glass cases down the centre of the room. I was shown various liturgical objects which, it is claimed, were saved from the sack of St. Sophia in 1453.

We then went down to the Church of St. George, which stands in a courtyard of the Phanar. It is a building in which the Patriarchs set up their throne only in 1603, having migrated from church to church for a variety of reasons, none of them happy ones. The present church is not a distinguished building and was reconstructed in 1720.

The priests showed me its treasures, which include the "Column of the Flagellation," taken, they said, from the old Church of the Holy Apostles, which was pulled down in the Middle Ages, and the body of St. Euphemius, the Third Patriarch of Constantinople, who died in A.D. 515. I was shown the Patriarchal Throne, an ornate ivory seat, which I was assured had once belonged to St. John Chrysostom. I suppose an expert would date it not earlier than the Fifteenth Century, but who knows? Such chairs, repaired and restored age after age, always retain the names of their great owners and, indeed, if one stick of the original object remains, the name is justified in the eyes of the pious.

The bishops and the priests accompanied me to the gate of the Phanar where we said good-bye, and I noticed how apprehensively they gazed into the street and how careful they were not to leave the doorstep. Priests in the street and a man in a fez are alike forbidden by the laws of Turkey.

So I left the territory of His All-Holiness, Benjamin I, "Archbishop of Constantinople, the New Rome."

GREECE

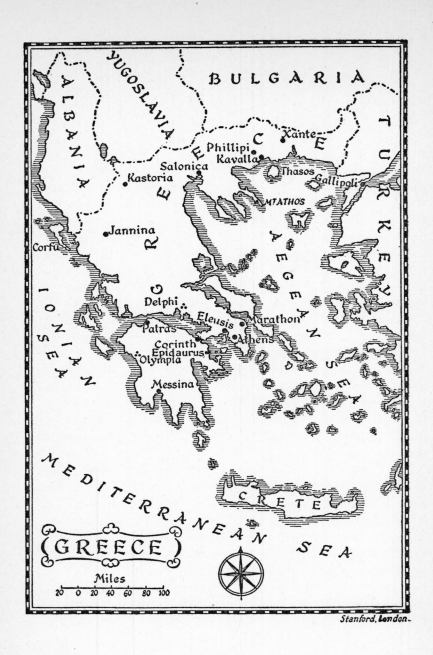

ALBANIA

YUGOSLAVIA

BULGARIA

TURKEY

GREECE

Xante

Phillipi
Kavalla

Salonica

Kastoria

Thasos

Gallipoli

Mt ATHOS

Jannina

Corfu

AEGEAN

IONIAN

SEA

Delphi

Eleusis

Marathon

Patras

Athens

Corinth
Epidaurus
Olympia

SEA

Messina

CRETE

MEDITERRANEAN

SEA

GREECE

Miles

20 0 20 40 60 80 100

Stanford, London.

I

KAVALLA

It was early morning and the sun was already warm. The ship rode at anchor on a sea like green glass. Looking shoreward, I saw a red and white town at the foot of a mountain. A high rock jutted out to sea, with houses rising in narrowing terraces to a summit crowned with the towers and walls of an ancient castle. This sea-girt rock was linked to the hills at the back by a Roman aqueduct of double arches. Such is Kavalla, the Neapolis of St. Paul's time, in whose little harbour the Apostle first set foot in Europe.

It was, in his day, a small roadstead in the shadow of a hill, almost an island, on whose crest was a temple modelled after the Parthenon at Athens. It held the statue of the Venus of Neapolis. The fleet of Brutus and Cassius had anchored in the bay during the Battle of Philippi, and it was to the lovely little island of Thasos, lying a few miles south of Kavalla, that Brutus had sent the body of Cassius for burial, so that his funeral would not disturb the morale of the army.

The Neapolis that Paul saw, as the ship from Troas came in with a following wind, must have been very like the Kavalla that I saw on that still, bright morning. The temple has disappeared from the top of the hill and a Byzantine-Turkish citadel takes its place, but the square white houses, dazzling in the sunlight, each house with a roof of red tiles, must have grouped themselves round the hill, tier above tier, the lowest reflected in the water, just as they do to-day.

The skyline is the same. The wild mountains of Macedonia have not changed. They rise from a sea of emerald

green, lifting themselves, mountain against mountain, to the
north, where only thirty miles away they meet the frontier
of Bulgaria. Far to the south, almost lost in the heat haze,
is the long, mountainous silhouette of Mount Athos. . . .

No departure has such an air of finality as that by rowing-
boat. When the traveller sees his suit-cases flung downward
to the arms of boatmen standing below in the shadow of a
ship's side, and when he prepares to descend the suicidal
ladders which are lowered at such moments, he has the feeling that the solid world is about to recede, and there comes
over him a loneliness which has been shared by all those
who have been marooned.

The two boatmen sang as their oars cut into the smooth
water. I could not catch one word of their chant. Though
the words were Greek, I was sure that the tune was Turkish. Stepping ashore on a little half-moon of sand packed
with men and donkeys, I watched brown, barelegged porters running up and down planks flung from the sterns of
sailing-ships, bearing on their backs bundles of firewood
from Thasos and sacks of charcoal from Mount Athos. These
were loaded upon donkeys and taken into the town.

A few yards away was the fish-market, evidently a centre
of importance. How fascinating it is to see the kind of fish
which men take from strange waters. There were fish in this
market whose destination should have been an aquarium
and not a kitchen: queer, flat, coloured fish, and long, thin,
silver fish. There were trays full of the black and green
octopi which are relished all over the Ægean and the Mediterranean, and there were calamare, or ink-fish, flaccid and
horrible in death. Most sinister of all were red oysters in
huge gnarled shells. Noticing my interest in these, a polite
fishmonger deliberately picked out one of the most deadly
looking and offered it to me with a charming bow. But my
courage failed me, whereon, with the boastful air of a man

performing a conjuring trick, he snicked the oyster with his knife and defiantly swallowed it.

I discovered that Kavalla, like many another coast-town in this part of the world, does not live up to its appearance from the sea. It proved to be a place without civic grandeur or plan, a new town full of big, stone warehouses on the waterfront, and an old town winding round the citadel hill, a warren of unmade roads and narrow streets.

I was fortunate enough to make the acquaintance of a young archaeologist, George Bakalakis, whose enthusiasm for Neapolis warmed my heart. How dreary the world would be without fiery young men who would pull down ten town halls to find one ancient inscription. He took me into a dusty shed where all that is left of the marble city of Paul's time lies about among the dust and the rats.

As we walked through the town, my companion told me that it is the centre of the Macedonian tobacco industry. The tobacco leaf is stored in the large warehouses which lie close to the harbour. Some of the best tobacco, still known as "Turkish," is grown in the district, and the tobacco workers are the only electors in Greece who send communist members to the Parliament in Athens.

A war memorial stands in the centre of a little public garden. It is not an inspired memorial, and the usual lion rampages on a stone cenotaph: but what interested me was the Greek inscription; "To those who died 1912–1922."

Our own war memorials, with 1914–1918 inscribed on them, cover a long period of suffering, but Macedonia knew ten years of war. When the first Balkan War broke out in 1912, the country was Turkish: when the Turks were driven out, Bulgarians occupied Kavalla: then came the second Balkan War, at the end of which the town became Greek. During the European War the Bulgarians again swooped down, committing frightful atrocities during their occupation, but in 1918 the Greeks resumed possession, and in 1921 plunged into war with Turkey.

We climbed the citadel hill, but I was disappointed to find that the castle, which looks so splendid from the sea, is just a hollow shell. On the top of the hill, on a terrace overlooking the open sea and the isle of Thasos, is the shrouded statue of a man on a horse. It is carefully concealed from view, and has been so for many a year. It is an equestrian statue of the great Mehemet Ali. The late King Fuad of Egypt promised to unveil it, but never managed to do so.

The only show-place in Kavalla is the house in which Mehemet Ali was born in 1769. It is now the property of the Egyptian Government, which maintains a caretaker in a fez. It is an interesting old Turkish house, with latticed harem windows and floor-boards which creak ominously. I had never realized that Mehemet Ali, who became Viceroy of Egypt, was, until the age of thirty or so, a humble tobacco merchant of Kavalla.

Descending the hill, we went to the little square near the harbour where, beneath matting stretched on poles, the male population of Kavalla not engaged in packing tobacco, unloading charcoal, or selling fish, was drinking coffee and proclaiming its Turkish traditions by playing tric-trac. To sit at a little table under the matting was, I discovered, to invite the attentions of small boys who cried shrilly, *"Loostro verneeki!"*, and, hitting a shoe-brush against a tray of polishes slung round their necks, flung themselves with violence on my feet. The number of young Greeks who begin life as *loostro-verneeki* boys must be prodigious.

Not far from the quay is a Greek church which has a curious history. It was once dedicated to St. Paul, then became a Turkish mosque, and has now become a church again, but dedicated to St. Nicholas.

The priest, a big, square-bearded Greek like a Hebrew prophet, sparkled up at once when I told him that it was a disgrace to Kavalla that his church should not be dedicated to St. Paul.

"Ah," he cried. "You are right. In the old days it used to be so. The holy Apostle Paul stepped ashore at this place, which in ancient times was the quayside; for the sea has gone back at this point. Come with me."

He led me round to the back of the church where, at the entrance to a little alley, is a round mark in the pavement.

"You are looking at the place where the Apostle Paul landed from the shores of Asia Minor. A big plane-tree once marked the spot."

His voice shook with indignation as he added:

"The Bulgarians cut it down."

"But you say that the church was once dedicated to St. Paul. Why is it now dedicated to St. Nicholas?"

He told me that when the Turks evacuated Kavalla, it was necessary to spend some money on the mosque in order to turn it again into a place of Christian worship. The fishermen agreed to find the money, but they would not hear of the re-dedication of the building to St. Paul. The continuity of the Christian tradition had, of course, been broken by centuries of Moslem occupation, and St. Paul meant little to the local fishermen, who, like all Greek sailors, placed their faith in St. Nicholas, their patron saint.

St. Nicholas, by the way, in addition to protecting sailors, children, travellers, and merchants, is also the patron saint of pawnbrokers. The story goes that a nobleman of the saint's native town, Parara in Asia Minor, had lost all his money, and did not know how he could endow his three beautiful daughters. St. Nicholas, hearing of his trouble, went by night and flung through the window three bags

of gold with which the nobleman was able to provide handsome dowries. These three bags are shown in all early ikons
as three gold apples, and the gold apples of St. Nicholas are
the origin of the pawnbroker's sign.

II

PHILIPPI

I HIRED an old car with torn celluloid side-screens and set off over the hills for Philippi, nine miles away.

The road leaps suddenly into the bleak fastness of Mount Symbolum, which stands like a barrier between the Plain of Philippi and the sea. This mountain is a continuation of the Pangaean range, famous in antiquity for its silver mines. The road twists to the summit, a height of 1,670 feet, and then slides down to an immense plain, green with crops and brown with marshland, as flat as an inland sea. The road was deep in dust. Every horseman, every ox-cart, every shepherd, moved in a little puff of brown cloud.

On those wide plains, and among those treacherous marshes, the Roman Republic came to an end forty-one years before Christ was born. It was there that the legions of Antony and young Octavius defeated the forces of Brutus and Cassius, and, to celebrate the victory, founded the colony of Philippi on the death-bed of the Republic.

I am sure that any one who in his schooldays has played the part of Brutus in Shakspere's *Julius Caesar* must look at the Plain of Philippi with more than usual interest. This, then, I told myself, was the reality behind the little platform in the governor's room at the end of term, this wide and desolate place so like my conception of it; and it was on these marshy levels that the real actors in one of the world's greatest dramas suffered and died. As I went on across the plain, I seemed to hear again the sepulchral voice of that Caesar who was to die so soon in France, warning me from

a patch of erratic limelight that I should see him again at
Philippi. . . .

After travelling for about eight miles I came to an inn on
the right of the road, remarkable only because a Roman
monument is built into the wall. It is a gigantic sepulchral
stone about twelve feet in height, and set on a plinth. It
bears the name and titles of a Roman officer named C. Vibius. As I was looking at it, a peasant came out of the inn
and, seeing my interest, began to show off the monument
and to point out a better vantage-point. I had read in Mr.
G. F. Abbot's *Macedonian Folklore* that the name of Alexander the Great is still remembered by the peasants, but I
did not expect to receive such a swift confirmation of this.

"What is this monument?" I asked.

"We call it the feeding-place of Bucephalus," he replied.

"And who was Bucephalus?" I asked, to see if he were
merely repeating a name parrot-like.

"Bucephalus was the horse of King Alexander," he replied
at once.

I asked him if he could tell me any stories of "King Alexander," but he shook his head.

In another mile or so I approached a conical hill with an
ancient tower on the top of it, and, almost before I was
aware of it, I found myself among the ruins of Philippi.
The modern road follows the line of the old Via Egnatia and
runs right through Philippi. The ruins lie ten or fifteen feet
below the modern level, and I walked down from the road
into the forum, where the bases of marble columns, rain-
gutters, and paving stones cover acres of ground which have
been excavated by French archaeologists.

The only modern building is a watchman's hut on the
side of the road: otherwise the city, which St. Luke described with pride as "a city of Macedonia, the first of the
district," is now desolate in the plain, its white bones shining

KAVALLA, MACEDONIA

wherever ten feet of soil have been removed.

The watchman came from his hut and took me through the dead city. Its most spectacular features are the piers and gateway of a Byzantine basilica. Before the French archaeologists began to dig, this church was the only ruin above ground. It stood in the fields, a landmark on the flat plain, and was wrongly described by the few writers who passed that way as a triumphal archway. It was a Greek cathedral dedicated, no doubt, to St. Paul. The caretaker told me that the local people have always called it "the palace of Alexander the Great."

The forum of Philippi has been excavated. The ground-plan is perfect. The stone rain-gutters that drained it in Roman times are so well preserved that they still carry off water in the wet season. Steps lead from the forum to higher levels, where marble floors and the bases of columns indicate the fine public buildings and temples that once lined the square.

Many inscriptions are lying about, just as they were taken from the earth. One, which was difficult to decipher, seems to describe the dedication of a temple, but others of a more personal character suggest that people did not live to a very great age in Philippi. Lying together in a room off the forum are two tombstones, one recording the deaths of Cassia Gemella and Antonius Alexander at the age of twenty-five, and the other commemorating Velleius Plato, who died aged thirty-six, after having made a tomb for himself and a relative, evidently a doctor.

The most interesting inscription is thirteen lines of Latin as clear cut as they were when they left the stonemason's hand centuries ago. They state that the statue was erected by soldiers under the command of L. Tatinius, who had begun his military career as a private in the footguards and had risen to the rank of centurion.

From the air of secrecy with which the caretaker led me to a certain ruined house, I sensed that he was about to show me the most precious relic of Philippi. He took a broom and swept away several inches of sand, revealing a beautiful pavement made of small red, white, and black tesserae.

"The walls of Philippi!" he said dramatically, and looking down as he swept away the sand, I saw that the sunlight was falling on a pictorial diagram of square fortified towers, arched gateways, and a machicolated wall.

I remembered the touch of local pride which seems to inspire St. Luke's mention of Philippi—"the first of the district." And here again was something of the same pride: the finest thing with which this long dead citizen of Philippi could decorate the pavement of his room were the walls and towers of his native town.

The caretaker asked my permission to cover the pavement, and it required little imagination to transform his broom into a scythe and himself into Father Time.

I took a farewell glance at the ruins lying in the shelter of the hill. Generations of men had grown up and had been harvested like corn and, like corn, had left no trace but that furrow on the plain. But the words of Paul's Epistles to the Philippians are as warm and as full of life as they were when the wagons creaked along the Via Egnatia; when streets, which now lie cold and open to the sky, rang to the sounds of men.

I drove on to the railhead at Drama. That dusty Macedonian town looked to me like the world's end. There were a few soldiers returning from leave, sitting under the roof of the station café while a patient Armenian tried to sell them a carpet.

I sat with them and waited two hours for the train to Salonica, drinking cup after cup of Turkish coffee and eating Turkish delight speared on little sticks.

The mountains changed colour, the dust swirled up under the roofs of approaching horsemen, and at last a bedraggled train puffed into the station.

III

SALONICA

SALONICA is about seventy miles from Philippi as the crow flies. St. Paul reached it in three days, travelling along the Via Egnatia, which went through Amphipolis and Apollonia, two cities which have now disappeared from the map. The train, winding between the mountains west of Drama, covers something like a hundred and fifty miles on the same journey. The track bends and twists in the valleys, making an immense detour in order to avoid the great mountain mass of Beshik Dagh, whose topmost summit wears snow until midsummer and is known locally as Pilaf Tepe from its fancied resemblance to a plate of rice.

Traversing the Struma Valley, the train runs for miles along the foot of the Bulgarian Mountains and almost enters Yugoslavia at Lake Doiran, where the frontier line between Macedonia and Yugoslavia passes across the water, dividing the lake between the two countries. For more than two years our troops held the Doiran Sector, fighting uphill all the time in every sense of the word. There is many a walled war cemetery on those lonely hills.

In Salonica I was given a room and a bath, which at that moment seemed to me the very apex of luxury. And there was a little balcony from which I could see, through a tangle of telegraph cables, the ships anchored in the harbour.

The charm of my surroundings was heightened by the fact that water actually ran from the bath-taps, that some one answered the bell, that there was a connection between the light-switch and the light and between the blind and its cord.

When I explored Salonica in the morning I saw a city that in ancient times must have been exquisite to look upon. It stands on a hill at the head of a blue gulf, mountains piled behind it, and to the far south rising from the sea is the snow-covered summit of Thessalian Olympus. Modern Salonica is a rather shabby reflection of two worlds. There is the new town built to European standards on the low ground which was swept by the great fire of 1917, and there is the old Turkish town which escaped the fire and climbs the hill, lying in picturesque disarray behind mighty Byzantine walls complete with square towers and gateways. The only features of interest in the new town are the Arch of Galerius, which spans the main street, and the Byzantine churches whose architecture and mosaics make Salonica as interesting as Istanbul to the student of this period.

The most interesting of these churches, dedicated to St. Demetrius, the patron and guardian of Salonica, was gutted by the fire, although happily some of the finest mosaics were undamaged. A Fourth Century crypt was discovered in 1919 at the east end of this church. It contains a round, marble baptismal font upheld by columns; and in graves near by were discovered the bodies of four bishops, sitting fully clothed in their state vestments. Unfortunately the bodies fell to dust when the tombs were opened. A workman led me to a contractor's hut in which all that is left of the metal decorations was lying among potsherds. I looked at a belt buckle and other fragments of Byzantine enamel, which, unless they are placed in a museum, may soon find their way into the pocket of a visitor.

The old town is a maze of narrow, crooked streets, unexpected trees, courtyards, and mosques disused since the Turks were expatriated under the Lausanne Treaty, leaving Salonica a city of Greeks, Armenians, and Spanish Jews. When the sun shines and the roads are dry, old Salonica exhibits the eccentric charm of intense individualism; but once the sun goes in, or, worse still, if rain falls, the old city is revealed as a squalid collection of ill-built and insanitary shanties.

In one of the streets leading steeply to the old city, I read a plaque on the wall of a humble little house over a potter's shop. It states that Ghazi Mustapha Kemal first saw the light of day there. The inscription is in French, Greek, and Turkish. A little higher up this street, I encountered a remarkable funeral. It came swaying from side to side down the steep, cobbled lane, led by two Greek priests, solemnly chanting. A man walked in front, holding the lid of the coffin; behind came a black hearse containing the coffin, and inside it, gruesomely exposed to every passer-by, was the body of a young woman. It was a distressing sight, but no one seemed to think anything of it. The children stopped playing and a few men took off their caps as the coffin went past.

I had been told that the custom of taking the exposed corpse to the cemetery is still observed in country places in Greece, but I was surprised to see it in such a big city as Salonica. The origin of this custom goes back to the Turkish occupation and to the days before Greece won her independence. The Turks, learning that Greeks were holding mock funerals in order to smuggle in arms and ammunition, brought in a law forbidding bodies to be buried in closed coffins.

A young student whom I met in Salonica gave me some details about Greek funeral customs. A candle is kept alight in the room of the departed for three days, because it is believed that the soul is sometimes lost for three days and returns to the place of its earthly associations.

"There is a special cake also put beside the candle," he said, "a cake spread with honey."

I thought of the honey jars which were placed on the pyre of Patroclus. No doubt many of such funeral rites go back to remote antiquity.

When three years have expired, the ceremony of "taking up the remains" is performed, an intensely gruesome ceremony to the Western mind, but one to which the Greeks attach great importance. They approach it also with a certain fear. Incorruptibility, which in the West has always been considered a proof of holiness, rouses in Greece the utmost horror and repugnance. It means that the dead person has been under a curse, or has become a vampire; and the evil spirit must be solemnly exorcised and the body destroyed. This, fortunately, does not often occur. The ceremony of "taking up the remains" is one in which members of the family go to the cemetery, bearing wine with which they wash the bones of the departed before packing them away in a wooden box. Every Greek cemetery has a special building for such boxes of bones. The priest is present at this ceremony ready, in case the body has not disintegrated, to release the soul of the dead person from the curse under which it is believed to lie.

A feature of Salonica that impresses the visitor are newspapers and advertisements printed in Hebrew characters. There is an enormous Jewish colony in the port, but I am told that it has decreased since the Greek occupation. In Turkish times Salonica was often called a Jewish city. The Jews, however, are a different race from the Jews who were present in New Testament times. They are Separdic Jews,

whose language was a corrupt kind of Spanish called La-
dino, and they settled in Salonica after their expulsion from
Spain under Ferdinand and Isabella.

I looked everywhere in Salonica for some memory of the
author of the Epistles to the Thessalonians. There is a street
leading up to the old town which is called in common speech
the "street of St. Paul." At the top of the hill is an attractive
monastery in a clump of cypress trees, called the Monastery
of Vlatadon, which seems to have some connection with the
Apostolic visit. There is a tradition that when Paul came
from Philippi to Thessalonica, he visited a house in that part
of the old city and knelt in the courtyard to pray. The spot
is marked by a circular marble from Thessaly, a dark stone
forming the centre of a white cross. I do not know whether
this is an early tradition.

The monastery is not very ancient, and I could find no one
who was able to tell me whether it was built on the site of
an early church. The founders of the monastery were two
Cretan brothers called Vlata, who lived in the Thirteenth
Century. Their monastery was the only one respected by
the Turks after the conquest of 1430, because the monks
offered to show the Turks how to capture Salonica if they
would promise to protect them and respect their rights when
the city was taken. They informed the besieging army that
the only way to subdue Salonica was to cut the water-pipes
that supplied the whole city with water from Mount Hor-
tiati. This advice was followed, and Salonica was forced to
capitulate. So great was the rage of the populace, however,
that the traitor monks had to be protected, and the Sultan
stationed a Chaoush, a Turkish officer, in the monastery for
this purpose. Since that time the place has been called locally the Chaoush Monastery.

Behind the municipal hospital is a small chapel dedicated

SNOW-CAPPED BELESH MOUNTAINS ON
THE YUGOSLAV-BULGARIAN FRONTIER

to St. Paul. The legend is that when the Apostle was driven from Thessalonica he spent the night there, outside the walls of the ancient city, and that from the tears shed by him on that occasion sprang a stream of holy water.

IV

ATHENS

I

WE entered a narrow channel stagnant as a village pond, which lay between two ranges of hills. There was not a ripple on the water. It was like green oil. Its surface was covered with countless yellow jelly-fish, which propelled themselves in a sinister and rather repellent way by sucking in and blowing out the water. Such was the Gulf of Lamia, in which we lay for some hours. There was a wooden jetty piled with barrels, the harbour of a small town called Stylis.

I went ashore, and was driven to Thermopylae in an old car which I found on the quayside. Summer had leapt on Greece and the heat was terrible. Men lay beneath olive trees as if dead; and the beasts in the field and the goats on the hill stood mournfully seeking the shade of walls, as they waited for the sun to set. The green hills had turned brown. The flowers had died. The earth was cracking in the heat. Over burning gullies of white stones strode high, pointless bridges, and above the helpless earth lay a sky across which, it seemed, no cloud would ever pass again.

Thermopylae looked like a salt desert in Arizona. The sun flickered over a plain dotted with hummocks of tough grass. It is now difficult to recognize the famous pass which Leonidas with his thousand Greeks defended against the Persian Army. Perhaps I might have been able to do so on a spring day, but the task was quite beyond me on this tropical forenoon. Earthquakes have changed the lie of the land, and silt brought down by the river Spercheius has built up

304

a wide plain between the mountains and the sea. There is certainly no obstacle at Thermopylae to-day which a battalion of Highlanders could not get round in half an hour. But it was worth the journey, if only to wonder where that famous hillock stood on which Leonidas and his heroes fell one by one, pierced by the arrows of the Medes; if only to say to myself in after years that I had stood upon the ground where Dienekes spoke a sentence that flew straight into immortality:

"The number of the barbarians is so great," he was told, "that when they shoot their arrows the sun will be darkened."

And Dienekes replied:

"So much the better, we shall then fight in the shade."

I walked to the sulphur springs which give Thermopylae its name. The day was so hot that no steam rose from them. They were warm and green and stank like parts of Harrogate. Under a burnt-up awning of vine boughs, I drank wine with a company of villagers. Then, summoning up my courage, I faced the heat again and went back to Stylis and the ship.

Night fell as we steamed through the narrow channel between the mainland and the island of Euboea. Early in the morning we came in close to Marathon.

I saw a little bay with flat land lying back to the hills. Somewhere there was the low mound beneath which lay the Athenians who died under the Persian arrows. From the hills at the back, ten thousand Athenians marched against the host of Darius, driving them seaward to their ships. In that same bay Cynaegirus, the brother of Aeschylus, held on to a galley with his right hand; when it was severed by a Persian scimitar, he held on with his left; and when that hand, too, was severed, he continued to hold on with his teeth. In the last century the mound of Marathon was opened and men saw the charred bones, and the pottery and other objects placed with the dead over two thousand four hundred years ago.

The ship then approached the rocky headland of Sunium. Behind that majestic cliff were the mines of Laurium, whose silver built the fleet that smashed the Persians at Salamis. Then, as we rounded the point, I saw a sight that remains in my mind for ever as one of the loveliest memories of Greece.

High on the crest of a cape stands the ruin of a white temple. It is all that is left of the Temple of Poseidon at Sunium, the most southerly point of Attica. In the old days, mariners coming from Asia Minor or from Egypt kept a look-out for the flash of sunlight on the temple at Sunium. It was built in remote ages to propitiate Poseidon, god of the sea, who was believed to have evil designs on all ships passing the cape.

When ships sailing westward had passed the Temple of Poseidon, the sailors would look along the hills for the first sign of Athens; and they would see the sunlight flashing from the gilded point of the spear which Athene held high above the Acropolis. They would explain to the voyagers that they were looking for the spearhead of Athena Promachos, whose helmet rose seventy feet above her sandals. And that mighty statue was standing there long after the glory of Athens had been humbled to the dust. Alaric the Goth saw it four centuries after Christ, and at the sight of it, men said, he turned his pirate ship and fled.

There are no words to express the first sight of Athens as a ship moves across Phaleron Bay towards the Piraeus. It is one of the supreme moments in travel.

The sun was sinking behind the island of Aegina. The last warm light was shining full on the slopes of Mount Hymettus. Five miles from the sea, and on ground that rose

KEMAL ATATURK'S BIRTHPLACE
IN SALONICA

only slightly, I saw a large city of brown-and-white houses, and from its centre, rising as abruptly as the rock of Stirling Castle springs from the Links of Forth, was a brown hill: and I knew that I was looking at the Acropolis. I could see the white pillars of the Parthenon in the clear light.

It did not matter now if Athens were to disappoint me; if she turned out to be a poor thing hiding behind a mighty name; for I had seen her in the light of evening as I had always imagined her to be: proud, splendid, and old.

No sooner had I stepped ashore in the morning and moved from the protective barrier of the dock gates, than a dark-visaged crowd of men swooped down upon me. Some held out brown sponges, others boxes of Turkish Delight; some imagined me to be the kind of man who wanted a doll dressed as an *efzone*, others offered me post-cards of the Acropolis and horrid little plaster replicas of the Venus de Milo. They all talked at the top of their voices, reducing their wares from fifty drachmae to forty and thirty and twenty without any encouragement on my part; and those who were not trying to sell something offered to guide me through Athens and to find the best car to take me there.

I looked at those men, if not with pleasure at least with appreciation. In an age that cheerfully accepts every kind of fake, they seemed to be delightfully authentic. They might have been a crowd out of Aristophanes.

Standing in the middle of this crowd, feeling rather like a bone that is being pulled to pieces by a pack of hungry dogs, I had sufficient detachment left to wonder if Sir Lawrence Alma-Tadema's well-washed, well-laundered and pleated Greece ever really existed outside the imagination of Victorian romanticists who saw in Periclean Athens everything that Victorian Sheffield was not. I have an idea that landing in Greece must always have been like this. I remembered how Lycinus, in the *Amores* of Lucian, says that as soon as he stepped ashore on the island of Rhodes "two or three people immediately hurried up, eager to tell me the history for a small fee. . . ."

Shaking myself free from the guides, I stepped into the nearest car and told the driver to take me to Athens. We had soon left the Piraeus behind us, and rounding Phaleron Bay, on whose waters rested an Imperial Airways seaplane, we entered the straight, five-mile motor road to Athens. This road is built on the site of the northern Long Wall of Themistocles, which, with its companion wall to the south, was in ancient times compared to a cable anchoring Athens to the coast. When we were within a mile or so of the city, I caught a fleeting glimpse of the Acropolis rising in a blaze of morning sunshine—one of the grandest sights in the world.

We plunged into the broad, straight streets of a modern European city, with good shops, green tramcars, murderous green motor omnibuses, a press of noisy cars, hundreds of cafés, whose tables overflowed to the pavement, newspaper kiosks, public gardens full of exotic trees (and German nurse-maids); and a great central place, the focus of modern Athens, Constitution Square, beneath whose pepper trees the modern Athenian gathers to discuss, with that passionate fervour which has always been a characteristic of the Greek, the latest political rumour.

The roof of my hotel was flat and accessible. From its height I looked over Athens. I saw the high, oblong rock of the Acropolis rising above the city, and I saw the wooded peak of Mount Lycabettus, the tame, domesticated volcano of Athens. And the size of Athens surprised me, for this big city is the creation of only a hundred years.

How strange it is to realize that Athens, so famous in antiquity and so vigorous to-day, disappeared from history

from the time of Pausanias, in the Second Century, until
comparatively modern days. Practically nothing is known
of Byzantine Athens, Latin Athens, or of Turkish Athens. It
disappeared as a mighty, but dying, classical city, to emerge
in 1675 as a Turkish village.

The first Englishman who expressed a wish to see Athens
was John Milton, but his wish was to remain unfulfilled. As
he was about to cross into Greece, the Civil War broke out
in England and he returned, because he "considered it base
that, while my fellow-countrymen were fighting at home for
liberty, I should be travelling abroad at ease for intellectual
culture."

The first Englishman actually to explore the site of ancient
Athens, and to give some measurements of the Parthenon,
was Francis Vernon, a Londoner. He was born in 1637 and
was afflicted with "an insatiable desire of seeing," which
curiosity caused him on one occasion to be captured and sold
by pirates and eventually, at the age of forty, to be murdered
by Arabs in Persia, during a quarrel about a penknife. Vernon's notes on Athens are embodied in a letter to a friend
in England and they are still, I believe, in the possession of
the Royal Society. So far as I know, they have never been
published.

The earliest published account in English is that of Sir
George Wheler, who in 1675 spent a month in Turkish
Athens. His book, *A Journey into Greece*, was printed in
1682. It is a delightful and valuable book, for the author was
an observant classical scholar and he was able also to describe with charm a journey through a country which at that
time was unknown and unexplored. Wheler discovered that
the Parthenon had become a Turkish mosque, with a minaret built beside it, to the top of which he climbed. Gunpowder was stored in the Temple of the Wingless Victory,
and he was not able to get into the Erechtheum "because

the Turk that lives in it hath made it his *Seraglio* for his Women."

Athens at that time was a town of about eight to ten thousand inhabitants, three parts of them Christians, the rest Turks. There were no walls, but the outermost houses were built close together and thus served as a wall, the approaches being closed at night with gates: for even at that time pirates were such regular visitors that the garrison patrolled the walls of the Acropolis all night, "making a great hallowing and noise to signify their watchfulness."

The Turks, contrary to the general conception of the race, have always been a tolerant, easygoing people, and Wheler counted about two hundred churches, fifty of which had regular priests in attendance.

He was shocked by the amount of paint used by the Greek women, who "looked very graceful in their manner of dress, but so horribly painted, that it was hard to conjecture what their natural complexion was by reason of the thick Vizard of Paint they had on." Again he noted that: "When a Virgin is to be married, she is brought to the church as richly attired as the fortunes of her relatives will bear, but her face is so bedaubed with gross paint that it is not easy to determine whether she be flesh and blood or a statue made of plaster. She returns home from the church to the house of her husband with a great crown of gilded metal on her head, accompanied by all the guests and her near relations with pipes and hand-drums and the best music they can make: whilst she in the meantime is conducted at so slow a pace that it is scarcely perceivable that she moveth. And so soon as she is entered into the house of her spouse they throw sugar-plums out of the windows upon the people, who are crowded and throng'd at the door."

The painted women of Athens invariably impressed the early travellers, and the fashion is, I think, of interest, because it may have been a survival from classical and Byzantine times. The classics are full of references to the eye-paint, the rouge, and the coats of white lead used by the women of Athens.

There is a big gap between the explorations of Wheler and the scientific travellers of the Eighteenth Century, who, beginning with Stuart and Revett in 1751, unconsciously prepared classical scholars in England to champion the cause of Greek Independence in the following century by causing them to identify modern Greeks with the heroes of their schooldays. Stuart and Revett's four mighty tomes, the *Antiquities of Athens,* give a splendid idea of the city as it used to be under Turkish rule.

The Acropolis was a warren of labyrinthine Turkish streets and gardens. Turbaned Turks in flowing draperies practised archery and exercised their horses in the shadow of the rock. When Wheler saw the Parthenon, the roof was still intact. But in 1687 the shells of the Venetian fleet fell on the building, igniting the powder stored there and killing three hundred Turks: the roof was blown off and many columns were destroyed. Characteristically, the Turks did not restore the Parthenon, but built a mosque and houses inside it. The Erechtheum, no longer a Turkish harem as in Wheler's time, was a roofless ruin with one of the Caryatides missing. An engraving of this building shows that the accumulation of earth on the Acropolis was so deep that the level of the roadway was about two feet below the Caryatides, so that nearly half this temple was below the ground.

In the following century it became the fashion to visit Athens. Byron first saw Greece in 1809—more than ten years before the War of Independence began—when, as a young man of twenty-two, he travelled across Europe with his Cambridge friend, John Cam Hobhouse, who afterwards became Lord Broughton. Hobhouse left a record of this tour in the form of a large volume entitled *A Journey through Albania and other Provinces of Turkey in Europe and Asia.* Byron recorded his impressions in the Second Canto of *Childe Harold.* The two friends saw everything that the early travellers had seen; but, to Byron's rage, they also saw Lord Elgin's agents sensibly engaged in taking down the metopes from the Parthenon and packing them for shipment to England. A lot of unkind things are said, perhaps naturally, about Lord Elgin in Greece, but any one who compares the two series of casts in the British Museum of those figures still in position on the Parthenon—one series taken by Lord Elgin and the other fifty years later—will realize that even in that time the frieze has suffered severe deterioration. Also, had Lord Elgin not taken the marbles, some one else certainly would have done so.

The Greek War of Independence began eleven years after Byron's visit, but it was not until 1833 that the Turkish garrison left Athens. In 1834 it was decided to create Athens the capital of the independent Kingdom of Greece.

A German architect, Schaubert, was employed to plan the wide streets, the squares, the boulevards: and so Athens, which in 1834 was a village of five thousand inhabitants, has become in 1936 a city of over four hundred and fifty thousand people.

II

I could sit for hours in Constitution Square—the agora of modern Athens—watching the Greek talking his eternal politics. The race has been diluted by Balkan blood, but some of the chief characteristics of the classical Greek remain. Was it not Demosthenes who pictured the Greeks bustling about the agora, asking, "Is there anything new?" or "What is the latest news?" And these same questions are asked to-day whenever the Athenians gather at the café tables under the pepper trees in Constitution Square.

"Well, and what is the latest news? Is there a recent development?"

Heads in black felt hats are obscured by one of the numerous newspapers, which is immediately flung aside when a boy comes along crying, so truly and delightfully, "*Ephemerides!*" with the latest crop of political discussion under his arm.

One side of the square is occupied by the huge yellow monstrosity of the old Palace of King Otho, now the Parliament House. The guard of tall *efzones* in their Albanian costumes—stiff white kilts, embroidered jackets, woollen tights, red upturned shoes with pom-poms on the toes—leans picturesquely on its rifles beside the Grave of the Unknown Warrior. Now and then a tourist steals up to take a photograph, and those good-looking young men instinctively adopt an heroic pose, because, like the Life Guards of Whitehall, they are used to it.

One of the first things the visitor notices about Athens is the clarity of the atmosphere. Plutarch somewhere speaks of air like spun-silk; and it is this silk-like air that covers Athens, creating in the mind a state of exhilaration and a sense of well-being. There is a sparkle and a happiness in the air of Athens which drive away ill-humour and depression.

The language of Aristophanes—let us not be pedantic about this—has kept abreast of the times. I look round at the hoardings and see that chocolate, cigarettes, and Dunlop tires are the best advertised objects . . . ΣΟΚΟΛΑΤΑ . . . ΣΙΓΑΡΕΤΤΑ . . . ΕΛΑΣΤΙΚΑ DUNLOP.

I see, inscribed above a door, the word tooth-doctor, ΟΔΟΝΤΙΑΤΡΟΣ, and, opening an Athens newspaper, I discover that the disciples of Asklepios, unlike their British colleagues, by no means deny themselves the pleasure of self-praise and advertisement. The cinema announcements, too, prove that Greece has been enriched by many new heroes. After a moment of indecision, I translate ΜΑΡΛΕΝ ΝΤΗΤΡΙΞ into Marlene

Dietrich. Greta Garbo is not, perhaps, any easier—ΓΚΡΕΤΑ ΓΚΑΡΜΗΟ; but it takes me some time to believe that ΚΛΑΡΚ ΓΚΕΙΜΠΛ is Clark Gable. High on a board, with the air of a battered and returned Odysseus, shines the word gramophone —ΓΡΑΜΜΟΦΟΝΑ.

It is good to sit among the eager, chattering crowds in this sunny place and to watch and listen. There is sometimes no need to listen, for the Greeks have a complete vocabulary of gesture. It is known to every one. What can be more significant than the gesture to distrust or dislike, a gesture also of warning? A man will lightly grasp the right-hand lapel of his coat with the first finger and thumb of his right hand and quietly, almost secretly, move the cloth back and forwards, saying at the same time, "Pup-pup-pup-pup." Or the gesture that denotes something fine and splendid and rare? The right hand is lifted shoulder high, first finger and thumb together, fingers curved, the palm of the hand towards the face of the gesturer, and the hand is brought down through the air several times in a very sharp, definite manner, only the hand and the forearm moving. Then there is the gesture inferring riches and splendour. The open right hand scoops the air in a luxurious way, as if shovelling invisible gold into the face of the speaker. Leisure and vitality describe Constitution Square as, I imagine, they would describe the agora of Athens in the time of Pericles.

It seems to me that rich and poor rub shoulders more intimately in Greece than in any other country I know. There are no titles, except a few old Venetian ones used locally in the Ionian Islands, and there is no feeling of social caste. The little bootblack, whose sharp rap of brush against his bootbox is one of the characteristic sounds of Athens, will glance up from polishing the shoes of a politician or an officer and, as equal to equal, give the usual Greek greeting?

"And what do you think of the political situation?"

The politician and the officer may smile with amusement, but they will answer gravely enough, as if to their own son.

There can be few countries where members of the Government are more readily accessible to every sort of suppliant and time-waster. In other countries secretaries and under-secretaries bar the way to Cabinet Ministers, but this would not work in Greece. Every one, if he has a grievance, regards it as his right personally to see the man who can remove it. Whether this innate sense of democracy is a legacy from ancient Greece I do not know, but it was one of the first things that impressed me. It is surprising to be told that when a man pushing a barrow of melons threatens to go and see the Prime Minister, he is probably making no idle boast.

George I, grandfather of the present King, understood this side of the Greek character. He would often walk in the streets and talk to any one. Once, meeting a fiery Republican, George I asked him:

"And do you still persist in wishing to hang me?"

"Certainly, Your Majesty," replied the deputy, "as long as you remain on the throne. If you abdicate and become a Republican, I should become your closest friend."

Naturally the Greeks have a word for it. It is *atomismós*—individuality. Every Greek, no matter how humble, prizes *atomismós* as his dearest possession. This means, of course, that the country is a difficult one to rule, but the free and independent expression of opinion. and the complete absence of any servility or feeling of inferiority between rich and poor, causes the little country of Greece to be a stimulating and sometimes incomprehensible place to visit.

The ambition of every Greek is to live in Athens. There is, consequently, no country life in Greece as we know it in England. There is a splendid peasantry, but few landed proprietors. There are no country houses such as those of England, or the châteaux of France, or the estates which once existed in Spain.

The dream of the average Greek is to sit in the cafés of Athens, reading the newspapers as they pour from the press. It has been estimated that every Greek reads ten newspapers a day. This may be true of Athens, and I am sure it would be true of the rest of Greece if ten different newspapers were obtainable outside the capital.

"Why is your political news so bad over the wireless?" a Greek asked me. "Whenever I manage to get London, what do I hear? Cricket! Football! Do you think of nothing else? If I want British political news, I must get Berlin or Rome."

"Well, you must understand that cricket and football occupy much the same position in my country that politics do in yours," I told him. "We have test matches and cup finals; and so do you. But *you* call them revolutions."

At first sight it would seem that Turkish Athens has vanished; but that is not so. At the foot of the Acropolis are a number of narrow lanes full of rickety old Turkish shops, owned, of course, by Greeks. The ambitious visitor can go to this place—the name is Shoe Lane—and buy as many fake tanagra figures, fake Greek vases, newly coined tetradrachms, and such-like, as he can afford; and they will not be cheap.

In those lanes lingers the last vestige of Turkish Athens. You will see an old man in European clothes turning over and over in his hand a string of amber beads, the *kombológion*, or rosary of the Orient; and, glancing inside a café, you will see a Greek sucking at the mouthpiece of a *narghile*, like any Turk or Syrian. In the markets, where peasants bring their fruits and vegetables, you will notice round the neck of mules and donkeys the little string of blue beads which Moslems believe to be a charm against the evil eye.

This faint flavour of the Orient, a note struck again by the

date-palms in the public gardens, by the presence of *pilaf*
on the restaurant menu, by the little glasses of *ouzo*, which
is the same as the *arak* of Syria and Palestine, and by the
vivid gestures of the Greeks, explains in some measure the
peculiar charm of Athens.

III

I paid my ten drachmae to the man in the little green office
on the side of the Acropolis, and began to mount the steps
to the Propylaea. We have all been familiar with pictures of
the Acropolis and the Parthenon since we were children. We
have seen them in books, in the vicar's study, in steamship
offices; and we have received them on postcards from every
friend who has gone on a Hellenic cruise.

I had been warned by Professor Mahaffy not to expect too
much. This is what he says, in *Rambles and Studies in Greece.*

"There is no ruin, all the world over, that combines so much
striking beauty, so distinct a type, so vast a volume of history,
so great a pageant of immortal memories. There is, in fact, no
building on earth which can sustain the burden of such greatness, and so the first visit to the Acropolis is and must be
disappointing. When the traveller reflects how all the Old
World's culture culminated in Greece—all Greece in Athens
—all Athens in its Acropolis—all the Acropolis in the Parthenon—so much crowds upon the mind confusedly that we look
for some enduring monument whereupon we can fasten our
thoughts, and from which we can pass as from a visible
starting-point into all this history and all this greatness. And
at first we look in vain. The shattered pillars and the torn
pediments will not bear so great a strain; and the traveller
feels forced to admit a sense of disappointment, sore against
his will."

With this warning fresh in my mind, I mounted the steps
leading to the Propylaea; and the sun blazed so violently over

the pillars of that exquisite entrance hall that my eyes ached as I looked. The ancient Athenians were so proud of this lovely building that, says a comedian of the period, "they are always belauding four things: their myrtle berries, their honey, the Propylaea, and their figs."

As I passed through the Propylaea, I saw before me a great space of rough rock rising upward, and on the summit of the rock the Parthenon stood against a blue sky.

I thought that never in my life had I seen anything so beautiful. I was almost afraid to go any nearer in case I was wrong. How Dr. Mahaffy could have written so strangely of the Parthenon puzzled and amazed me; for if there is one sight that seems to me to exceed the most ardent expectation, it is the Parthenon. Lifted high above Athens, with nothing behind it but the blue sky of summer, far larger than I had ever imagined it to be, yet looking queerly weightless, the Parthenon, even in ruin, looks as if it has just alighted from heaven upon the summit of the Acropolis.

Why can no picture or photograph succeed in portraying the Parthenon? It is not an easy question to answer. There is something about the balance of that temple, something purely Greek in its rejection of the unnecessary, which is almost impossible to convey on canvas, because it appeals not so much to the eye as to the mind. I can best describe it by saying that to me the Parthenon has a quality of life which suggests a bird alighting from the air in that brief moment as it closes its wings and is still poised and balanced.

The pillars of Pentelic marble have yellowed with time to a colour that is generally described as gold; but it is not: it is an uneven milky brown, the colour of crust on Devonshire cream.

I wonder if we should have considered the Parthenon as beautiful in the days of its glory. I think not. Instead of

THE THESEUM FROM THE ACROPOLIS,
ATHENS

the cream-coloured marble now worn and weathered by the years, many of the statues and much of the architecture shone with gold and with colour. The Greeks loved colour and brilliance. Their statues were often painted and gilded: hair was red; draperies were green, blue, or red; spears, sandals, crowns, bridles, and chains were of bronze or of gilded bronze. In the gloom of the Parthenon stood the forty foot high statue for whom all this splendour was devised, the great wooden figure of Athena, helmeted, standing with her left hand touching her shield, and in her right hand a figure of Winged Victory.

This statue by Pheidias was one of the most remarkable works of antiquity. Although made of wood, because it was the traditional material for statues, not an inch of wood was visible. The face and hands were plates of ivory. The eyes were of precious stones, and tresses of gold hair fell from a gold helmet.

Even in times when men could combine to make so perfect a thing as the Parthenon and all that it contained, envy was at work, and human nature was not always noble. Pericles, knowing that the time would come when Pheidias might be in trouble with the citizens, insisted that the gold plates on this statue, weighing forty talents, should be removable.

True enough the time came when enemies charged Pheidias with stealing part of the gold which the State had entrusted to him. The artist was able to detach the plates and order them to be weighed and the charge was at once proved to be false.

The abiding memory of Athens is the Parthenon, high above the modern city, the sea far off between the columns, and sunlight touching the creamy marble. No men have ever found a more exquisite stage for their genius; and no stage was more fortunate in its artists.

IV

Perhaps more nonsense has been written about the "mystery" of woman than about almost any other subject on earth. The smile of Leonardo da Vinci's Mona Lisa, which has enchanted so many men, and has inspired so many admirable essays, is really an integral part of a face such as hers. It is a thing not of the mind, but of the mouth and the eyelids. She is probably wondering what to order for dinner.

Many a woman endowed with that curved mouth, full cheeks, and heavy eyes looks as if she is pondering problems of eternity when, in reality, she is wondering how much the milk bill will be on Monday. Even incredibly stupid women, given that particular cast of feature, could establish a reputation for mystery, if only they would keep their mouths closed and continue to smile.

I have sat, and stood, in front of that "smile" in Paris more times than I care to count; and, therefore, I do claim to know it. I also know all the stories that have been put forward to explain it. Whenever I hear people trotting out the old "marvellous," "mysterious," "spiritual," and "incalculable," I feel like the husband of a society beauty when he hears people praising a face which he knows perhaps only too well in a hideous plaster of beauty preparations. . . . However . . .

If you wish to encounter real mystery in woman, and to see smiles that are really incalculable, you must go to the little museum on the Acropolis at Athens and look at the statues of the Korae.

A Kore is a "young woman," and the name has been given to these statues because learned professors and archaeologists do not really know who they were or what they were. All we know is that they are statues of women who lived in Athens about six hundred years before Christ. And the mystery which is frozen on their lovely lips has followed them into this modern world.

It is a pity that plaster casts of the Korae cannot be given to every museum in the world. All museums are anxious to have them, but it is impossible to cast them without destroying the trace of ancient colour that still clings to their faces and their garments. If some method could be devised of casting them without injury, they would be recognized everywhere as the most exquisite group of women that has come down to us from the ancient world.

They are not only beauty frozen in marble for all to see, beauty tricked out with every elegance of fashion, but also beauty of a kind which is in itself a rebuke to the lack of poise and dignity, the over-assertion and the vulgar vivacity which characterize too many women in the world to-day.

Before I describe these lovely creatures, I must say something of their history. When the Persians sacked Athens in 480–479 B.C., they burnt the Acropolis and its temples. The Athenians returned to a smoking ruin. We do not know what this earlier Acropolis was like to look at: all we know is that it held a temple to Athena.

When the Persians had been defeated, a glorious Athens carved in marble rose under Pericles. The treasury was crammed with the spoil of the Persian wars and with the silver of the Delian League, and Pericles set the whole state to work to create a group of buildings that would have no rival in the world.

First, however, it was necessary to clear the ruined site. Until the year 1885 no one knew how that was done. In that year excavators, digging on the Acropolis, unearthed a great number of archaic statues, all of them broken, and some stained by the smoke of the Persian sack of Athens fourteen centuries before.

It was then discovered that the contemporaries of Pericles,

finding the old statues of a previous age broken beyond repair, simply used them as packing for the platforms of new buildings. In that way the art of an older period was preserved and rendered up to the gaze of modern men. Among the statues were seventeen exquisite Korae.

These maidens belong to a period hundreds of years before the creation of the well-known Greek beauty, with her straight nose and her curved limbs. They belong to a time when sculptors, who had previously worked in wood, were groping their way towards marble, and therefore the statues are a little stiff and formal.

They all have much the same bland expression and more or less the same draperies. All of them observe the same pose. Their pleated garments cling to the figure, outlining a graceful curve of the leg from the thigh to the knee and fitting closely above the ankle.

There are slight variations in fashion which suggest a difference in period. Some wear short pleated tunics falling below the waist; others wear an elaborate *himation,* which drapes itself gracefully over the bust in folds.

All the Korae stand alike: bolt upright, one hand delicately lifting the folds of long garments, the other bent outward from the elbow holding some gift or flower. The hair of these ancient maidens suggest that twenty-five centuries ago women spent more time, and took more trouble, before their mirrors even than a woman of to-day.

Their hairdressing is, one might say, architectural. On the forehead, and almost to the crown of the head, are small curls in rows, while the long hair falls behind in tresses, some of which, almost like plaits, are brought forward on each side of the head to fall over the breast.

It must have taken hours to prepare such heads. One is reminded of the ancient Greek poet who sang:

"They comb the curls of their hair to go to the sanctuary

of the goddess; they put on beautiful garments and their tunics sweep the ground; their braided hair waves in the wind in their gilded chains, and gold ornaments shine on the top of their heads."

The poet, lucky man, had evidently seen the Korae on their way to the temple.

Perhaps the most remarkable thing about the Korae is the impression they give of perfect poise and dignity. They are women who are completely sure of their personal charm. They are not anxious to make an impression. There is no need for such effort. They are like goddesses sure of worshippers.

Charm and grace describe them better than beauty. The "Venus Calliphige" in Naples has great beauty, but she has no charm, and neither has the "Venus de Milo." They are just good-looking, rather heavy, female shapes. But the Korae stand in hieratic subtlety, their full lips curved in a slight smile, their almond eyes gazing straight before them.

One is reminded of Archilochus of Paros, who lived at this time, and declared that in his day men valued gracefulness more than life. And to study the Korae is to understand that their spell is what the ancient Greeks called *charis*, or gracefulness developed into an art and practised as a cult. It is something that has vanished from the world, and something that cannot be imitated.

It is strange that while most men appreciate the Korae, few women appear to do so; yet I am not conscious that their appeal is that for which most film actresses strive so tediously.

When I was last in the museum a crowd of English tourists flocked in, and I heard a woman say:

"How frightful. They are just like a herd of cows! What foolish faces! What idiotic smiles!"

A husband, who ventured to remark that he thought they were rather good-looking, was cut short with:

"Don't be a fool, George. They're perfectly *hideous*. . . ."

I think the Korae are the most attractive women in the world; and I wish I could go and look at them every day.

v

"I have noticed in Athens," I said, "many eating-places tucked away in side streets. There is generally an old vine growing over trellis-work, and through the open door you see a yard where a man in shirt-sleeves is always drawing wine from a barrel. Let us go and dine in one of those taverns."

"As you wish," replied Sophocles.

It was about 9 p.m., the hour that Athens dines. The heat of the day still lay over the city, but the ghost of a sea wind was beginning to blow from Phaleron.

We left the brightly lit main street and dived into one of the many dark side-roads where the big wine carts and the empty market wagons were trundling over the stones. We passed through an open door into a paved courtyard piled with barrels.

A cheerful individual in shirt-sleeves, trousers, and carpet slippers, was sitting beside a wire fence, feeding a pet sheep with herbs while a small dog sat up and begged for attention.

The courtyard was roofed, like most Greek taverns, with vine-covered trellis-work, in spring a welcome green shade, but in summer burnt by the sun into a roof of crackling brown. Round the courtyard were three or four simple little white-washed rooms with tables and chairs set ready for dinner. An appetizing odour of food came from the opposite end of the courtyard, where, through glass windows, I could see the cook busy over an enormous fire.

"You will eat here?" asked the proprietor, who shook

hands with me in the friendly Greek fashion. "Come and choose your dinner."

He led the way into the kitchen.

It is the admirable custom in Greek taverns to inspect the food you order before it is cooked. The kitchen was full of wine, meat, fish, and vegetables. There were langoustes, there were red mullet, which they call *barbouni,* and there were the horrid ink-fish which are eaten stewed in oil.

After we had ordered our meal, the proprietor, followed by his pet sheep and his dog, led the way into one of the alcoves, where the three of us sat down together. The sheep nibbled our trousers and had to be turned out, much to the delight of the dog.

Little glasses of *ouzo* were produced, accompanied by the assortment of hors-d'œuvre which generally comes with it, for the Greeks never drink without eating. There were squares of bread covered with red caviar, crisp potatoes, pistachio nuts, and slices of cucumber.

The proprietor lifted his glass, said how much he admired England and the English, and how complimented he was that a stranger should have decided to dine in his tavern: then, rising, he went out to superintend the dinner.

"The Government," began Sophocles, "is said to have decided . . ."

"Do you mind, Sophocles," I said gently, "not talking politics to-night? Talk about food instead. It is so much healthier. Tell me what the Greeks eat. . . ."

As he described the favourite dishes, I realized that there is scarcely a Greek dish that is not Turkish in its origin. It is my firm conviction that the Turks borrowed their cuisine from the Greeks, as they borrowed so much; but the names are Turkish, with the addition of a Greek affix. *Pilaf* becomes *pilafi, dolma* becomes *dolmades.* Nearly all the sweets of Greece are the well-known Turkish sweets and pastries.

The proprietor entered, bearing slices of red melon.
"Where does this come from?" I asked.
"It comes from Larissa, the capital of Thessaly," he said.

I remembered the great hills of Thessaly, piled up round
Mount Olympus, that I had seen from the ship; and Larissa,
I thought, was the town that centuries ago placed on its sil-
ver coins a copy of the lovely head of Kimon's Arethusa.

"All the best red melons come from Larissa," continued
the proprietor, "and all the best yellow melons from Argos."

He placed on the table a jug of resinated wine.

"This is in your honour," he said to me with a bow. "It is
made from my own grapes."

Resinated wine, called *retsinata* or *retsina*, is the *vin ordi-
naire* of Greece. Most strangers, I am told, dislike it, and
think it tastes of turpentine. When the wine is young, resin
tapped from pine-trees is placed in it as a preservative; and
that has been the method of making wine in Greece from
remote ages. There is probably no more authentic relic of
antiquity in the life of modern Greece. The wand which
Dionysus carries in a thousand statues and reliefs, and on a
thousand vases, is the *thyrsus*, a sceptre surmounted by a
pine-cone.

"Good health."

We all touched glasses and drank. The Greek is always
flattered and delighted when a foreigner drinks *retsinata*
without a shudder.

When we had finished our Thessalian melon, we were
given langouste cut into slices and covered with a vinaigrette
sauce. This shell-fish, I was told, had come that morning
from Oropos, which faces the island of Euboea. We then
ate veal and a salad of tomatoes and cucumber.

While Sophocles and I sat talking over the ruins of this
romantic meal, the door opened to admit a thin, cadaverous

man who had not shaved for some time. He regarded us
with burning eyes. Silently he advanced into the room, half
closed his eyes, and, stretching out an arm dramatically,
began to declaim in a high, sing-song voice.

"Who is he?" I asked.

"He is a wandering poet," whispered Sophocles. "He goes
from tavern to tavern."

"I cannot understand him. What is he saying?"

"It is a poem he has made about the political situation.
It is very clever. It suits both sides, so that no one can take
offence at it."

"He cannot be a Greek, then."

"Oh, yes, he is," said Sophocles earnestly. "I can tell from
his accent that he is an Athenian."

The poet finished, and asked me for a cigarette. He lit it
and recited a poem in which life was compared to the smoke
of a cigarette. He apostrophized the cigarette, blew clouds
of smoke into the air, and at the end, with a terrific gesture
of finality, he stamped the cigarette beneath his feet and
ground the life out of it on the stone flags.

When the oration ended, the poet came up to our table
and accepted a glass of wine. A crowd of workmen and
artisans, each one with his evening paper, came in and ordered wine. They plunged into violent political argument.

When they had drunk their wine, Sophocles asked them
to share our enormous jug of *retsinata*. They gathered round
and each one, before he drank his glass, toasted me—"the
stranger"—coupled with the United States of America. Many
Greeks are unable to tell the difference between an American and an Englishman. When I corrected them, they rose
to their feet and toasted England. America, they said, "very
nice," but England—ah, England!

Then followed such a series of varied toasts, first one and

then another rising and proposing something, that I felt the situation contained all the germs of a violent political discussion. I was glad when one man rose to his feet and asked us to drink to the health of "Vyron."

How Byron would have delighted in the sight of us standing under the scorched vine that hot night, dramatically drinking his health as the saviour of modern Greece.

"Vee-ron!" they cried, lifting their glasses in the air.

I could think of no Greek statesman whose name would have been received with unanimous approval, therefore I weakly sought refuge in Philhellenism:

"To Pericles," I cried.

"What does he say?" I could hear them asking.

When it was explained, they rose out of sheer politeness and emptied their glasses.

The door opened to admit three musicians, who sang a number of songs in a curiously high-pitched tone.

"Let us escape now," said Sophocles, "or we shall be here all night."

"Are all Greeks as friendly?" I asked him. "Have all Greeks the same flood of talk? Do you all know the recipe for a happy Greece?"

"That is the curse of my country," said Sophocles. "We all know. We all think we could do so much better than the people in charge. We all believe that if we were in control of the country everything would be all right. Every Greek rules Greece in his own mind."

The proprietor stood at the door of the tavern, accompanied by his dog and his sheep. He poured out a glass of *retsinata.*

"This," he said, "is something particularly good. Will you please taste?"

I lifted my glass.

"Long live England," said the proprietor.

"Thank you," I replied, "and long live Greece."

And with a last handshake we plunged into the side-streets of Athens.

V

OLYMPIA

THE ruins of Olympia lie in a pine-wood in the Valley of the Alpheus. The flat land with the river winding through it, in winter a torrent, in summer a stony track, rises to surrounding hills except on the west, where the river enters the sea.

In this ghostly wood, where every footfall is hushed by a bed of pine-needles, you come across the white bones of temples, baths, and altars, and the ruins of the immense gymnasium in which athletes trained for the most famous contest of antiquity.

I know of few other relics of ancient Greece which are so sadly maligned by the camera. The photographs which I have seen of Olympia make that glorious spot look like a stonemason's yard. In fact, so dreary and uninteresting are these photographs, that I almost decided to save myself the difficult and fatiguing journey there.

As soon, however, as I set foot inside the magic wood I saw that Olympia and Delphi are the most romantic ruins in Greece.

I have heard it said that the Olympic Games are the only festival of antiquity which a modern crowd would have understood. And this may be true. Could we borrow the time-machine which H. G. Wells invented in a novel years ago, it would be interesting to attend the festival at Olympia with a Cup Final crowd from the North of England.

I wonder what they would have thought of the Games? Apart from the sacrifice of boars at the beginning of the festival and the sacrifice of oxen at the end of it, there was nothing about the Olympic Games which a spectator from Huddersfield would not have appreciated as readily as a spectator from Ithaca or Thessaly.

He might, it is true, have been a little surprised by the nudity of the competitors, but as the ancient Greek males were burnt almost black by the sun and by repeated applications of oil, their nudity might not have embarrassed him.

It is perhaps strange that dark bodies should be less embarrassing than pale ones, as the Greeks themselves discovered when the soldiers of Agesilaus stripped the Persian captives and were shocked by their whiteness.

Lucian says in one of his dialogues that the first duty of an athlete is to expose his naked body to the elements and to endure all weathers. And this convention, which shocked the Romans as well as the barbarians, was responsible for the perfection of Greek sculpture, for the artists of those days haunted the gymnasia and were familiar, as no artists have ever been, with the human form in movement.

The modern visitor to Olympia would have seen nothing remarkable in the foot races and the various jumping contests. Hollywood in its more lavish moments would no doubt have prepared him for the excitement of the chariot races in the Hippodrome. He would even recognize in the terrible physical ordeal of the Pancratium—a sight that probably would have horrified our bull-baiting ancestors of the last century—nothing more remarkable than our modern all-in wrestling.

He would not have been surprised by the partisanship and by the tremendous local enthusiasm, for is not the same thing happening at every football match to-day?

But surely he would have been astonished by the strange mixture of religion and athletics, the queer blend of a pilgrimage atmosphere with that of the Derby, which must have characterized the great festival in the Valley of the Alpheus.

Every four years heralds proclaimed a sacred peace throughout the Greek world. Warring States laid down their arms and turned their attention to the Olympic Games.

The various States specialized in different sports. The Spartans loved to excel in all those contests which demanded endurance and stamina. The Ionians, on the other hand, shone in the more graceful sports. Boeotia provided the most famous wrestlers, Aegina the toughest boxers, and so on.

Along all the roads that led to Olympia great crowds pressed in the dust and heat of summer: runners, wrestlers, boxers, horsemen, charioteers, and also thousands of spectators anxious to watch their team, or champion, win the crown of wild olive.

Athletes who competed in the Olympic Games had to prove that they had been trained for ten months in a recognized gymnasium. They were then obliged to take up residence at Olympia and exercise for thirty days under the observation of the judges. Magnificent baths and gymnasia were provided for this purpose.

No man who could not pass this preliminary test was allowed to take part, but once the names of the chosen were announced on a white board at Olympia there was no drawing back. If, for any reason, a man withdrew his name, he was branded as a coward, and was fined as heavily as for the detestable crime of bribery.

Boxing was a violent sport in ancient Greece. An epigram written in ancient times ran:

"After twenty years Ulysses was recognized by his dog, Argos, but as for you, Stratophon, after four hours' boxing you are unrecognizable not only by a dog but also by your fellow citizens."

Perhaps the most disfiguring of all contests was the all-in-boxing-wrestling matches called Pancratium. In those contests all tactics were admissible, and many a match ended with the death of one of the competitors.

In Olympia to-day you can see the platform of the great temple of Zeus almost as perfect as it was in ancient times. Bits of its pavement are still visible. Its columns lie all around it as they fell during an earthquake one thousand four hundred years ago.

This temple housed the colossal statue of Zeus by Phidias, one of the seven wonders of the ancient world. Its flesh was of ivory, its garments of various shades of gold. An ancient writer wrote this beautiful tribute to it:

"A man whose soul is utterly immersed in toil, who has suffered many disasters and sorrows, and cannot even enjoy sweet sleep, even such an one, I think, if he stood face to face with this statue, would forget all the dangers and difficulties of this mortal life. . . ."

What happened to that marvellous work of art? How one wishes that it might have been preserved from the wreck of the ancient world. It seems, however, that when the Olympic Games were abolished in A.D. 394, the statue was carried off to Constantinople, where, later, it perished in a fire.

But the Germans who excavated the ruins of Olympia from twenty feet of earth had the good fortune to discover one of the greatest treasures of the old world still lying broken and splintered in the ruins. That is the exquisite Hermes of Praxiteles. It is to be seen in the museum near the ruins, and no reproduction or picture can convey the beauty and delicacy of the young marble god as he stands holding the infant, Bacchus, on his arm.

One memory of Olympia which I took away with me is not of temples or of gods, but of a shallow marble trench lying in a pine-wood near a twenty foot high bank.

This trench was the starting-place where the runners

lined up for the races. Facing it to-day, like a wall, is a high bank of earth beneath which lies the great stadium.

Not far away I found a wild olive tree. Is it, I wonder, a cultivated tree that has gone back to nature or is it a descendant of the famous *kotibos* which once grew in the sacred grove of Altis and was reaped with a golden sickle for the making of the Olympic crowns?

The wreath of wild olive was the only prize given in antiquity to the victors at Olympia. In the silence of the pine-wood its leaves still cast their shadow on ruined altars.

AN ARCADIAN SHEPHERD

VI

EPIDAURUS

THE old man was standing beside the road, and around him towered the mountains which divide Arcadia from Argolis.

He was an Arcadian shepherd who for the best part of a century has been roaming the mountains with his sheep, a gun on his shoulder to protect them from wild animals.

I saw him at the end of a wearying day which had begun long before sunrise, and he seemed ample compensation for three punctures, magneto trouble, and a faulty rear spring. He combined the austerity of great age with the dignity of those who have never had any contact with cities. There was nothing on him except the ancient double-barrelled muzzle-loader, that was not produced in or about his mountain cabin. Every bit of his clothing was homespun, his moccasins were made of sheepskin, and his crook was cut from mountain ash.

He submitted with patient dignity to the ordeal of the camera. He had none of the Albanian's semi-Oriental fear of the lens, and—although I discovered that he had never before been photographed—he posed with the easy skill of a film actor. It would have been insulting to have offered him money, so I asked him to accept the only thing I could think of at the moment: a half-empty tin of fifty English cigarettes.

One of the swiftest ways to the heart of a city Greek is a gift of Virginian cigarettes; but this old man had no use for them. But when he saw the flat tin box his eyes lit with pleasure. He opened it, handed back the cigarettes, and began to polish the tin on his sleeve, holding it up and smiling with pleasure like a girl with a jewel.

It was strange to see that dignified old Nestor treasuring an empty cigarette tin! I went back to the car and discovered two more tins in my luggage, which I gave him; and his delight was unbounded.

We shook hands and I went on over the break-neck mountain road that winds down to the Devon-red plain of "thirsty, horse-breeding Argos." To the east, near the sea, lie the ruins of Epidaurus.

Epidaurus contains what I believe to be the ruin of the earliest hospital ward in existence. People go there, however, not to see this, but to inspect the magnificent theatre, the best preserved in Greece.

It is also the most attractively situated Greek theatre I know, with the exception, perhaps, of the theatre at Delphi and the exquisite theatre at Jerash in Trans-Jordania.

The rather incoherent ruins of the huge medical establishments, the baths, the gymnasia, the concert halls, clubs, and temples which centuries ago made Epidaurus a kind of Greek Harrogate (or perhaps Lourdes) are really more interesting.

A good deal of imagination is necessary to visualize this town as it was in classical times, because it has suffered severely from despoilers and those insatiable people in search of building-stone, who will mop up temples, roads, aqueducts, as the red ant eats wood.

Nothing preserves an ancient site better than an earthquake just bad enough to drive away the population and to prevent rebuilding; statues, houses, and temples are then neatly buried and sealed, as it were, pending the arrival of a French or a German archaeologist.

Epidaurus, however, was gradually pulled to pieces century after century, its statues, marbles, and pillars carried away, so that to-day hardly anything remains but the ground-plan.

To any one interested in medicine Epidaurus is, of course, the most fascinating site in Greece. It was the chief seat of the cult of Asklepios, the God of Healing, who in later times migrated to Rome and in due course bequeathed to the British medical profession, and also to the Royal Army Medical Corps, the symbol of his staff and his sacred serpent.

As I explored those ruins I wondered whether Epidaurus had been purely a faith-healing centre, or if scientific medicine had also been practised there.

Many of the inscriptions discovered are similar to the published accounts of the cures at Lourdes. There are records of persons suffering from maladies which had defied the best doctors in Greece who, after a night spent in the temple of Epidaurus, claimed to be instantly cured.

"O Blessed Asklepios, god of healing," reads one account, "it is thanks to thy skill that Diophantes hopes to be relieved from his incurable and horrible gout, no longer to move like a crab, no longer to walk upon thorns, but to have a sound foot as thou hast decreed."

I hope that a faith great enough to inspire a patient to set up a tablet before he had been cured received its reward!

The usual procedure was that so delightfully sketched by Aristophanes in *Plutus*. The patient spent the night in the temple of the god, who visited him in a dream. The dream was interpreted by the priests who prescribed treatment.

A survival of this procedure exists to-day at the miracle-working shrine on the isle of Tenos. Every year great crowds of suffering people visit the miraculous ikon of the Madonna, but it is essential to spend a night in the church before the cures begin.

I know a Greek who swore to me that after sleeping in this church and praying before the ikon he was cured of cancer.

I have met with another relic of dream-cures in Syria and

Trans-Jordania where churches dedicated to St. George (the patron saint of England and also of lunatics!) are said to cure insanity if the sufferer is taken to them and chained all night to a pillar set apart for this purpose.

In spite of the superstition underlying the cult of Asklepios —the tame serpents that were taught to lick the patient, the dogs that performed the same function, the dreams, and so on—sound medical knowledge must also have been dispensed there, otherwise surely its reputation could not have endured for centuries.

Greek medical knowledge was more advanced than many people imagine and, as the lesser of two evils, I think I would rather have had a leg amputated in ancient Greece than at the Battle of Trafalgar.

One of the most interesting exhibits in the Athens Museum are the cases full of amazingly modern-looking medical implements which were in use centuries before Christ. The Greeks used forceps, probes, directors, syringes. They also employed anaesthetics.

Homer mentions the anaesthetic effects of nepenthe. Herodotus describes a Scythian hemp that induced anaesthesia, and other writers say that mandragora was used by surgeons as an anaesthetic.

Doctors tell me that the two treatises on fractures and dislocations in the Hippocratic Collection, written about 600 B.C., are, with certain reservations, as good as any modern work on the same subject. One wonders, therefore, whether scientific medicine and medical superstition existed side by side at Epidaurus.

What, for instance, is the mysterious circular maze under the temple of the god? Some scholars believe that it was a snake-pit into which the patient was led in pitch darkness. While he lay trembling, it is supposed, one of the harmless yellow snakes that still exist around Epidaurus came to him and flickered its tongue over him—the sign that the god would heal him.

It is easy to laugh at such superstition.

"How incredible," said an English tourist who was visiting the ruins, "that a race which produced Plato and Pericles could have believed such rubbish."

"But," I asked him, "have you ever studied a modern chemist's shop? Surely the cult of Asklepios does not argue greater credulity than the countless quack remedies in which millions of us believe to-day. And, by the way, do you know how many fortune-tellers there are in London?"

I think he was annoyed. He moved away with a superior nose in the air, and whenever we met again he pretended not to see me.

VII

DELPHI

I

SOME ONE was playing a pipe in the afternoon heat. There was no other sound but the snapping of cicadas in the olive groves.

Like all near-Eastern music, this tune was plaintive, though pathetic, sad but not gloomy, wild without being savage. It had also the queer flavour of antiquity, just as a glass of resin wine or the bean soup of Sparta has it.

It was like some old, old sound welling up through a crack in the thirsty soil of Greece, the cry of some buried urn or old sword, or a ring from a woman's hand.

Who could be playing in the heat of afternoon? Perhaps it was Pan whistling to his goats! It could not be Orpheus. The music was too rough, too childish, too earthy. It was, moreover, just the place in which you might surprise Pan, his thick lips opened on the pipe-stem and his shaggy fingers on the stops: a blazing afternoon on the hill-slopes of Delphi, the yellow mountains rising into the sky, their flanks like furnace walls, the eagles Parnassus slowly flying in circles against the distant blue, the goats drawn into the shadow of the olive trees, the green lizards lying on hot stones with open mouths, as if gasping for air.

Each little pipe-note moved in the heat, and broke, a cool bubble of sound.

Behind a breastwork of rocks I saw an old man sitting on a stone with a pipe to his lips. He was alone. He wore the long smock of the Greek highlander. A small round cap was tilted against his white hair. I watched him for some time before he noticed me. Then he bowed gravely, removing his pipe for a second, and instantly resumed his music. It is not usual for an old man to play a pipe in the blaze of afternoon. Young goat-herds sometimes do so in the shade of the olive trees to pass the time; but old men sleep in the shade. I asked him why he was playing in the sun.

"For the rich strangers who will come from the sea," he replied, pointing with his pipe-stem down the mountain-side to the port of Itea, which shone far off on the edge of the Corinthian Gulf.

"Rich strangers from the *sea?*"

Then I understood. A cruising ship was coming to Itea. Hundreds of people would drive through the olive groves up into the mountains. The solitude of Delphi would be shattered for an afternoon. The visitors would wander about the ruins, then depart as suddenly as they had come, leaving Delphi more silent, more lonely than ever.

I could not help smiling at the thought of this seemingly artless old man carefully posed on the path to the ruins.

"Oh, my dear," I could already hear the tourists saying, "look at this dear old man! Isn't he perfectly sweet? Where's your camera, Marjorie? Is ten drachmae too much to give him?"

Then, the last visitor departing, the "dear old man" would swiftly put away his pipe—until the time came when the next tourists would climb painfully to the mountain fastness.

I left him and explored, as I have done in spring and summer, by the light of sun and of moon, the most magic and exquisite relic of Ancient Greece; the sanctuary of the Delphic Oracle.

A century ago the village of Kastri stood above the ruins. When Dodwell toured Greece in 1806 he looked in vain for

Delphi, yet all the time it lay beneath the very cottages in which he slept. The first thing the French excavators did when they decided to discover Delphi was to move the entire village to another place. Then, one by one, the hidden beauties sprang to light. They discovered the Sacred Way running up the hill-side between the once-splendid shrines given by the States of Ancient Greece in reverence and gratitude to the Oracle. They discovered the mysterious temple in which the Priestess delivered her riddles. They discovered the beautiful little theatre in which plays were acted during the Pythian Games.

High above the ruins, cut in the side of the mountain, is the Stadium of Delphi. It is nearly six hundred feet in length, and the thousands of stone seats that line one side, rising tier above tier, are almost as perfect as they were when great crowds filled them during the Pythian Games centuries ago.

I sat watching the sun blaze down on the grass-grown arena. I thought that few ruins in the world could be more magic than this, few sights more eerie than the thousands of empty seats waiting for an audience. Century has followed century across the world, empires have been born, have flourished and have fallen into dust since the last Pythian Games filled the stadium. Yet I defy any one to sit there on a summer's afternoon without feeling that he is the advance guard of a crowd that will soon come shouting up the hill.

I looked down on the arena. Was I mad? Had the sun gone to my head? Two young athletes stood gazing at the tiers of empty seats as if acknowledging the plaudits of the crowd. They laughed and tossed to each other the heavy stone weights, like cannon-balls, which still lie in the grass. They flung them through the air with skill.

"I'll race you once round!" one of them cried.

THE GORGE AT DELPHI

"Right!"

They stripped off their shirts and stood clothed only in white shorts. Their bodies were bronzed by the sun of a Mediterranean cruise.

Standing at the starting-point, they set off at an easy pace, swinging round the empty amphitheatre with the sun shining on their brown bodies. And it seemed to me that all the ghosts of Ancient Greece watched them from the stone galleries. Seriously and solemnly they ran, as if each seat were occupied, and when at length they drew up, panting and laughing, opposite the throne where the judge awarded the laurel wreath, I felt that the spirit of the place had materialized in the bodies of two young Englishmen.

I felt that I, too, had a part to play. Rising from my hidden seat in the shadow of a fig tree, I clapped my hands; and the sound of applause once more echoed among the hills.

"Good heavens, what's that?" exclaimed one of the athletes; and, looking up, they saw me.

"You seem very solid and muscular," I said, "but nevertheless you are suspiciously ghostly."

"Yes," they agreed, "it is rather a ghostly spot."

We went together down through the ruins of the temple of the Delphic Apollo, and at the end of the Sacred Way, where once embassies had brought their gold and silver to the shrine of Pythia, we came upon an old man playing a pipe.

"Oh, my dear, isn't he sweet? Have you taken his picture?"

A group of girls and women surrounded him. And his cap was full of silver.

II

To sit alone in the ruins of Delphi, to study that lonely spot at leisure and, above all, to see it by the light of a full moon is an experience no man can forget. Dr. Farnell said that "no other spot in Europe has been framed by Nature to work so strongly as the hollow ravine of Delphi on the religious temperament."

It is true, as he says, that the place seems haunted, and that even modern men fall under the influence of its spell. If this is so to-day, when Delphi is merely the skeleton of a town spread out on a mountain-side, what must have been the effect on the minds of those who came in its glory, convinced that the Pythia, the voice of the Oracle, could answer the riddles of existence?

Those travellers climbed out of a plain dark with olive trees into the hot sunlight of the mountains below Parnassus. There two thousand feet above the plain, they saw a town of marble carved in the mountain-side, its temples shining in the sun, its statues of gold, silver, bronze, and coloured marble glittering in the light. The air of Delphi was described by Plutarch to be as "fine as silk"; in that clarity the town shone against the stupendous background of yellow mountains towering to the sky.

In gratitude to the Oracle, all the States of Greece had contributed to the beauty of Delphi. The Sacred Way curved up to the Temple of Apollo between shrines full of gold and silver and flanked by hundreds of statues.

Temples and votive statues were crowded together, each seeking to be richer and more beautiful than the next, expressing the rival glories of States. There was no Phidias at Delphi to demand artistic co-operation. The Sacred Way was a vast treasure-trove in which the piety of centuries jostled and fought for recognition. Beautiful it undoubtedly was, for the greatest artists in the world had made it, but it must have suggested the overcrowded detachment of a cemetery rather than the ordered design of the Acropolis.

Above the national treasury stood the Temple of Apollo,

where Pythia, mounted on her tripod, specialized in the art of ambiguity.

What was the Delphic Oracle? In remote times, it was said, a shepherd, passing over those mountains, came to a cavern which emitted intoxicating vapours. He fell into a trance and began to prophesy. Others who came also prophesied, but in their trance fell into the cavern and perished.

Therefore, in order to save the lives of those who fell under the influence of the vapour, a tripod was erected above the cavern.

In historic times the Temple of Apollo was built over the cavern and a priestess, called the Pythia, seated on a tripod, went into a trance and spoke words which, translated by the priests, were regarded as the inspired words of Apollo—the god of prophecy.

The Pythia, in early times always a virgin of Delphi, was not allowed to marry. After, however, an unfortunate love affair between a Pythia and a young Thessalian visitor, the priestess was always a woman over fifty, but she had to dress like a young girl.

For three days before the Pythia went into her trance she prepared herself by fasting. On the appointed day she descended into the cavern below the temple.

She burnt laurel leaves, flour of barley, and perhaps myrrh, in the never-dying flame of the altar. Then she mounted the tripod above the chasm. In a short time her body would begin to twitch, her face would become contorted, and strange cries would come from her lips. Her symptoms, as described by ancient writers, suggest those of a medium in a state of trance. Beside the tripod stood a priest who wrote down and interpreted the frenzied ravings of the Pythia and these, rendered in the form of hexameter verse, were delivered to the suppliants in a sealed vase.

The message was usually a riddle. No explanation was

ever given. The visitor had to go away and puzzle it out for himself.

The Delphic Oracle may sound like superstition in its most deplorable form. But how can we explain the fact that for over a thousand years this Oracle exercised a beneficent effect on one of the most quick-witted races in history and also earned the respect of some of the greatest thinkers of antiquity? It is an historical fact that the colonial expansion of Greece was directed by the Oracle. No Greek colony was ever founded without a consultation at Delphi.

Kings and emperors toiled up the rocky slopes to ask the Pythia's advice on matters of state. And the Oracle was no respecter of persons. Pythia generally spoke straight from the shoulder. She was also often on the side of the weak. She frequently championed slaves.

Even when her advice destroyed the inquirer, her authority was never questioned. Croesus, for instance, worried by the Persian invasion, went to Delphi to seek advice. He was told that "if he crossed the Halys he would destroy a great empire." Encouraged by this advice, he crossed the Halys; but it was his own empire that was destroyed! Pythia was extraordinarily skilful in giving a message with a double meaning.

I am sure that if the true history of the Delphic Oracle could be written we would learn of a first-class spy system throughout the countries of the ancient world. The priests of Delphi were probably men of outstanding attainments who interpreted the ravings of Pythia in the light of their own intimate knowledge of politics. No doubt their archives contained useful data about every one who was likely to consult the Oracle. If some one came unheralded to Delphi, surely there must have been time during the preliminary purification ceremonies to find out what he had come for? Much that must have seemed miraculous to the believer was probably only the efficient working of a clever intelligence department.

There is a touch of real grandeur and pathos in the last recorded oracle from Delphi. It was in the Fourth Century after Christ when the Emperor Julian the Apostate, who hated Christianity, sent an emissary to Delphi with the idea of rebuilding the Sanctuary and restoring the Oracle to its ancient fame.

The Emperor's messenger saw only a pale shadow of the ancient Delphi. It had been plundered for centuries. Its wealth and its authority had departed. Oracles were no longer in fashion. Delphi counted for nothing in the world. But the fire of prophecy burned up in a last flame as Pythia wearily and sadly mounted the sacred tripod:

"Go tell the Emperor," she said, "that the carved work of the sanctuary is cast down upon the ground, and the God thereof hath no longer where to lay his head. And the laurel of his divination is withered, and the waters that spoke with voices are dried up."

In those words—the most pathetic in all antiquity—the Delphic Oracle recognized the victory of Christianity.

As I wandered about the ruins of Delphi I thought that the Oracle has still a message for Mankind. In the vestibule of the Temple, plain for all to read who consulted Pythia, were three sentences.

They were: "Know thyself"; "Nothing too much"; "Moderation in all things."

III

In the early morning the peasants of Delphi tramp down to the Vale of the Pleistos where olive trees cast a cool shade on the hottest day. The women, sitting sideways on pack saddles, skilfully guide their mules, ponies, or donkeys down the break-neck slopes. The men tramp behind with the young boys. Each family is accompanied by a cheerful little dog of indefinite ancestry, and often by a couple of goats or a pet sheep.

One of the prettiest sights to be seen in Greece is a dog at Delphi that was brought up with a goat who has taught him how to butt. Though he is now an old and sober dog, and his friend the goat is an old and sober goat, you can see them leaping about and butting each other on their way down to the olive groves.

Although I have watched them perform this pretty act many a time, I have never seen either of them take a mean advantage; the goat has never attempted to horn his friend, and the dog has never given way to the great temptation of grasping his opponent by the beard. So they go their happy way in the morning sunlight. Every time I see them I think of some frieze from a Greek vase.

The dogs of Delphi are, I am sure, the happiest in Greece. They are remarkable even in a country which is not, on the whole, cruel to animals.

They strut about with their tails up, confident, busy, and well fed. Even when the moon is full you are not kept awake half the night, as in so many places, by a savage barking. The moon rides over Delphi in a silence broken only by the cry of an owl. The reason is that all the dogs of Delphi, tired out after their day in the plain, are fast asleep in the houses with the family, the pet sheep, and the goats.

I, who have come to estimate very shrewdly the temper of a village by the conduct of its dogs, took one glance at those little creatures and knew that in Delphi I would find no mules with saddle galls, no lame donkeys plodding under their burdens, no skeleton ponies. I was right.

The mountaineers round Delphi are a happy and self-contained community. They are extraordinarily clannish and regard the man from the next district as a foreigner. Their kindness and hospitality to a stranger—especially to any wandering Englishman—is almost reckless.

Walking one day with a Greek friend on the hills round Delphi, I came across a picturesque individual who wore the national dress: a knee-length smock, thick woollen tights strapped at the knee, and heelless hide slippers with pompoms on the upcurving toes. His lined brown face sprouted prawn-like whiskers. His head was covered with a crop of short wiry hair like a cap of coco-nut matting. Like so many mountain Greeks, he was partly Albanian. The true Greek is not a farmer; he is mercantile by nature, and a born shopkeeper. He gravitates instinctively to the town. The Albanian, on the other hand, is naturally a farmer and a herdsman.

We sat down near the peasant. My friend asked him questions about the olive crop and the price of olives and olive oil. He answered courteously, and introduced his sons, who were going down to the groves armed with twelve-foot switches to whip the olives from the trees. Then the following conversation took place:

"Your companion," said the peasant. "Is he from Europe?"

"He is from England."

"What does he do?"

"He is a writer."

He gave me a glance of brief respect, then, crossing his legs and nursing a foreleg in an easy attitude, he asked:

"How much money does he make?"

His next questions were even more remarkable.

"Did he get those clothes in England?" "How much did he pay for them?" "Has he got any children?" "Are they boys or girls?" "What age are they?"

He insisted that we should drink a bowl of milk. His manner was that of an Eighteenth Century *grand seigneur* inviting distinguished guests to his château. We followed him up the mountain path to a little cabin.

The peasant's house in Greece is merely a sleeping-place. The family are out of doors all day long. The bedding, which is piled in a corner during the day, is spread out on the floor at night and the family retire to sleep in their clothes. Of comfort, furniture, decoration there is nothing.

But the family is self-supporting. They live on coarse bread, olives, garlic, eggs. On a feast day, such as Easter, a lamb is sometimes killed. If they grow vines, they make their own wine. Tubular bee-hives give them honey, which all over Greece replaces sugar. Beside many a cabin is a loom on which the women make cloth. Some peasants even keep silkworms and produce enough silk to make festal dresses and scarves for the women.

Such families are, in the only true sense of the word, independent.

It is people like the Greek peasant and the Arab of Syria, who survive the crash of Empires.

While we stood outside the cabin the peasant disappeared to return with a bowl of goat's milk. My friend drank. I drew a deep breath and followed his example.

The peasant offered to cook eggs for us. We promised to return some day. Then, the formalities having been observed, we shook hands and made to go. But that was not in order. The mountaineer insisted on escorting us to the dusty road, where he stood waving until we passed from sight.

GIRLS OF THASOS

VIII

ELEUSIS

THE wine-shop on the Sacred Way was full of brigand-like men sitting under a vine, drinking and puffing rank smoke into the air. Mules tethered to the awning posts threatened, as they moved, to pull down the frail canvas over the heads of the drinkers. It was cool and dark under the vine: white and hot outside where the sun palpitated upon miles of rock and olive groves.

As I approached, powdered from head to foot in the white dust of Attica, the brigands welcomed me with that reverence for eccentricity which becomes more pronounced the farther one travels to the East. I was a foreigner and therefore rich. How incredible that any man rich enough to ride should choose to walk! I could see them thinking this.

No sooner had I sunk gratefully on a chair than two bearded muleteers sent over a glass of resin wine from their table.

It is in such acts of kindness and good breeding that the Greek peasant endears himself to the traveller, and I have noticed that the fiercer-looking the Greek, the kinder he is to a stranger.

I rose to my feet and thanked them, drinking the wine, and they smiled, bowed, and wagged their heads with the effusive friendliness of shaggy dogs. I sent over to them wine from my table and some little cubes of Turkish Delight. We were friends. The ancient courtesies had been observed.

I sat in the shade, looking out into a great furnace of heat where the white road ran onward to Eleusis, and thinking what a fool I was to try and walk the thirteen miles from

Athens on a day like this. It was asking for sunstroke or apoplexy.

Meanwhile it was good to sit and drink the pungent *retsinata* in the wine-shop. The flies were horrible, the place stank of sweat, of dust, of stale garlic-soup, and sour wine; but at least it was shady under the vine.

Through the dusty olive grove opposite, a goat-boy brought his tinkling herd to a fountain by the roadside. A pretty girl from the inn, her bare legs brown as an Arab's, went to the fountain to fill, not a pitcher, alas, but an empty petrol tin. And over the white road, moving in puffs of white dust, came market carts going to Athens with piles of cabbages and aubergines and huge red water-melons.

It is among the common people of Greece, among the fishermen, the muleteers, the shepherds, the hillmen, and the peasants, that one seems to catch the echo of the hospitality of the Homeric age and the simplicity of Theocritus. These people are very like the ancient Greeks, gentle, moderate people, neither great eaters nor great drinkers, but mighty in talk, fierce in argument, proud, vain, individualistic, and keen to bargain.

So I sat watching the Sacred Way, a broad highway leading from Athens to Eleusis, one of the best roads in Greece. It follows more or less the old route taken every year by the great crowds of ancient times who went at night by torch-light to attend the Mysteries of Eleusis.

As I drank the pine-scented wine beside this road, I thought how strange it is that in spite of all the hundreds of thousands of men and women who were initiated into these Mysteries, not one ever dared to divulge them. There were scoffers and sceptics in ancient times. There were indiscreet satirists like Lucian. Yet not one of them has betrayed the vows of secrecy which were imposed on all who were admitted into the Mysteries, not one has left us an account of the scene that took place by night in the temple at Eleusis. The greatest of Greek thinkers, even Plato, professed a respect and reverence for a ceremony which, in the words of Cicero, taught men "not only to live happily, but to die with a fairer hope."

The temple of the Mysteries at Eleusis enshrined the lovely story of Persephone, in which the Greeks explained the miracle of spring and the rebirth of Nature after the death of winter. It seems certain that those who attended the Mysteries were given hope of happiness beyond the Shades.

They gathered at Athens in the autumn. They had been previously prepared in the spring by teachers to fit them for the Greater Mysteries. All save murderers and barbarians might participate.

Heralds proclaimed a sacred peace. The crowds of *mystae* went down to the sea and purified themselves. They each sacrificed a pig. Then on the appointed night they formed the sacred procession and went by foot along the Sacred Way, stopping to sacrifice at the various altars that lined the road from Athens to the sacred city.

Chanting and by torchlight, they came over the hill at Daphni and marched down to the plain, where the waters of the Bay of Eleusis shone in the starlight. Ancient writers called that ceremony "the night of torches," and one of them, breaking the silence which surrounds everything to do with the Mysteries, mentioned the torches moving like fireflies round the margin of the bay.

While the crowd rested, the priests took into the sanctuary the "Sacred Objects," always carried veiled in the procession, always exhibited on the night of initiation, but—*never spoken about by the thousands who had seen them.*

While I was thinking of these things beside the Sacred Way, the muleteers got up and stamped off into the sunlight, others came and formed new groups at the tables. Among the newcomers was a young man in a reach-me-down suit and a felt hat who bore himself with the slick superiority of the Greek who has been to America. He came over to me and said:

"Say, boss, these guys want to know whether you're English or American."

It turned out that he had worked in New York hotels, in a sea-food shop on Broadway, and in various Greek restaurants. It had given him a contempt for his own country. "They don't know how to work over here," he kept saying. He had saved up enough money to return and marry, and buy a taxi-cab on the instalment system. By the greatest good fortune the cab was in a shed at the back.

"Take me to Eleusis," I said.

"Sure!" he replied.

And in twenty minutes we were running downhill to the lovely blue Bay of Eleusis, which looks like an inland lake, because the isle of Salamis seems to close the outlet to the sea.

Far off, shining in the white heat, we saw the little town of Eleusis lying on the edge of blue waters.

The ruins cover a large area of level ground at the foot of the hill. Until about fifty years ago they were hidden by a modern village which had been built on the ruins. Now you can see hundreds of columns, and bases of pillars and blocks of marble lying about in puzzling confusion. I came to the ruin of one of the gates and saw, cut sharply on the pavement, the wheel-ruts of the chariots that had passed that way centuries ago.

The chief feature, of course, is the ruin of the great Temple of the Mysteries. It is unlike any other Greek temple. In Ancient Greece worship and sacrifice took place in the open air, and the temple was merely a shrine for the divinity. In

Eleusis, however, the temple is built to hold a congregation of perhaps three thousand people.

Standing in the great hall of the Mysteries, I wondered what secrets had been imparted to the worshippers in this place. Before the ruins were excavated, scholars believed that the priests led the initiates through underground tunnels in which horrible apparitions were encountered, symbolic of the terrors of Hades. It was also believed that elaborate machinery was employed to produce terrifying spectacles. But not a trace of underground tunnels or of pits has been discovered in the ruins. Whatever happened in the Temple of the Mysteries seems to have occurred in full view of the congregation as they sat round like people in a theatre.

What was it they saw? Was it merely a mystery play showing the descent of Persephone into the Shades and her resurrection? The ruins give no answer. They guard their secret as closely as it was guarded for thousands of years by all those who, having visited this temple, for ever afterwards remained silent.

The young man from America was lounging in the shade. We went back together over the long white road to Athens.

IX

MARATHON

THE first road made in Greece, when the War of Independence freed the country from the Turk over a century ago, was the thirty-mile road between Athens and Marathon. It was made because every intelligent traveller in Greece wants to see the site of the famous battle. Few battles have become household words, but Marathon is one of them. Thermopylae is another. Waterloo is a third.

Marathon occupies a remarkable place in the history of the world. It has been written about, talked about, and argued about in all the languages of Europe for so many centuries that the very word now stands for an encounter of a small heroic force against overwhelming odds.

> The mountains look on Marathon
> And Marathon looks on the sea.

Those resounding lines are probably as well known as any written by Byron. And many who could tell you nothing about Marathon, except that it had something to do with a long-distance race, are familiar with Wordsworth's:

> The man of abject soul in vain
> Shall walk the Marathonian plain.

As recently as before the War the Plain of Marathon was a difficult place to get at. It meant a day or two on horseback, and travellers were advised to take food and blankets with them. To-day, hailing any taxi in Athens, you can order the driver to go to Marathon; and you can do the journey, there and back, between noon and dusk.

I set out one morning with a young Greek journalist who knows the history of his country.

Once you get clear of the outskirts of Athens the road runs between two great mountains, Hymettus to the right, and Pentelicus to the left. I had a magnificent view of the high, tree-clad slopes of Pentelicus, and through field-glasses I could see—or rather I thought I saw—the marble quarries which the Greeks worked in ancient times.

"You must go up to those quarries," said my young friend. "You will see drums and portions of marble pillars cut nearly two thousand years ago still waiting to be taken down to temples which are now in ruins or have completely vanished. You can see also the slopes made by the ancient Greeks for sliding the marble to the foot of the mountain. . . ."

We now entered a purely pastoral country where flocks of sheep grazed under the olive trees. The shepherds were the most picturesque figures I had seen in Greece. They might have stepped from an ancient frieze or from a Greek vase. They were tall, fierce-looking fellows draped in hooded cloaks made of brown goat-hair.

I stopped the car and jumped out, much to the alarm of my Greek friend. And I soon realized why. Two enormous and infuriated dogs came leaping towards me with bared fangs. They were not the gentle strategists of the British sheepfold, but savage monsters which, in Macedonia, guard the flock from wolves.

Just as I was thinking of retreat, the nearest shepherd called one word and the dogs, dropping their tails, ran to him and lay at his feet, subdued but watchful. We talked to the shepherds, but my Greek friend had some difficulty in understanding them.

"These men are the most mysterious and interesting people in Greece," he explained. "They are Vlach shepherds. They have a language of their own, which is said to be an older and purer Greek than we speak to-day. Its syntax is strange and some scholars believe that the original tongue was Latin. There is a tradition that the Vlachs are descendants of Roman legionaries planted in Dacia by Trajan in A.D. 106. No one knows much about them. They dislike strangers. In the spring the Vlachs live with their flocks on the plains, and in summer they move to the hills. They have their own laws."

As we went on, I explained to my friend that the word given by Germanic tribes to these nomads is Vlach or Wallach, which means "foreigner."

When the Saxons invaded England they gave the same name to the Romanized Britons who were living there—the Welsh. It is the same word. Just as the ancient Britons were driven from civilized Roman towns into the mountains of Wales, so these Romans in Greece were driven into the hills to become nomads and shepherds.

"How interesting," said my Greek friend. "So Lloyd George is a Vlach?"

Start a conversation in Greece on botany or bee-keeping, and it will swing round to politics! Fortunately our arrival at Marathon prevented our talk from taking its predestined course.

The plain of Marathon is a flat expanse of green fields and red ploughland running to the sea. There were miles of olive groves and vineyards, the small gnarled vines lying in neat rows on the red soil. And how right Byron was. "The mountains look on Marathon, and Marathon looks on the sea."

We walked towards the famous mound which covers the bones of the one hundred and ninety-two Athenians who were slain by the Persians in 490 B.C. The heroes were buried where they fell, and when the mound was excavated in the last century their burnt bones were discovered with the pottery and other objects placed with them in the grave over two thousand four hundred years ago.

The mound, apart from its association, is not impressive. It is only about forty feet in height and about two hundred feet in circumference. A wild pear tree was in full bloom at its foot, and asphodel were growing in clusters all over it.

"Now let's see how much we can remember of the Battle of Marathon," I said, as we stood on the top of the hill. "You begin."

"It was in September, 490 B.C.," said the Greek.

"No," I objected, "you must begin two years earlier. The Persians were conquering the world. The Greeks had rebelled in Asia and the Athenians sent twenty ships to help their kinsfolk. In return, the Persians sent a fleet to subdue Athens. That fleet was wrecked off the coast of Mount Athos two years before the battle of Marathon. The Persians then built a new fleet, and for two years the great King Darius made his servant sit beside him and say every day, 'Remember the Athenians.' In September, 490 B.C., this new fleet came into the bay over there to subdue Athens, the little State that had dared to defy the might of Darius. . . . Your turn!"

"When the Athenians heard that the Persians had landed they, as you say in England, 'had the wind up.' They sent the runner Pheidippides to Sparta to beg help. This man ran one hundred and thirty-five miles in two days; and the road is all up and down mountains. The Spartans refused to help until the moon was full. Then the Athenians—ten thousand of them against twice as many Persians—marched to Marathon along more or less the same road we have taken from Athens. . . . You go on."

"The Persians were astonished to see the Athenians. It was the habit of the Greeks, when invaded, either to stay in their cities and be besieged, or to fight outside the walls. They rarely marched distances to fight. The Persians were on the plain with their backs to the sea. The Athenians were on the higher ground near the hills. When the Persians saw the heavy, armed Athenian infantry coming at them, they thought their enemies had gone mad. The Persians were not used to infantry charges. They liked to skirmish up like Arabs, discharge their arrows, and gallop off.

"The Greek tactics upset them. They were driven back to the ships. The Greeks fought them in the water. The courage, the charge, and the Greek spear were superior to Persian cavalry, Persian numbers, and Persian bows. That was Marathon."

"And," interrupted the Greek, with spirit. "Do you remember the story of Cynaegirus, the brother of Aeschylus, who was holding on to a Persian galley with his right hand? When his hand was cut off he continued to hold on with his left, and when that hand was severed he clung to the side of the ship with his teeth."

So the mound of Marathon, lonely in the plain, covered with asphodel and with a wild pear tree at its foot, will ever remind men of the undying memories of Greece.

X

SUNIUM

LIFTED high above the sea, upon a hill at Sunium, the Temple of Poseidon awakens vague memories of something else. "What is it?" you ask yourself, as you listen to the beat of the waves upon the rocks beneath. Through the wind-worn columns of the temple you see lying to the south the outline of the islands of the Cyclades. But what is absent? The scene lacks slow music. It lacks also a ballet. The temple at Sunium, transcending the limits of Nature, has invaded the perilous realm of Art.

Only at Drury Lane or Covent Garden could one see a ruin so perfect, so much as every romantic poet and as every artist thinks a Greek temple should be. It is almost self-conscious in its rightness as it stands against the slow-moving clouds, its graceful Doric columns really "snow white"; the bright daisies springing from the broken pavement. Indeed the Temple of Poseidon might have been designed by a committee of stage painters, and, to make it all too good to be true, one of the pillars has been autographed by Byron.

The promontory of Sunium is the most southerly point of Attica, and so wild and tempestuous are the tide-races round this thrust of land that in classical times sailors believed that Poseidon, god of the sea, had evil designs on ships that went that way. Therefore, inspired by fear, and a courteous desire to avert evil by flattery and offerings, they erected on the hill a lovely temple of white marble, which, even now in its decay, looks as though it might fly away into the sky.

My first impression of Sunium was, however, of a less spiritual character; it was of the finest baked red mullet I have eaten in Greece.

A friendly little inn stands at the foot of the hill, maintained, I believe, by the Greek Government. It is a credit to them, and the traveller in Greece must wish that there were many more like it. The whole family rushed at me when I entered, took my hat and stick, and then, chattering brightly in the friendly Greek way, followed me into the little dining-room and began to quarrel about feeding me.

A daughter wanted to slay a hen. Some one else suggested bean stew. While all this was being argued with force and eloquence, a girl of greater charm and sense than her companions appeared silently with a jug of resin wine, which she poured out for me. It is extraordinary how the woman who just does things instead of making a fuss about them impresses herself upon the mind.

While the argument was at its height and I was resigned to eat anything that was given to me, the door opened and a boy came into the room, holding a huge red mullet. It had just been drawn from the sea below the Temple of Poseidon. I said in fairly good Greek that this was indeed the gift of the sea god, but, as nobody could understand me, the remark fell flat.

However, I was delighted to find that they intended to bake this fish for me. The mother embraced the fisherman with passion, kissed him on both cheeks, which seemed to surprise him; and then they all went off to cook the red mullet.

All I can say about the result of their combined action is that until you have eaten this fish baked as the Greeks do it, a fish straight from the sea at Sunium, you have no right to talk about red mullet.

Feeling in a perfect mood for reverie, I said good-bye to that kindly family and, climbing through the myrtle bushes and grape-hyacinths, came to the white temple on the hill.

I lay in the shade of a marble column. It was a hot, lazy afternoon. There was not a living thing in sight except a goat with a long black beard that lifted its Pan-like face towards me and then fell to cropping the grass; bees droned in the flowers, and I could hear the waves breaking on the rocks below. . . .

I must have fallen asleep. I would like to have been able to say that unto me a vision was granted of white-robed maidens coming up the hill to offer the first-fruits of the year. But, alas, my awakening was one which must be painfully familiar to any one who has dozed for a moment in a Greek temple. Two sharp female voices were speaking in English. One said: "It's here!" The other said: "No, it isn't." Then the first voice asked: "Where is it? We *must* find it. It's ridiculous to come all this way and not find it."

I peeped round the corner of the pillar and saw that the worst had happened. Two elderly women were pointing with umbrellas, and, as they pointed, the Temple of Poseidon seemed to vanish and to be replaced by the main street of Cheltenham.

There are elderly Englishwomen of so strong and definite a type that wherever they go about the world, two by two, clad in tweed, pince-nez on nose, umbrella in hand, they take with them a little bit of England. They make dignified allowances for the regrettable peculiarities of foreign nations, and their rigidity of mind and behaviour induces an awed respect in the minds of all who encounter them. They have tremendous courage. They will, without a thought, interrupt the largest and most violent man who is beating a donkey and threaten to report him to the local R.S.P.C.A., whether such a society exists or not. They will wash the faces of dirty children at public fountains and deliver, with passion, concise lectures on infant welfare to startled mothers, who cannot understand a word of English.

On those rare occasions when, in charge of a licentious guide, they appear accidentally at "dancings" or "cabarets," sitting bolt upright and sipping black coffee, their presence casts an aura of respectability over the most unfortunate occasion, turning the mind instantly to some memory of a meeting in a parish hall at home in England.

Such were the women who were standing in the Temple of Poseidon, pointing with their umbrellas and looking for something. Seeing me lying there, one of them, putting on a forced expression and an unnatural voice, said:

"Pardon, monsieur, mais voulez vous avoir l'obligeance . . ." Then, noticing, perhaps, my old flannel trousers and tweed coat, she smiled in an embarrassed way as if caught in the act of doing something undignified, and apologized for mistaking me for a foreigner:

"I'm so sorry." Then, in her natural voice, she said: "We wonder whether you could tell us where Lord Byron wrote his name."

I had not the slightest idea. I had not troubled to find out. Byron, always a schoolboy, was always writing his name on something. All I knew was that it was somewhere, carved among the hundreds of other names on one of the columns.

It seemed to me so strange that two people from a distant country could come to this lovely place to find a man's name carved on a stone. They were not in the least interested in the lovely temple or in the little bay below, where in olden times the Grecian corn ships took shelter. They were probably not much interested in Byron. They kept looking at their watches and peering sharply about as if they had lost a passport or a purse.

At last we found it—"BYRON" carved with admirable force and strength. He must have carried a special knife about with him, for the letters were a quarter of an inch deep.

"Ah, how interesting," said the ladies. "Thank you so

much. Good day!"

I wanted to ask whether they had ever read Byron, and if they could remember any of his poems. I think it would have pleased the shade of Byron if two elderly English women in tweed costumes and brogues had sat down on "Sunium's marbled steep" to recite even his more hackneyed verse. But one does not ask such women questions of that kind.

Feeling their way among the marble chips with the tips of their umbrellas, they descended the hill towards a waiting car. I had the extraordinary delusion that a curate had cycled past into the myrtle bushes.

I saw the sunset from Sunium. I watched the gold clouds gather, and I saw the isles of the Cyclades fade into the mist of evening. A boy herding goats came over the hill, and for a moment the white temple was full of the sound of bells.

THE END

INDEX